for
Networking
Technologies
CNE

Joel Stegall
David Johnson

The Coriolis Group, LLC
14455 N. Hayden Road, Suite 220
Scottsdale, Arizona 85260

480/483-0192
FAX 480/483-0193
http://www.coriolis.com

Library of Congress Cataloging-in-Publication Data
Stegall, Joel
      Exam Cram for networking technologies CNE / by Joel Stegall and David Johnson
            p.   cm.
      Includes index.
      ISBN 1-57610-351-X
      1. Electronic data processing personnel--Certification.   2. Novell software--Examinations--Study guides.   3. Computer networks   I. Johnson, David.   II. Title.
QA76.3.S745   1999
004.6--dc21   99-13177
                                                                   CIP

Printed in the United States of America
10 9 8 7 6 5 4 3 2 1

Publisher
Keith Weiskamp

Acquisitions Editor
Shari Jo Hehr

Marketing Specialist
Cynthia Caldwell

Project Editor
Toni Zuccarini

Technical Reviewer
Dean Hardy

Production Coordinator
Meg E. Turecek

Cover Design
Jody Winkler

Layout Design
April Nielsen

CORIOLIS

14455 North Hayden Road, Suite 220 • Scottsdale, Arizona 85260

Coriolis: The Training And Certification Destination ™

Thank you for purchasing one of our innovative certification study guides, just one of the many members of the Coriolis family of certification products.

Certification Insider Press™ has long believed that achieving your IT certification is more of a road trip than anything else. This is why most of our readers consider us their *Training And Certification Destination*. By providing a one-stop shop for the most innovative and unique training materials, our readers know we are the first place to look when it comes to achieving their certification. As one reader put it, "I plan on using your books for all of the exams I take."

To help you reach your goals, we've listened to others like you, and we've designed our entire product line around you and the way you like to study, learn, and master challenging subjects. Our approach is *The Smartest Way To Get Certified*™.

In addition to our highly popular *Exam Cram* and *Exam Prep* guides, we have a number of new products. We recently launched Exam Cram Live!, two-day seminars based on *Exam Cram* material. We've also developed a new series of books and study aides—*Practice Tests Exam Crams* and *Exam Cram Flash Cards*—designed to make your studying fun as well as productive.

Our commitment to being the *Training And Certification Destination* does not stop there. We just introduced *Exam Cram Insider*, a biweekly newsletter containing the latest in certification news, study tips, and announcements from Certification Insider Press. (To subscribe, send an email to **eci@coriolis.com** and type "subscribe insider" in the body of the email.) We also recently announced the launch of the Certified Crammer Society and the Coriolis Help Center—two new additions to the Certification Insider Press family.

We'd like to hear from you. Help us continue to provide the very best certification study materials possible. Write us or email us at **cipq@coriolis.com** and let us know how our books have helped you study, or tell us about new features that you'd like us to add. If you send us a story about how we've helped you, and we use it in one of our books, we'll send you an official Coriolis shirt for your efforts.

Good luck with your certification exam and your career. Thank you for allowing us to help you achieve your goals.

Keith Weiskamp
Publisher, Certification Insider Press

About The Authors

Joel Stegall has a master's degree in Biomechanics from The University of Texas at Austin. He taught Physics and Human Anatomy & Physiology, and coached track and field in Austin, Texas, for 18 years. He became a CNE/CNI in 1993 and has been teaching Novell certified curricula since then. In addition, he was instrumental in setting up one of the first Secondary NEAP programs in the country. The program is designed to train high school students to manage Novell-based networks and targets Novell certification as a training objective. He is currently an MCNE/MCNI.

David Johnson is a manager at a large systems integration and maintenance company in Austin, TX. He served many years in the networking trenches, working his way up the food chain. When not working or writing, DJ enjoys billiards, food, cigars, and wine. DJ can be reached at **count0@texas.net**.

Acknowledgments

First, I want to thank my wife and children for their endless patience and support. Without their constant understanding, I wouldn't have been able to complete this project. I would also like to thank Blake Williams for helping me type things out at the last minute. And finally, I want to thank Ed Tittel of LANWrights for giving me this opportunity and Mary Burmeister for keeping everyone sane, and making us all sound good with her excellent editing skills.

—*Joel Stegall*

As always, thanks to the staff at LANWrights for the opportunity to do something I enjoy. Special thanks to Mary Burmeister for handling this project and my own special deadlines. And, of course, thanks to Mama for reminding me that a cat's life is always best.

—*David Johnson*

Contents At A Glance

Table Of Contents

Introduction

Welcome to *Exam Cram for Networking Technologies CNE*! This book aims to help you get ready to take—and pass—Novell certification Test 050-632, titled "Networking Technologies." This Introduction explains Novell's certification programs in general and talks about how the *Exam Cram* series can help you prepare for Novell's certification tests.

Exam Cram books help you understand and appreciate the subjects and materials you need to pass Novell certification tests. *Exam Cram* books are aimed strictly at test preparation and review. They do not teach you everything you need to know about a topic (such as the ins and outs of TCP/IP protocols and routing trees, or everything there is to know about cabling schemes). Instead, we (the authors) present and dissect the questions and problems we've found that you're likely to encounter on a test. We've worked from Novell's own training materials, preparation guides, and tests, and from a battery of third-party test preparation tools. Our aim is to bring together as much information as possible about Novell certification tests.

Nevertheless, to completely prepare yourself for any Novell test, we recommend that you begin by taking the Self-Assessment included in this book immediately following this Introduction. This tool will help you evaluate your knowledge base against the requirements for a CNE under both ideal and real circumstances.

Based on what you learn from that exercise, you might decide to begin your studies with some classroom training or by reading one of the many study guides available from Novell Press (an imprint of IDG Books Worldwide) or third-party vendors. We also strongly recommend that you install, configure, and fool around with any software that you'll be tested on—especially NetWare 5 itself—because nothing beats hands-on experience and familiarity when it comes to understanding questions you're likely to encounter on a certification test. Book learning is essential, but hands-on experience is the best teacher of all!

Novell Professional Certifications

Novell's various certifications currently encompass six separate programs, each of which boasts its own special acronym (as a would-be certificant, you need to have a high tolerance for alphabet soup of all kinds):

➤ **CNA (Certified Novell Administrator)** This is the least prestigious of all the certification tracks from Novell. Candidates can demonstrate their skills in any of a number of areas of expertise. This certification requires passing one test in any of five tracks (three are specific to NetWare versions 3.x, 4.x, and 5; two are specific to GroupWise versions; for the purposes of this book, we assume the NetWare 5 track is the one for you). Table 1 shows the required test for the CNA certification. For more information about this program and its requirements, visit **http://education.novell.com/cna/**.

➤ **CNE (Certified Novell Engineer)** This is the primary target for most people who seek a Novell certification of one kind or another. Candidates who wish to demonstrate their skills in installing and managing NetWare networks make up its primary audience. This certification is obtained by passing six or seven tests, including five or six (depending on which track you pursue) required core tests and a single elective. Table 1 shows the required and elective tests for CNE certification in the NetWare 5 track. For more information about this program and its requirements, visit **http://education.novell.com/cne/**.

➤ **MCNE (Master CNE)** Candidates for this certification program must first prove their basic expertise by obtaining CNE certification. To obtain MCNE status, candidates must pass four to six additional tests in any of seven specialized areas. This is Novell's most elite certification. For more information about this program and its requirements, visit **http://education.novell.com/mcne/**.

➤ **CIP (Certified Internet Professional)** This certification program is designed for individuals who seek to step into one or more of a variety of professional Internet roles. These roles include that of Certified Internet Business Strategist, Certified Web Designer, Certified Web Developer, Certified Internet Manager, and Certified Internet Architect. To qualify, candidates must pass anywhere from one to five required tests, depending on which role they seek to fill. For more information about this program and its requirements, visit **http://www.netboss.com**.

Table 1   Novell CNA And CNE Requirements*

CNA

Only 1 test required	
Test 050-639	NetWare 5 Administration

CNE

All 5 of these tests are required	
Test 050-639	NetWare 5 Administration
Test 050-632	Networking Technologies
Test 050-640	NetWare 5 Advanced Administration
Test 050-634	NDS Design and Implementation
Test 050-635	Service and Support
Choose 1 elective from this group	
Test 050-629	Securing Intranets with BorderManager
Test 050-628	Network Management Using ManageWise 2.1
Test 050-641	Network Management Using ManageWise 2.6
Test 050-636	intraNetWare: Integrating Windows NT
Test 050-618	GroupWise 5 Administration
Test 050-633	GroupWise 5.5 System Administration

* This is not a complete listing. We have included only those tests needed for the NetWare 5 track. If you are currently a CNE certified in NetWare 4, you need only take the CNE NetWare 4.11 to NetWare 5 Update test (Test 050-638) to be certified in NetWare 5.

➤ **CNI (Certified Novell Instructor)** Candidates who wish to teach any elements of the Novell official curriculum (and there is usually an official class tied to each of the Novell certification tests) must meet several requirements to obtain CNI certification. They must take a special instructor training class, demonstrate their proficiency in a classroom setting, and take a special version of the test for each certification topic they wish to teach, to show a higher level of knowledge and understanding of the topics involved. For more information about this program and its requirements, visit **http://education.novell.com/cni/**.

Novell also offers a Master CNI (MCNI) credential to exceptional instructors who have two years of CNI teaching experience, and who possess an MCNE certification as well.

➤ **CNS (Certified Novell Salesperson)** This is a newer Novell certification and focuses on the knowledge that sales professionals need to master to present and position Novell's various networking products accurately and professionally.

To obtain this certification, an individual must pass a self-study class on sales skills and Novell products, as well as take regular product update training when it becomes available. This level of certification is intended to demonstrate a salesperson's ability to position and represent Novell's many products accurately and fairly. For more information about this program and its requirements, visit **http://education.novell.com/powersell/**.

Certification is an ongoing activity. Once a Novell product becomes obsolete, Novell certified professionals typically have 12 to 18 months during which they may recertify on new product versions. If individuals do not recertify within the specified period, their certifications become invalid. Because technology keeps changing and new products continually supplant old ones, this should come as no surprise to anyone. Certification is not a one-time achievement, but rather a commitment to a set of evolving tools and technologies.

The best place to keep tabs on Novell's certification program and its various certifications is on the Novell Web site. The current root URL for all Novell certification programs is **http://education.novell.com/certinfo/**. But if this URL doesn't work, try using the Search tool on Novell's site with "certification" or "certification programs" as a search string. You will then find the latest, most up-to-date information about Novell's certification programs.

Taking A Certification Exam

Alas, testing is not free. Each computer-based Novell test costs $95, and if you don't pass, you may retest for an additional $95 for each additional try. In the United States and Canada, tests are administered by Sylvan Prometric and by Virtual University Enterprises (VUE). Here's how you can contact them:

➤ **Sylvan Prometric** Sign up for a test through the company's Web site at www.slspro.com. In the United States or Canada, call 800-233-3382; outside that area, call 612-820-5706.

➤ **Virtual University Enterprises** Sign up for a test or get the phone numbers for local testing centers through the Web page at www.vue.com. In the United States or Canada, call 800-511-8123 or 888-834-8378; outside that area, call 612-897-7370.

To sign up for a test, you need a valid credit card, or contact either company for mailing instructions to send them a check (in the U.S.). Only when payment is verified, or a check has cleared, can you actually register for a test.

To schedule a test, call the number or visit either of the Web pages at least one day in advance. To cancel or reschedule a test, you must call before 7 P.M. pacific standard time the day before the scheduled test time (or you may be charged, even if you don't show up for the test). When you want to schedule a test, have the following information ready:

➤ Your name, organization, and mailing address.

➤ Your Novell Test ID. (Inside the U.S., this means your Social Security number; citizens of other nations should call ahead to find out what type of identification number is required to register for a test.)

➤ The name and number of the test you wish to take.

➤ A method of payment. (As we've already mentioned, a credit card is the most convenient method, but alternate means can be arranged in advance, if necessary.)

Once you sign up for a test, you'll be informed as to when and where the test is scheduled. Try to arrive at least 15 minutes early. You must supply two forms of identification—one of which must be a photo ID—to be admitted into the testing room.

All tests are completely closed-book. In fact, you will not be allowed to take anything with you into the testing area, but you will be furnished with a blank sheet of paper and a pen or, in some cases, an erasable plastic sheet and an erasable pen. We suggest that you immediately write down on that sheet of paper all the information you've memorized for the test. In *Exam Cram* books, this information appears on a tear-out sheet inside the front cover of each book. You'll have some time to compose yourself, to record this information, and even to take a sample orientation test before you begin the real thing. We suggest you take the orientation test before taking your first test, but because they're all more or less identical in layout, behavior, and controls, you probably won't need to do this more than once.

When you complete a Novell certification test, the software will tell you whether you've passed or failed. Results are broken into topical areas that map to the test's specific test objectives. Even if you fail, we suggest you ask for—and keep—the detailed report that the test administrator should print for you. You should use this report to help you prepare for another go-round, if needed.

If you need to retake a test, you'll have to schedule a new test with Sylvan Prometric or VUE and pay another $95.

The first time you fail a test, you can retake the test the next day. However, if you fail a second time, you must wait 14 days before retaking that test. The 14-day waiting period remains in effect for all retakes after the first failure.

Tracking Novell Certification Status

As soon as you pass one of the applicable Novell tests, you'll attain Certified NetWare Administrator (CNA) status. Novell also generates transcripts that indicate which tests you have passed and your certification status. You can check (or print) your transcript at any time by visiting the official Novell site for certified professionals at **http://certification.novell.com/pinlogin.htm**. As the name of the Web page (pinlogin) is meant to suggest, you need an account name and a Personal Identification Number (PIN) to access this page. You'll receive this information by email about two weeks after you pass any exam that might qualify you for CNA or CNE status.

At the Novell certification site, you can also update your personal profile, including your name, address, phone and fax numbers, email address, and other contact information. You can view a list of all certifications that you've received so far and check a complete list of all exams you've taken.

Benefits Of Novell Certification

Once you pass the necessary set of tests (one for CNA, six or seven for CNE, four to six more for the MCNE), you'll become certified (or obtain an additional certification). Official certification normally takes anywhere from four to six weeks, so don't expect to get your credentials overnight. When the package for a qualified certification arrives, it includes a set of materials that contain several important elements:

➤ A certificate, suitable for framing, along with an official membership card.

➤ A license to use the appropriate Novell certified professional logo, which allows you to use that logo in advertisements, promotions, and documents, and on letterhead, business cards, and so on. As part of your certification packet, you'll get a logo sheet, which includes camera-ready artwork. (Note: Before using any artwork, individuals must sign and return a licensing agreement that indicates they'll abide by its terms and conditions.)

➤ A subscription to the *NetWare Connection* magazine, which provides ongoing data about testing and certification activities, requirements, and changes to the program.

➤ Access to a special Web site, commensurate with your current level of certification, through the **http://certification.novell.com/pinlogin.htm** login page. You'll find more than your own personal records here—you'll also find reports of new certification programs, special downloads, practice test information, and other goodies not available to the general public.

Many people believe that the benefits of Novell CNA or CNE certification go well beyond the perks that Novell provides to newly anointed members of these elite groups. For years, job listings have included requirements for CNA, CNE, and so on, and many individuals who complete the program can qualify for increases in pay and/or responsibility. As an official recognition of hard work and broad knowledge, any of the Novell certifications is a badge of honor in many IT organizations, and a requirement for employment in many others.

How To Prepare For An Exam

Preparing for any NetWare-related test (including "Networking Technologies") requires that you obtain and study materials designed to provide comprehensive information about the product and its capabilities that will appear on the specific test for which you are preparing. The following list of materials will help you study and prepare:

➤ The objectives for the course that relates to Test 050-632 appear in the information that Novell provides for Course 565: Networking Technologies. You can read these objectives on the Novell Web site at **http://education.novell.com/testinfo/objectives/565tobj.htm**. These will also define the feedback topics when you take the test, so this document should be an essential part of your planning and preparation for the exam. You might even want to print a copy and use it along with your other study materials.

➤ General information about Novell tests is also available, including what type of test will be delivered for each topic, how many questions you'll see on any given test, the minimum passing score (which Novell calls a "Cut Score") for each test, and the maximum amount of time allotted for each test. All this information is compiled in a table called "Test Data" that you can read at **http://education.novell.com/testinfo/testdata.htm**.

In addition, you'll probably find any or all of the following materials useful as you prepare for the "Networking Technologies" test:

➤ **Novell Course 565: Networking Technologies** Novell Education offers a three-day class that covers the materials for this test at a level intended to sufficiently acquaint students with networking concepts, such as protocols, design, installation, and maintenance, so they can handle the materials that will appear on the related 050-632 test.

➤ **Novell Press Study Guide** Novell Press offers a book titled *Novell's CNE NetWare 5 Study Guide*, by David James Clarke IV (ISBN 0-7645-4543-4) that covers all the objectives for Test 050-632 in complete detail. The Novell study guides are a terrific complement to this book, and we highly recommend them.

➤ **The Novell Support Connection CD** This monthly CD-based publication delivers numerous electronic titles on topics relevant to NetWare and other key Novell products and topics, primarily, "Monthly Update" CDs (there are two at the time of this writing). Offerings on these CDs include product facts, technical articles and white papers, tools and utilities, and other information.

A subscription to the Novell Support Connection costs $495 per year, (a $100 discount is available to all CNEs and MCNEs as one of the benefits of certification), but it is well worth the cost. Visit **http://support.novell.com** and check out the information under the "Support Connection CD" menu entry for more details.

➤ **Classroom Training** Although you'll find Novell Authorized Education Centers worldwide that teach the official Novell curriculum, unlicensed third-party training companies (such as Wave Technologies, American Research Group, Learning Tree, Data-Tech, and others) offer classroom training on Networking Technologies as well. These companies aim to help you prepare to pass Test 050-632. Although such training runs upwards of $350 per day in class, most of the individuals lucky enough to partake (including your humble authors, who've even taught such courses) find them to be quite worthwhile.

➤ **Other Publications** You'll find direct references to other publications and resources in this book, but there's no shortage of information available about Networking Technologies. To help you sift through the various offerings available, we end each chapter with a "Need To Know More?" section that provides pointers to more complete and exhaustive resources covering the chapter's subjects. This should give you some idea of where we think you should look for further discussion and more details, if you feel like you need them.

By far, this set of required and recommended materials represents a nonpareil collection of sources and resources for Networking Technologies and related topics. We anticipate that you'll find that this book belongs in this company. In the next section, we explain how this book works, and we give you some good reasons why this book counts as a member of the required and recommended materials list.

About This Book

Each topical *Exam Cram* chapter follows a regular structure, along with graphical cues about important or useful information. Here's the structure of a typical chapter:

➤ **Opening Hotlists** Each chapter begins with a list of the terms, tools, and techniques that you must learn and understand before you can be fully conversant with that chapter's subject matter. We follow the hotlists with one or two introductory paragraphs to set the stage for the rest of the chapter.

➤ **Topical Coverage** After the opening hotlists, each chapter covers a series of topics related to the chapter's subject title. Throughout this section, we highlight topics or concepts likely to appear on a test using a special Exam Alert layout, like this:

> This is what an Exam Alert looks like. Normally, an Exam Alert stresses concepts, terms, software, or activities that are likely to relate to one or more certification test questions. For that reason, we think any information found offset in Exam Alert format is worthy of unusual attentiveness on your part. Indeed, most of the information that appears on The Cram Sheet appears as Exam Alerts within the text as well.

Pay close attention to any material flagged as an Exam Alert. Although all the information in this book pertains to what you need to know to pass the exam, we flag certain items that are especially important. You'll find what appears in the meat of each chapter to be worth knowing, too, when preparing for the test. Because this book's material is highly condensed, we recommend that you use this book along with other resources to achieve the maximum benefit.

In addition to the Exam Alerts, we have provided tips that will help you build a better foundation for Networking Technologies knowledge. Although the information may not be on the exam, it's certainly related and will help you become a better test-taker.

> This is how tips are formatted. Keep your eyes open for these, and you'll become a Networking Technologies expert in no time!

➤ **Practice Questions** Although we talk about test questions and topics throughout each chapter, this section presents a series of mock test questions and explanations for both correct and incorrect answers. We also try to point out especially tricky questions by using a special icon, like this:

Ordinarily, this icon flags the presence of a particularly devious inquiry, if not an outright trick question. Trick questions are calculated to be answered incorrectly if not read more than once, and carefully, at that. Although they're not ubiquitous, such questions make occasional appearances on the Novell tests. That's why we say test questions are as much about reading comprehension as they are about knowing your material inside out and backwards.

➤ **Details And Resources** Every chapter ends with a "Need To Know More?" section, which provides direct pointers to Novell and third-party resources offering more details on the chapter's subject. In addition, this section tries to rank or at least rate the quality and thoroughness of the topic's coverage by each resource.

If you find a resource you like in this collection, use it, but don't feel compelled to use all the resources we cite. On the other hand, we recommend only resources we use on a regular basis, so none of our recommendations will be a waste of your time or money. But purchasing them all at once probably represents an expense that many network administrators and would-be CNAs, CNEs, and MCNEs might find hard to justify.

The bulk of the book follows this chapter structure slavishly, but there are a few other elements that we'd like to point out. Chapter 20 includes a sample test that provides a good review of the material presented throughout the book to ensure you're ready for the exam. Chapter 21 is an answer key to the sample test that appears in Chapter 20. We suggest you take the sample test when you think you're ready for the "real thing," and that you seek out other practice tests to work on if you don't get at least 76 percent of the questions correct. In addition, you'll find a Glossary, which explains terms, and an index that you can use to track down terms as they appear in the text.

Finally, the tear-out Cram Sheet attached next to the inside front cover of this *Exam Cram* book represents a condensed and compiled collection of facts and tips that we think you should memorize before taking the test. Because you can dump this information out of your head onto a piece of paper before taking the exam, you can master this information by brute force—you need to remember it only long enough to write it down when you walk into the test room. You might even want to look at it in the car or in the lobby of the testing center just before you walk in to take the test.

Novell Terms

While studying for your Networking Technologies test, you may come across terms that we represent a certain way in our material, but that are represented differently in other resources. Some of these are as follows:

➤ **Network board** A network board is also called a network interface card (NIC), network adapter, network card, and network interface board. Novell uses the term *network board* most often. However, the network board vendors usually refer to network boards as NICs.

➤ **NDS tree** The NDS tree is also called the Directory tree and sometime it's simply referred to as the Directory (with a capital D).

One general source of confusion (as is the case with NDS) is that sometimes an "N" in an acronym is thought to stand for "NetWare" when it really stands for "Novell". As long as you know the specifics of the utility itself, you should be okay—the name isn't going to be a huge issue.

How To Use This Book

If you're prepping for a first-time test, we've structured the topics in this book to build on one another. Therefore, some topics in later chapters make more sense after you've read earlier chapters. That's why we suggest you read this book from front to back for your initial test preparation. If you need to brush up on a topic or you have to bone up for a second try, use the index or table of contents to go straight to the topics and questions that you need to study. Beyond helping you prepare for the test, we think you'll find this book useful as a tightly focused reference to some of the most important aspects of the "Networking Technologies" test.

Given all the book's elements and its specialized focus, we've tried to create a tool that will help you prepare for—and pass—Novell Test 050-632, "Networking Technologies." Please share your feedback on the book with us, especially if you have ideas about how we can improve it for future test-takers. We'll consider everything you say carefully, and we'll respond to all suggestions.

Send your questions or comments to us at **cipq@coriolis.com** or to our series editor, Ed Tittel, at **etittel@lanw.com**. He coordinates our efforts and ensures that all questions get answered. Please remember to include the title of the book in your message; otherwise, we'll be forced to guess which book you're writing about. Also, be sure to check out the Web pages at **www.certificationinsider.com** and **www.lanw.com/examcram**, where you'll find information updates, commentary, and certification information.

Thanks, and enjoy the book!

Self-Assessment

Based on recent statistics from Novell, as many as 400,000 individuals are at some stage of the certification process but haven't yet received a CNA, CNE, or other Novell certification. We also know that easily twice that number may be considering whether to obtain a Novell certification of some kind. That's a huge audience!

The reason we included a Self-Assessment in this *Exam Cram* book is to help you evaluate your readiness to tackle CNE (and even the MCNE) certification. It should also help you understand what you need to master the topic of this book—namely, Exam 050-632, "Networking Technologies." But before you tackle this Self-Assessment, let's talk about concerns you may face when pursuing a CNE, and what an ideal CNE candidate might look like.

CNEs In The Real World

In the following section, we describe an ideal CNE candidate, knowing full well that only a few real candidates will meet this ideal. In fact, our description of that ideal candidate might seem downright scary. But take heart: Although the requirements to obtain a CNE may seem pretty formidable, they are by no means impossible to meet. However, you should be keenly aware that it does take time, requires some expense, and consumes substantial effort to get through the process.

More than 150,000 CNEs are already certified, so it's obviously an attainable goal. You can get all the real-world motivation you need from knowing that many others have gone before, so you'll be able to follow in their footsteps. If you're willing to tackle the process seriously and do what it takes to obtain the necessary experience and knowledge, you can take—and pass—all the certification tests involved in obtaining a CNE. In fact, we've designed these *Exam Crams* to make it as easy on you as possible to prepare for these exams. But prepare you must!

The same, of course, is true for other Novell certifications, including:

➤ **MCNE (Master CNE)** This certification is like the CNE certification but requires a CNE, plus four to six additional exams, across eight different tracks that cover topics such as network management, connectivity, messaging, Internet solutions, plus a variety of hybrid network environments.

➤ **CNA (Certified Novell Administrator)** This entry-level certification requires passing a single core exam in any one of the five possible NetWare tracks, which include NetWare 3, NetWare 4/intraNetWare, and NetWare 5, plus GroupWise 4 and GroupWise 5.

➤ **Other Novell certifications** The requirements for these certifications range from two or more tests (Certified Novell Instructor, or CNI) to many tests, plus a requirement for minimum time spent as an instructor (Master CNI).

The Ideal CNE Candidate

Just to give you some idea of what an ideal CNE candidate is like, here are some relevant statistics about the background and experience such an individual might have. Don't worry if you don't meet these qualifications, or don't come that close—this is a far from ideal world, and where you fall short is simply where you'll have more work to do:

➤ Academic or professional training in network theory, concepts, and operations. This includes everything from networking media and transmission techniques through network operating systems, services, protocols, routing algorithms, and applications.

➤ Four-plus years of professional networking experience, including experience with Ethernet, token ring, modems, and other networking media. This must include installation, configuration, upgrade, and troubleshooting experience, plus some experience in working with and supporting users in a networked environment.

➤ Two-plus years in a networked environment that includes hands-on experience with NetWare 4.x and, hopefully, some training on and exposure to NetWare 5 (which only started shipping in August 1998, so nobody outside Novell has years of experience with it—yet). Some knowledge of NetWare 3.x is also advisable, especially on networks where this product remains in use. Individuals must also acquire a solid understanding of each system's architecture, installation, configuration, maintenance, and troubleshooting techniques. An ability to run down and research information about software, hardware components, systems, and technologies on the Internet and elsewhere is also becoming an essential job skill.

➤ A thorough understanding of key networking protocols, addressing, and name resolution, including Transmission Control Protocol/Internet Protocol (TCP/IP) and Internetwork Packet Exchange/Sequenced Packet Exchange (IPX/SPX). Also, some knowledge of Systems Network Architecture (SNA), DECnet (Digital Equipment Corporation Network), Xerox Network System (XNS), Open Systems Interconnection (OSI), and NetBEUI is strongly recommended.

➤ A thorough understanding of Novell's naming, directory services, and file and print services is absolutely essential.

➤ Familiarity with key NetWare-based TCP/IP-based services, including Hypertext Transfer Protocol (HTTP) Web servers, Dynamic Host Configuration Protocol (DHCP), Domain Name System (DNS), plus familiarity with one or more of the following: BorderManager, NetWare MultiProtocol Router (MPR), ManageWise, and other supporting Novell products and partner offerings.

➤ Working knowledge of Windows NT is an excellent accessory to this collection of facts and skills, including familiarity with Windows NT Server, Windows NT Workstation, and Microsoft implementations of key technologies, such as Internet Information Server (IIS), Internet Explorer, DHCP, Windows Internet Name Service (WINS), and Domain Name Service (DNS).

Fundamentally, this boils down to a bachelor's degree in computer science, plus three or more years of work experience in a technical position involving network design, installation, configuration, and maintenance. We believe that less than half of all CNE candidates meet these requirements, and that, in fact, most meet less than half of these requirements—at least, when they begin the certification process. But because all 150,000 people who already have been certified have survived this ordeal, you can survive it too—especially if you heed what our Self-Assessment can tell you about what you already know and what you need to learn.

Put Yourself To The Test

The following series of questions and observations is designed to help you figure out how much work you must do to pursue Novell certification and what types of resources you may consult on your quest. Be absolutely honest in your answers, or you'll end up wasting money on exams you're not yet ready to take. There are no right or wrong answers, only steps along the path to certification. Only you can decide where you really belong in the broad spectrum of aspiring candidates.

Two things should be clear from the outset, however:

➤ Even a modest background in computer science will be helpful.

➤ Hands-on experience with Novell products and technologies is an essential ingredient to certification success. If you don't already have it, you'll need to get some along the way; if you do already have it, you still need to get more along the way!

Educational Background

1. Have you ever taken any computer-related classes? [Yes or No]

    If Yes, proceed to question 2; if No, proceed to question 4.

2. Have you taken any classes on computer operating systems? [Yes or No]

    If Yes, you'll probably be able to handle Novell's architecture and system component discussions. If you're rusty, brush up on basic operating system concepts, especially virtual memory, multitasking regimes, program load and unload behaviors, and general computer security topics.

    If No, consider some basic reading in this area. We strongly recommend a good general operating systems book, such as *Operating System Concepts*, by Abraham Silberschatz and Peter Baer Galvin (Addison-Wesley, 1997, ISBN 0-201-59113-8). If this title doesn't appeal to you, check out reviews for other, similar titles at your favorite online bookstore.

3. Have you taken any networking concepts or technologies classes? [Yes or No]

    If Yes, you'll probably be able to handle Novell's networking terminology, concepts, and technologies (brace yourself for occasional departures from normal usage). If you're rusty, brush up on basic networking concepts and terminology, especially networking media, transmission types, the OSI reference model, networking protocols and services, and networking technologies, such as Ethernet, token ring, Fiber Distributed Data Interface (FDDI), and wide area network (WAN) links.

    If No, you might want to read several books in this topic area. The two best books that we know of are *Computer Networks, 3rd Edition*, by Andrew S. Tanenbaum (Prentice-Hall, 1996, ISBN 0-13-349945-6) and *Computer Networks and Internets*, by Douglas E. Comer (Prentice-Hall, 1997, ISBN 0-13-239070-1). We also strongly recommend the Laura Chappell book, *Novell's Guide to LAN/WAN Analysis* (IDG/Novell Press,

1998, ISBN 0-7645-4508-6), for its outstanding coverage of NetWare-related protocols and network behavior. In addition, Sandy Stevens and J.D. Marymee's *Novell's Guide to Bordermanager* (IDG/Novell Press, 1998, ISBN 0-7645-4540-X) is also worth a once-over for those who wish to be well-prepared for CNE topics and concepts.

Skip to the next section, "Hands-On Experience."

4. Have you done any reading on operating systems or networks? [Yes or No]

   If Yes, review the requirements stated in the first paragraphs after questions 2 and 3. If you meet those requirements, move on to the next section, "Hands-On Experience." If No, consult the recommended reading for both topics. A strong background will help you prepare for the Novell exams better than just about anything else.

Hands-On Experience

The most important key to success on all of the Novell tests is hands-on experience, especially with NetWare 4.x, intraNetWare, and NetWare 5, plus the many system services and other software components that cluster around NetWare—such as GroupWise, Novell Directory Services (NDS), and the Netscape FastTrack Server—which appear on many of the Novell certification tests. If we leave you with only one realization after taking this Self-Assessment, it should be that there's no substitute for time spent installing, configuring, and using the various Novell and ancillary products upon which you'll be tested repeatedly and in depth.

5. Have you installed, configured, and worked with:

   ➤ NetWare 3.x? NetWare 4.x? NetWare 5? [Yes or No]

      The more times you answer Yes, the better off you are. Please make sure you understand basic concepts as covered in Test 050-639 and advanced concepts as covered in Test 050-640.

      You should also study the NDS interfaces, utilities, and services for Test 050-634, and plan to take Course 580: Service and Support, to prepare yourself for Test 050-635. To succeed on this last exam, you must know how to use the Micro House Support Source product, which costs more than $1,000 for a yearly subscription, but to which you'll have a week's exposure and after-hours access in Course 580.

You can download objectives, practice exams, and other information about Novell exams from the company's education pages on the Web at **http://education.novell.com**. Use the "Test info" link to find specific test information, including objectives, related courses, and so forth.

If you haven't worked with NetWare, NDS, and whatever product or technology you choose for your elective subject, you must obtain one or two machines and a copy of NetWare 5. Then, you must learn the operating system and IPX, TCP/IP, and whatever other software components on which you'll be tested.

In fact, we recommend that you obtain two computers, each with a network board, and set up a two-node network on which to practice. With decent NetWare-capable computers selling for under $600 apiece these days, this shouldn't be too much of a financial hardship. You can download limited use and duration evaluation copies of most Novell products, including NetWare 5, from the company's Web page at **www.novell.com/catalog/evals.html**.

For any and all of these Novell exams, check to see if Novell Press (an imprint of IDG Books Worldwide) offers related titles. Also, David James Clarke IV is working on NetWare 5 upgrades to his outstanding *CNE Study Guide* series. When they become available, they should become essential items in your test preparation toolkit.

6. For any specific Novell product that is not itself an operating system (for example, GroupWise, BorderManager, and so forth), have you installed, configured, used, and upgraded this software? [Yes or No]

If the answer is Yes, skip to the next section, "Testing Your Exam-Readiness." If it's No, you must get some experience. Read on for suggestions on how to do this.

Experience is a must with any Novell product test, be it something as simple as Web Server Management or as challenging as NDS installation and configuration. Here again, you can look for downloadable evaluation copies of whatever software you're studying at **www.novell.com/catalog/evals.html**.

If you have the funds, or your employer will pay your way, consider checking out one or more of the many training options that Novell offers. This could be something as expensive as taking a class at a Novell Authorized Education Center (NAEC), to cheaper options that include Novell's Self-Study Training programs, their video and computer based training options, and even classes that are now available online. Be sure to check out the many training options that Novell itself offers, and that it authorizes third parties to deliver, at **http://education.novell.com/general/trainopt.htm**.

Before you even think about taking any Novell test, make sure you've spent enough time with the related software to understand how it may be installed and configured, how to maintain such an installation, and how to troubleshoot that software when things go wrong. This will help you in the exam, and in real life!

Testing Your Exam-Readiness

Whether you attend a formal class on a specific topic to get ready for an exam or use written materials to study on your own, some preparation for the Novell certification exams is essential. At $95 a try, pass or fail, you want to do everything you can to pass on your first try. That's where studying comes in.

We have included a practice test in this book, so if you don't score that well on the first test, you need to study more and then locate and tackle a second practice test. If you still don't hit a score of at least 76 percent after two or more tests, keep at it until you get there.

For any given subject, consider taking a class if you've tackled self-study materials, taken the test, and failed anyway. The opportunity to interact with an instructor and fellow students can make all the difference in the world, if you can afford that privilege. For information about Novell courses, visit Novell Education at **http://education.novell.com** and follow the "Training options" link.

If you can't afford to take a class, visit the Novell Education page anyway, because it also includes pointers to a CD that includes free practice exams (it's called the Guide CD, and you can read more information about it at **http://education.novell.com/theguide/**). Even if you can't afford to spend much at all, you should still invest in some low-cost practice exams from commercial vendors, because they can help you assess your readiness to pass a test better than any other tool. The following Web sites offer practice exams online for less than $100 apiece (some for significantly less than that):

➤ **www.bfq.com** Beachfront Quizzer

➤ **www.certify.com** CyberPass

➤ **www.stsware.com** Self Test Software

➤ **www.syngress.com** Syngress Software

7. Have you taken a practice exam on your chosen test subject? [Yes or No]

If Yes, and your score meets or beats the Cut Score for the related Novell test, you're probably ready to tackle the real thing. If your score isn't above that crucial threshold, keep at it until you break that barrier.

If No, obtain all the free and low-budget practice tests you can find (see the previous list) and get to work. Keep at it until you can break the passing threshold comfortably.

 Taking a good-quality practice exam and beating Novell's minimum passing grade, known as the Cut Score, is the best way to assess your test-readiness. When we're preparing ourselves, we shoot for 10 percent over the Cut Score—just to leave room for the "weirdness factor" that sometimes shows up on Novell exams.

Assessing Readiness For Exam 050-632

In addition to the general exam-readiness information in the previous section, there are several things you can do to prepare for the "Networking Technologies" exam. As you're getting ready for Exam 050-632, visit the Novell Education forums online. Sign up at **http://education.novell.com/general/forumlogin.htm** (you'll need to agree to the terms and conditions before you can get in, but it's worth it). Once inside these forums, you'll find discussion areas for certification, training, and testing. These are great places to ask questions and get good answers, or simply to watch the questions that others ask (along with the answers, of course).

You should also cruise the Web looking for "braindumps" (recollections of test topics and experiences recorded by others) to help you anticipate topics you're likely to encounter on the test. The Novell certification forum at **http:// www.saluki.com:8081** is a good place to start, as are the forums at **www. theforums.com**, and you can produce numerous additional entry points by visiting Yahoo! or Excite and entering "NetWare braindump" or "Novell braindump" as your search string.

When using any braindump, it's OK to pay attention to informa-tion about questions. But you can't always be sure that a braindump's author will also be able to provide correct answers. Thus, use the questions to guide your studies, but don't rely on the answers in a braindump to lead you to the truth. Double-check everything you find in any braindump.

Novell exam mavens also recommend checking the Novell Support Connec-tion CDs for "meaningful technical support issues" that relate to your test's topics. Although we're not sure exactly what the quoted phrase means, we have also noticed some overlap between technical support questions on particular products and troubleshooting questions on the tests for those products. For more information on these CDs, visit **http://support.novell.com** and click on the "Support Connection CD" link on that page.

Onward, Through The Fog!

Once you've assessed your readiness, undertaken the right background studies, obtained the hands-on experience that will help you understand the products and technologies at work, and reviewed the many sources of information to help you prepare for a test, you'll be ready to take a round of practice tests. When your scores come back positive enough to get you through the exam, you're ready to go after the real thing. If you follow our assessment regime, you'll not only know what you need to study, but when you're ready to make a test date at Sylvan or VUE. Good luck!

Novell
Certification Exams

Terms you'll need to understand:

√ Radio button

√ Checkbox

√ Exhibit

√ Multiple-choice question formats

√ Careful reading

√ Process of elimination

√ Adaptive tests

√ Form (program) tests

√ Simulations

Techniques you'll need to master:

√ Assessing your exam-readiness

√ Preparing to take a certification exam

√ Making the best use of the testing software

√ Budgeting your time

√ Guessing (as a last resort)

Exam taking is not something that most people anticipate eagerly, no matter how well prepared they may be. In most cases, familiarity helps offset test anxiety. In plain English, this means you probably won't be as nervous when you take your fourth or fifth Novell certification exam as you'll be when you take your first one.

Whether it's your first exam or your tenth, understanding the details of exam taking (how much time to spend on questions, the environment you'll be in, and so on) and the exam software will help you concentrate on the material rather than on the setting. Likewise, mastering a few basic exam-taking skills should help you recognize—and perhaps even outfox—some of the tricks and snares you're bound to find in some of the exam questions.

This chapter, besides explaining the exam environment and software, describes some proven exam-taking strategies that you should be able to use to your advantage.

Assessing Exam-Readiness

Before you take any more Novell exams, we strongly recommend that you read through and take the Self-Assessment included with this book (it appears just before this chapter, in fact). This will help you compare your knowledge base to the requirements for obtaining a CNE, and it will also help you identify parts of your background or experience that may be in need of improvement, enhancement, or further learning. If you get the right set of basics under your belt, obtaining Novell certification will be that much easier.

Once you've gone through the Self-Assessment, you can remedy those topical areas where your background or experience may not measure up to an ideal certification candidate. But you can also tackle subject matter for individual tests at the same time, so you can continue making progress while you're catching up in some areas.

Once you've worked through an *Exam Cram*, have read the supplementary materials, and have taken the practice test, you'll have a pretty clear idea of when you should be ready to take the real exam. We strongly recommend that you keep practicing until your scores top 77.5 percent; you may want to give yourself some margin for error, though, because in a real exam situation, stress will play more of a role than when you practice. Once you hit that point, you should be ready to go. But if you get through the practice exam in this book without attaining that score, you should keep taking practice tests and studying the materials until you get there. You'll find more information about other practice-test vendors in the Self-Assessment, along with even more pointers on how to study and prepare. But now, on to the exam!

The Exam Situation

When you arrive at the testing center where you scheduled your exam, you'll need to sign in with an exam coordinator. He or she will ask you to show two forms of identification, one of which must be a photo ID. After you've signed in and your time slot arrives, you'll be asked to deposit any books, bags, cell phones, pagers, or other items you brought with you. Then, you'll be escorted into a closed room. Typically, the room will be furnished with anywhere from one to half a dozen computers, and each workstation will be separated from the others by dividers designed to keep you from seeing what's happening on someone else's computer.

You'll be furnished with a pen or pencil and a blank sheet of paper, or, in some cases, an erasable plastic sheet and an erasable pen. You're allowed to write down anything you want on both sides of this sheet. Before the exam, you should memorize as much of the material that appears on The Cram Sheet (in the front of this book) as you can, so you can write that information on the blank sheet as soon as you are seated in front of the computer. You can refer to your rendition of The Cram Sheet anytime you like during the test, but you'll have to surrender the sheet when you leave the room.

Most test rooms feature a wall with a large picture window. This allows the exam coordinator to monitor the room, to prevent exam-takers from talking to one another, and to observe anything out of the ordinary that might go on. The exam coordinator will have preloaded the appropriate Novell certification test—for this book, that's Test 050-632—and you'll be permitted to start as soon as you're seated in front of the computer.

All Novell certification exams allow a certain maximum amount of time in which to complete your work (this time is indicated on the exam by an on-screen counter/clock, so you can check the time remaining whenever you like). Test 050-632, "Networking Technologies," is what Novell calls a *form test* or a *program test*. This means it consists of a set of 79 questions. You may take up to 105 minutes to complete this exam. The Cut Score, or minimum passing score, for this test is 620 out of 800 (or 77.5 percent).

All Novell certification exams are computer-generated and use a combination of questions, including several multiple-choice formats, interacting with illustrations (sometimes called exhibits), and operating simulations. In short, Novell provides plenty of ways to interact with the test materials, and not only check your mastery of basic facts and figures about networking technologies, but also require you to evaluate multiple sets of circumstances or requirements. Sometimes, you'll be asked to give more than one answer to a question (but in these cases, Novell almost always tells you how many answers you'll need to choose).

Sometimes, you'll be asked to select the best or most effective solution to a problem from a range of choices, all of which may be correct from a technical standpoint. Taking such a test is quite an adventure, and it involves real thinking. This book shows you what to expect and how to deal with the potential problems, puzzles, and predicaments.

Many Novell tests, but not the "Networking Technologies" exam, employ more advanced testing capabilities than might immediately meet the eye. Although the questions that appear are still multiple choice, exhibit, and so forth, the logic that drives them is more complex than form or program tests (like this exam), that use a fixed sequence of questions. Most Novell tests that cover specific software products employ a sophisticated user interface, which Novell calls a *simulation*, to test your knowledge of the software and systems under consideration in a more or less "live" environment that behaves just like the original (this exam does not).

Eventually, most Novell tests will employ *adaptive testing*, a well-known technique used to establish a test-taker's level of knowledge and product competence. Adaptive exams look the same as form tests, but they interact dynamically with test-takers to discover the level of difficulty at which individual test-takers can answer questions correctly. Normally, when new tests are introduced in beta form (and for some time even after the beta is over), they are form tests. Eventually, most of these tests will be switched over to an adaptive format. That is, once Novell has run its question pool past enough test-takers to derive some statistical notion of how to grade the questions in terms of difficulty, it can then restructure the question pool to make a test adaptive.

On adaptive exams, test-takers with differing levels of knowledge or ability see different sets of questions. Individuals with high levels of knowledge or ability are presented with a smaller set of more difficult questions, whereas individuals with lower levels of knowledge are presented with a larger set of easier questions. Even if two individuals answer the same percentage of questions correctly, the test-taker with a higher knowledge or ability level will score higher because his or her questions are worth more.

Also, the lower-level test-taker will probably answer more questions than his or her more knowledgeable colleague. This explains why adaptive tests use ranges of values to define the number of questions and the amount of time it takes to complete the test. Sooner or later, we expect this test, 050-632, to become adaptive as well.

Adaptive tests work by evaluating the test-taker's most recent answer. A correct answer leads to a more difficult question (and the test software's estimate of the test-taker's knowledge and ability level is raised). An incorrect answer leads to a less difficult question (and the test software's estimate of the test-taker's knowledge and ability level is lowered). This process continues until the test determines a test-taker's true ability level (presenting a minimum of 15 questions to all test-takers). A test concludes when the test-taker's level of accuracy meets a statistically acceptable value (in other words, when his or her performance demonstrates an acceptable level of knowledge and ability) or when the maximum number of items has been presented (in which case, the test-taker is almost certain to fail; no adaptive Novell test will present more than 25 questions to any test-taker).

Novell tests come in one format or the other—either they're form tests or they're adaptive. Thus, you must take the test in whichever format it appears; you can't choose one format over another. But if anything, it pays off even more to prepare thoroughly for an adaptive test than for a form test: The penalties for answering incorrectly are built into the test itself on an adaptive test, whereas the layout remains the same for a form test, no matter how many questions you answer incorrectly.

In the following section, you'll learn more about what Novell test questions look like and how they must be answered.

Exam Layout And Design

Some exam questions require you to select a single answer, whereas others ask you to select multiple correct answers. The following multiple-choice question requires you to select a single correct answer. Following the question is a brief summary of each potential answer and why it's either right or wrong.

Question 1

Which network class is reserved for multicast addresses?

○ a. Class A

○ b. Class B

○ c. Class C

○ d. Class D

○ e. Class E

The correct answer is d. Class D networks are reserved for multicast addresses. Class A, B, and C networks contain assignable addresses, and Class E networks are reserved for future and experimental use as well as for broadcasts. Therefore, answers a, b, c, and e are incorrect.

This sample question format corresponds closely to the Novell certification test format—the only difference on the test is that questions are not followed by answers. In the real test, to select an answer, you would position the cursor over the radio button next to the correct answer, item d. Then, you would click the mouse button to select the answer.

Let's examine a question that requires choosing multiple answers. This type of question provides checkboxes rather than radio buttons for marking all appropriate selections.

Question 2

> At which two layers of the OSI model are switches able to establish VLANs? [Choose the two best answers]
>
> ❏ a. Physical
>
> ❏ b. Data Link
>
> ❏ c. Network
>
> ❏ d. Transport

Answers b and c are correct. Depending on the type of switch used, VLANs can be established at either the Data Link or Network layer. The Physical and Transport layers are not involved in VLAN creation. Therefore, answers a and d are incorrect.

For this type of question, more than one answer is required. As far as the authors can tell (and Novell won't comment), such questions are scored as wrong unless all the required selections are chosen. In other words, a partially correct answer does not result in partial credit when the test is scored. For Question 2, you have to check the boxes next to items b and c to obtain credit for a correct answer. Notice that picking the right answers also means knowing why the other answers are wrong!

Although these two basic types of questions can appear in many forms, they constitute the foundation on which most of Novell's certification test questions rest. More complex questions include exhibits, which are usually diagrams of some kind of network or topology. These exhibit questions may use charts or network diagrams to help document a workplace scenario that you'll be asked to troubleshoot or configure. Careful attention to such exhibits is the key to success. Be prepared to toggle frequently between the exhibit and the question as you work.

Test-Taking Strategy For Form And Adaptive Tests

When it comes to either kind of Novell test—be it a form test or an adaptive test—one principle applies: Get it right the first time. You cannot elect to skip a question and move on to the next one when taking either of these types of tests. In the form test, the testing software forces you to go on to the next question, with no opportunity to skip ahead or turn back. In the adaptive test, the adaptive testing software uses your answer to the current question to select whatever question it plans to present next. In addition, you can't return to a question once you've answered it on an adaptive test, because the test software gives you only one chance to answer each question.

On an adaptive test, testing continues until the program settles into a reasonably accurate estimate of what you know and can do, taking anywhere between 15 and 25 questions. On a form test, you have to complete an entire series of questions, which usually takes an hour or longer and involves many more questions than an adaptive test (79 for Test 050-632).

The good news about adaptive tests is that if you know your stuff, you'll probably finish in 30 minutes or less; in fact, Novell never schedules more than 60 minutes for any of its adaptive tests. The bad news is that you must really, really know your stuff to do your best on an adaptive test. That's because some questions are difficult enough that you're bound to miss one or two, at a minimum, even if you do know your stuff. So the more you know, the better you'll do on an adaptive test, even accounting for the occasionally brutal questions that appear on these exams.

Of course, it's also true on a form test that you must know your stuff to do your best. But for us, the most profound difference between a form test and an adaptive test is the opportunity to cover a broader range of topics and questions on the form test, versus the randomness of the adaptive test. If the adaptive test engine happens to hit a hole in your knowledge base early on in the testing process, that can make it harder for you to pass, as the test engine probes your knowledge of this topic. On a form test, if some questions hit a hole, you can assume that other questions will appear that you'll be able to answer.

Either way, if you encounter a question on an adaptive test or a form test that you can't answer, you must guess an answer immediately. Because of the way the adaptive software works, you may have to suffer for your guess on the next question if you guess right, because you'll get a more difficult question next! On a form test, at least, a lucky guess won't cost you in terms of the difficulty of the next question (but that may still not prevent that next question from being a real skull-buster, either).

Test-Taking Basics

The most important advice about taking any test is this: Read each question carefully! Some questions may be ambiguous, whereas others use technical terminology in incredibly precise ways. Your authors have taken numerous Novell exams—both practice tests and real tests—and in nearly every instance, we've missed at least one question because we didn't read it closely or carefully enough.

Here are some suggestions on how to deal with the tendency to jump to an answer too quickly:

➤ Make sure you read every word in the question. If you find yourself jumping ahead in the question impatiently, read the question again.

➤ As you read, try to restate the question in your own terms. If you can do this, you should be able to pick the correct answer(s) much more easily.

➤ Some questions may be long and complex, to the point where they fill up more than one screen's worth of information. You might find it worthwhile to take notes on such questions and to summarize the key points in the question so you can refer to them while reading the potential answers to save yourself the effort of ping-ponging up and down the question as you read.

➤ Some questions may remind you of key points about networking terms or technologies that you might want to record for reference later in the test. Even if you can't go back to earlier questions, you can indeed go back through your notes.

Above all, try to deal with each question by thinking through what you know about the various networking technologies and protocols, and the OSI model. By reviewing what you know (and what you've written down on your information sheet), you'll often recall or understand things sufficiently to determine the answer to the questions you'll encounter on the test.

Question-Handling Strategies

Based on exams we have taken, some interesting trends have become apparent. For those questions that take only a single answer, usually two or three of the answers will be obviously incorrect, and two of the answers will be plausible—of course, only one can be correct. Unless the answer leaps out at you (if it does, reread the question to look for a trick; sometimes those are the ones you're most likely to get wrong), begin the process of answering by eliminating those answers that are most obviously wrong.

Things to look for in obviously wrong answers include spurious utility names and terminology you've never seen. If you've done your homework for an exam, no valid information should be completely new to you. In that case, unfamiliar or bizarre terminology probably indicates a totally bogus answer. In fact, recognizing unlikely answers is probably the most significant way in which preparation pays off at test-taking time!

Mastering The Inner Game

In the final analysis, knowledge breeds confidence, and confidence breeds success. If you study the materials in this book carefully and review all the practice questions at the end of each chapter, you should become aware of those areas where additional learning and study are required.

Next, follow up by reading some or all of the materials recommended in the "Need To Know More?" section at the end of each chapter. The idea is to become familiar enough with the concepts and situations you find in the sample questions that you can reason your way through similar situations on a real test. If you know the material, you have every right to be confident that you can pass the test.

You should also visit (and print or download) the Test Objectives page for Course 565, "Networking Technologies" (**education.novell.com/testinfo/objectives/565tobj.htm**). Here, you'll find a list of 46 specific test objectives that will help guide your study of all the topics and technologies that Novell thinks are relevant to the 050-632 test. In fact, you can use this as a kind of road map to help guide your initial studying and to help you focus your efforts as you gear up to take your practice test(s)—and then, for the real thing when you're ready.

After you've worked your way through the book and the Test Objectives, take the practice test in Chapter 20. This will provide a reality check and help you identify areas to study further. Make sure you follow up and review materials related to the questions you miss on any practice test before scheduling a real test. Only when you've covered all the ground and feel comfortable with the whole scope of the practice test should you take a real one.

If you take the practice test and don't score at least 77.5 percent correct, you'll want to practice further. Novell provides free practice tests on its "The Guide" CD. To obtain this CD, you must contact a local NetWare Authorized Education Center (NAEC) and request that one be sent to you. For more information on how to obtain this CD, you can use the Training Locator on the Novell certification pages at **education.novell.com** to locate the NAEC(s) nearest you.

Armed with the information in this book and with the determination to augment your knowledge, you should be able to pass the "Networking Technologies" test. However, you need to work at it, or you'll spend the exam fee more than once before you finally pass. If you prepare seriously, you should do well. Good luck!

Additional Resources

A good source of information about Novell certification tests comes from Novell itself. Because its products and technologies—and the tests that go with them—change frequently, the best place to go for test-related information is online.

If you haven't already visited the Novell Education site, do so right now. The Novell Education home page resides at **education.novell.com** (see Figure 1.1).

> *Note: This page might not be there by the time you read this, or it may be replaced by something new and different, because things change on the Novell site. Should this happen, please read the sidebar titled "Coping With Change On The Web."*

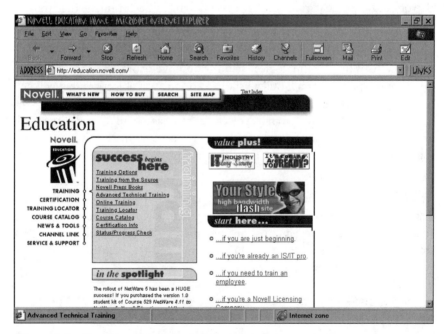

Figure 1.1   The Novell Education home page.

The menu options on the left side of the home page point to the most important sources of information in these pages. Here are some suggestions of what
to check out:

➤ **Training** Use this link to locate an NAEC in your vicinity, to learn
more about available training, or to request The Guide CD (which
includes practice tests, among other materials).

➤ **Certification** This option is the ultimate source of all information about
the various Novell certifications. Use this menu entry to find a list of the
courses and related tests, including test objectives, test data, a testing
FAQ (a list of frequently asked questions about Novell's testing policies,
strategies, and requirements), and more.

➤ **News & Tools** Check this item to get news about new tests, updates to
existing tests, retirement of obsolete tests, and information about
software and practice tests.

These are just the high points of what's available on the Novell Education
pages. As you browse through them—and we strongly recommend that you
do—you'll probably find other informational tidbits mentioned that are every
bit as interesting and compelling.

The following vendors offer practice tests for Novell certification topics:

➤ www.certify.com is the Cyber Pass Web site. This company makes
"CNEQuizr."

➤ www.stsware.com is the Self Test Software Web site. This company
makes practice tests for most of the Novell curriculum.

➤ www.bfq.com is the Beach Front Quizzer Web site. This company
makes practice tests for most of the Novell curriculum.

➤ www.syngress.com is the Syngress Software Web site. This company has
a set of NetWare 5 practice exams in the works. Visit the Web site for
more information.

You can find still more sources of practice exams on the Internet if you're willing to spend some time using your favorite search engines.

Here's the bottom line about testing readiness: If you don't score 77.5 percent
or better on the practice test in this book, you'll probably be well served by
buying one or more additional practice tests to help get you ready for the real
thing. It may even be cheaper than taking the Novell test more than once, and
it will certainly increase the pool of potential questions to use as practice.

Coping With Change On The Web

Sooner or later, all the information we've shared with you about the Novell Education pages and the other Web-based resources mentioned throughout the rest of this book will go stale or be replaced by newer information. In some cases, the URLs you find here might lead you to their replacements; in other cases, the URLs will go nowhere, leaving you with the dreaded "404 File not found" error message. When that happens, don't give up.

There's always a way to find what you want on the Web if you're willing to invest some time and energy. Most large or complex Web sites—and Novell's qualifies on both counts—offer a search engine. On all of Novell's Web pages, a Search button appears along the top edge of the page. As long as you can get to Novell's Web site (it should stay at **www.novell.com** for a long time), use this tool to help you find what you need.

The more focused you can make a search request, the more likely the results will include information you can use. For example, you can search for the string

```
training AND certification
```

to produce a lot of data about the subject in general, but if you're looking for the objectives for Test 050-632, "Networking Technologies," you'll be more likely to get there quickly if you use a search string similar to the following:

```
050-632 AND objectives
```

Also, feel free to use general search tools—such as **www.search.com**, **www.altavista.com**, and **www.excite.com**—to look for related information. Although Novell offers great information about its certification tests online, there are plenty of third-party sources of information and assistance that need not follow Novell's party line. Therefore, if you can't find something where the book says it lives, start looking around. If worse comes to worst, you can always email us. We just might have a clue.

Networking
And The OSI Model

Terms you'll need to understand:

√ Protocol

√ Physical topology

√ Transmission media

√ Frame

√ Header

√ Logical topology

√ Connectionless

√ Connection oriented

√ Nonreliable

√ Reliable

√ Datagram

Techniques you'll need to master:

√ Explaining the function of and need for networking protocols

√ Understanding the OSI reference model

√ Listing the major networking tasks performed at each layer of the OSI reference model

√ Comparing and contrasting the characteristics of physical and logical topologies employed in computer networks

√ Mapping functions of common network connectivity devices to specific layers of the OSI reference model

This chapter introduces you to the Open Systems Interconnection (OSI) reference model for networking. The OSI reference model, or OSI model, is used as the conceptual framework for identifying and organizing the basic tasks associated with computer networking. It also serves as the central reference for understanding the relationship between the basic networking tasks and the standards and protocols that define how they are implemented.

Networking Standards And The OSI Model

Networking standards provide the infrastructure that enables network communication and allows the sharing of resources among groups of networked computers. The standards, applicable to the entire range of networking tasks, are specified by the rules (called *protocols*) and families of rules (called *protocol suites*) that are implemented in hardware and software designed to accomplish each networking task.

The OSI model, which is based on the concept of promoting interoperability between heterogeneous systems, was developed by the International Standards Organization (ISO) as a tool to better the understanding of how networking and data communication protocols work. It provides a "blueprint-level" set of guidelines for the development of standards that fulfill the growing need for cross-platform interoperability. It also gives vendors and developers a common point of reference as they work to produce new network applications and products.

The OSI model also serves as the point of reference for all topics covered in this book. A working familiarity with the model and how it can be used will prove to be a valuable resource as you add to your understanding of networking principles.

A Layered Approach

The OSI model represents networking with seven groups of functionally related networking tasks. The groups appear in the model as named layers arranged vertically in a hierarchy. In the hierarchy, tasks performed in upper layers are dependent on the tasks in the lower layers for their operation. A layer's name is based on the general level of functionality that can be associated with any of the tasks in that layer.

The following list shows the layers in the OSI model, arranged in order from top to bottom:

➤ Application

➤ Presentation

➤ Session

➤ Transport

➤ Network

➤ Data Link

➤ Physical

 The mnemonic "(P)lease (D)o (N)ot (T)hrow (S)ausage (P)izza (A)way" provides an easy way to recall the names and order of the seven layers. It's based on the layer names listed from the bottom (Physical layer) of the model to the top (Application layer).

In the model, communication within the layered stack occurs only between adjacent layers in the form of service requests directed to the layer below, and service responses directed to the layer above through service ports or sockets. The requests and responses accompany inbound and outbound data as it's moved vertically up or down the stack.

Communication across the network occurs between processes operating within peer layers on other networked entities. The communication is encapsulated in a protocol-specific header that's constructed by a layer process and attached to the front of each data transmission. Additional protocol headers are appended at each lower layer as outbound data is moved downward through the stack. Because each header is protocol specific, the information it contains can only be interpreted by a peer process (the same networking task) using the same protocol. The rest of the transmission—without the header—is treated by each process as pure data. When a peer stack receives a data transmission, the headers are read and removed by the peer processes at each layer, in order, as the data moves up the stack. The accompanying data is handled along the way in accordance with the instructions specified in each header.

Layer Associated Tasks

Networking tasks are associated with specific layers of the OSI model. At some of the layers, the tasks provide a "class of service" for the communication they handle. The communication service classes are broadly categorized as either *connection oriented* or *connectionless*, and *reliable* or *nonreliable*. More information on service classes is included in later discussions of individual protocols.

You need to be able to readily associate specific network tasks with individual OSI layers. In addition, you should know a key word or words to associate with each layer. In the Practice Questions sections, you'll find that key words often provide a link to the correct choice when you're faced with the dilemma of selecting the *best* answer when two or more choices appear to be correct.

Tasks at several layers are dependant on addresses used to identify devices, networks, and/or network services. You need to be familiar with how these addresses are used, the devices that use them, and the layers to associate with their use.

The three address levels are summarized as follows:

➤ **Physical address** Also called the node address, hardware address, NIC address, or MAC address, this address uniquely identifies a device on the network. Typically, the manufacturer encodes the physical address into the chipset of a network board.

➤ **Network address** An administratively assigned (logical) address that identifies the network segment to which a device is connected.

➤ **Service address** An assigned (logical) number that identifies the port or socket used by a specific service on a service provider (server).

Note: A network board is also called a network interface card (NIC), network adaptor, network card, and network interface board. Novell uses the term network board most often. However, the network board vendors usually call it a NIC.

The following sections provide you with a brief summary of tasks to associate with each OSI layer; they include key words, service classes, and address information where applicable.

The Physical Layers

Protocols at this layer define the following:

➤ The encoding and timing of *bit* transmissions

➤ The transmission media, which is the mechanical and electrical specifications for cable, wire, repeaters, and so on

➤ The physical topology, or structural layout, of the network

Data at this level is a bit stream; therefore, the concepts of communication service class and addressing do not apply.

The key word to associate with the Physical layer is *bits*.

The Data Link Layer

Protocols for tasks at this layer define the following:

➤ How bits sent from the Physical layer are arranged into logical groups, called *frames*.

➤ The layout and type of control information (source and destination address, frame length, upper-layer protocol information, and so on) that's attached to the front of each frame as a frame header.

The key word to associate with the Data Link layer is *frames*.

The Data Link layer is divided into two functional sublayers: the Media Access Control (MAC) sublayer and the Logical Link Control (LLC) sublayer. The MAC sublayer lies between the Physical layer and the LLC sublayer. These two sublayers are discussed in the following sections.

Understanding The MAC Sublayer

The processes operating at the MAC sublayer follow rules that define methods for accessing the transmission media (media access methods) and moving data on the physical topology (logical topology). The physical address (an ID unique to a device on the network) is incorporated into the Data Link frame header and is used to identify the source and destination devices for each frame of data.

The key terms to associate with the MAC sublayer are *media access*, *logical topology*, and *physical address*.

Understanding The LLC Sublayer

Protocols for tasks at the LLC sublayer define the following:

➤ **Connection services** Whether a process uses connection-oriented or connectionless services

Typically, in a local area network (LAN) environment, Data Link layer processes are connectionless and nonreliable. However, many of the older wide area network (WAN) protocols are connection oriented, and some newer WAN protocols (such as Frame Relay and ATM) define connection-oriented and reliable services.

➤ **Error control (reliability)** Whether protocols include rules for handling missing frames, retransmission of frames, flow control, and so on

➤ **Frame synchronization** How the data is framed and where each frame starts and ends

The Network Layer

Protocols at the Network layer define the following:

➤ How messages from upper layers are organized into datagrams

➤ How datagrams are routed to their proper destination through the internetwork

Protocols at the Network layer typically define a connectionless, nonreliable service, called a *datagram service*, that has a low overhead and is dependent on upper-layer processes to supply reliability when needed.

Key words to associate with the Network layer are *datagrams* and *routing*.

The Transport Layer

Transport layer protocols define processes that deal with end-to-end control and error checking to determine whether all packets of data have arrived. Connection services at this layer are connection oriented and reliable.

The key term to associate with the Transport layer is *reliability*.

The Session, Presentation, And Application Layers

Connection services above the Network layer are generally connection oriented and reliable.

The Session Layer

The Session layer includes processes that establish, maintain, and release connections.

The best term to associate with the Session Layer is *dialog*.

The Presentation Layer

The Presentation layer processes are the only network processes that actually transform data. The transformation process may involve formatting, compressing, translating, and/or encrypting data.

The best term to associate with the Presentation Layer is *format*.

The Application Layer

Shared services, including email, file and print services, and file format translation, are defined by the protocols at this layer.

Associate the term *shared* with the Application layer.

Network Topologies

Network topology refers to the physical layout of the network transmission media as well as its attached nodes (physical topology) and the methods used to place, retrieve, and move data on the media (logical topology). Common physical and logical topologies in current use are summarized in the following lists.

The five physical topologies are:

➤ **Bus** Uses a single long cable to which all networked devices are attached

➤ **Cellular** Uses wireless media to connect networked devices to a central hub in a star-like configuration

➤ **Mesh** Uses point-to-point connections to attach every device to every other device on the network

➤ **Ring** Uses a series of point-to-point connections to connect all devices in a closed loop

➤ **Star** Uses one or more central hubs to which all networked devices are attached

The two logical topologies are:

➤ **Bus** Signals generated are propagated in all directions simultaneously to all devices on the network, regardless of the intended recipient.

➤ **Ring** Signals generated travel a specific path from station to station in one direction, generally counterclockwise.

Network Connectivity Devices And The OSI Model

Network components that connect devices to the network and connect networks together are generally classified as *network connectivity devices*. These devices operate under instructions placed in the frame header by a process operating at a single layer of the OSI model. The following sections provide a summary of the connectivity devices with which you need to be familiar. Notice that each type of device is associated with a specific layer of the OSI model.

Physical Layer Devices

Connectivity devices operating at the Physical layer are used to extend the network. Repeaters and active hubs do this by regenerating or repeating all received transmissions to all other ports on the device. Because repeaters and active hubs do this on a purely mechanical level, they're considered Physical layer devices.

Data Link Layer Devices

Devices that provide connectivity at the Data Link layer are capable of providing frame-filtering functions based on physical address information contained in the Data Link header. The following list summarizes the characteristics of three Data Link layer devices:

➤ **Network boards** Network boards, in conjunction with their drivers, enter their own hardware address as the source address in the Data Link header of every frame they transmit. In addition, they're able to accept or reject incoming frames based on the destination address field entries in the headers of the incoming frames.

➤ **Bridges** Bridges connect LAN segments that use the same communication protocol stack. The bridge creates and maintains a table that maps all devices on the network to a specific LAN segment directly connected to one of its ports. Data Link header information is used to build the table by associating source and destination addresses of incoming frames with the bridge's ports.

➤ **Switches** A switch chooses a path or circuit for sending data to its destination based on Data Link header information. It forwards data to one of its ports, where the data is then directed to the correct destination device. Switches function as either circuit switches or packet switches:

   ➤ **Circuit switches** Circuit switches use common media to set up a dedicated path that is used by two or more parties for the duration of the connection. A different switched path may be used to connect a different set of parties or even the same parties at another time.

   ➤ **Packet switches** Packet switches are typically used in LANs to split messages into packets and direct the packets along a path that may vary over the duration of the connection. Because the length of the paths traversed by different packets may vary as the actual path changes, it's possible for packets to arrive at the destination out of order. The packet switch functions include the collection, reorder, and reassembly of the packets into the original message at the destination.

Network Layer Devices

Routers are the primary Network layer connectivity devices. They use network address information located in the Network layer header to direct data to a particular network. Routers reference information maintained in dynamically or administratively created tables that map the address of every known network to one of the router's ports. Route distance or cost, based on the table information, is used to determine the direction that data is forwarded.

Gateways are devices that translate between the protocol stacks used in different networking platforms. Although they can operate at the Network layer and higher, they are generally associated with the Network layer.

Practice Questions

Question 1

> At which OSI layer would you expect data compression and decompression to occur?
>
> ○ a. Physical layer
>
> ○ b. Data Link layer
>
> ○ c. Presentation layer
>
> ○ d. Application layer

The correct answer is c because data transformation occurs at the Presentation layer only. Answers a, b, and d are incorrect.

Question 2

> Which of the following connectivity devices use information in the Data Link header to accomplish their tasks? [Choose the two best answers]
>
> ❏ a. Router
>
> ❏ b. Network board
>
> ❏ c. Active hub
>
> ❏ d. Bridge

The correct answers are b and d. Network boards insert their hardware address in the source address fields of the Data Link header for every frame they transmit. Therefore, answer b is correct. Bridges associate the hardware address contained in the source address field of the Data Link header with the port that incoming frames arrived on. Therefore, answer d is correct. Answer a is incorrect because routers are Network layer devices and as such do not have access to Data Link headers. Active hubs, operating at the Physical layer, deal with a bit stream that is not organized into logical frames. Therefore, answer c is incorrect.

Question 3

> Which physical topology uses point-to-point connections to attach every device to every other device on the network?
>
> ○ a. Bus
>
> ○ b. Mesh
>
> ○ c. Ring
>
> ○ d. Cellular

The correct answer is b. In a mesh topology, every device is directly connected to every other device via a point-to-point connection. Both the bus and cellular topologies use multipoint connections. Therefore, answers a and d are incorrect. A ring topology uses point-to-point connections to attach a device to the devices on either side, not to every other device. Therefore, answer c is incorrect.

Question 4

> Which of the following statements concerning the relationships between layer processes is not true?
>
> ○ a. Network layer processes depend on Data Link layer processes for their operation.
>
> ○ b. Network layer processes handle service requests made by the Data Link layer.
>
> ○ c. Transport layer processes request Network layer services.
>
> ○ d. Transport layer processes provide services to the Session layer.

The correct answer is b. The relationship between layers requires that the processes in a layer request services from the layer below, and provide services to the layer(s) above. The statement in answer b does not support this relationship and is therefore the correct choice. The statements in a, c, and d support the relationship. Therefore a, c, and d are incorrect.

Question 5

> End-to-end control and error-checking tasks are commonly asso-
> ciated with which OSI layer?
>
> ○ a.   Network layer
>
> ○ b.   Data Link layer
>
> ○ c.   Transport layer
>
> ○ d.   Physical layer

The correct answer is c. The Transport layer processes perform tasks associated with ensuring reliability. Because end-to-end control and error checking imply connection-oriented and reliable service, answer c is correct. Layers below the Transport layer are generally characterized as connectionless and unreliable. Therefore, answers a, b, and d are incorrect.

Question 6

> Which of the following sequences correctly represents the OSI
> layer relationships from bottom to top?
>
> ○ a.   Network layer-Transport layer-Session layer
>
> ○ b.   Physical layer-Data Link layer-MAC layer
>
> ○ c.   Transport layer-Network layer-Data Link layer
>
> ○ d.   Physical layer-MAC sublayer-Data Link layer

The correct answer is a. The correct layer sequence from bottom to top is Physical, Data Link, Network, Transport, Session, Presentation, Application. The only answer that matches this sequence is a. Therefore, answers b, c, and d are incorrect.

Question 7

> Which of the following connectivity devices is used to extend a
> network on a purely mechanical basis?
>
> O a. Repeater
>
> O b. Router
>
> O c. Switch
>
> O d. Bridge

The correct answer is a. Repeaters operate at the Physical layer on a purely
mechanical basis. The devices in answers b, c, and d are capable of recognizing
addresses and require some intelligence. Therefore, answers b, c, and d are
incorrect.

Question 8

> At which layer of the OSI model do you find connection-oriented
> services for older WAN protocols?
>
> O a. Network layer
>
> O b. Data Link layer
>
> O c. Transport layer
>
> O d. Physical layer

The correct answer is b. Although most LAN protocols at the Data Link layer
are connectionless, the older WAN protocols and some of the newer WAN
protocols are connection oriented and reliable. Therefore, answers a, c, and d
are incorrect.

Question 9

> Which of the following connectivity devices creates and maintains a table that maps all devices on the network to a specific LAN segment directly connected to one of its ports?
>
> ○ a. Network board
>
> ○ b. Active hub
>
> ○ c. Router
>
> ○ d. Bridge

The correct answer is d. This is a trick question because answers c and d may both appear to be correct if you don't notice that the question refers to a single network and not a group of networks. Both bridges and routers build and maintain tables, but bridges connect LAN segments on a network together, whereas routers connect networks to networks. Therefore, answer c is incorrect. Answers a and b are incorrect because neither of these devices builds or maintains tables.

Need To Know More?

 Lewis, Chris. *Cisco TCP/IP Routing Professional Reference, 2nd Edition.* McGraw-Hill. New York, 1998. ISBN: 0-07-041130-1. Chapter 2 of this book provides a very good overview of the OSI reference model and the Department of Defense (DoD) networking model.

 Parker, Timothy. *Teach Yourself TCP/IP in 14 Days, 2nd Edition.* Sams Publishing. Indianapolis, IN, 1998. ISBN: 0-672-30885-1. Chapter 1 includes additional information on the topics of standards and protocols that is pertinent to this chapter.

 www.garlic.com/~lynn/rfcietff.htm contains everything you need to know about protocols and standards. This is a very detailed site, with information on what RFCs are and links to RFC-related sites. It includes both frames and no-frames versions, with RFCs listed by author, date, category, and number. Search by keyword.

Lower-Layer Networking Protocols And The OSI Model

Terms you'll need to understand:

- √ Institute of Electrical and Electronics Engineers (IEEE)
- √ IEEE 802.x
- √ Thicknet
- √ Thinnet
- √ Autonomous Unit Interface (AUI)
- √ Media Independent Interface (MII)
- √ AutoNegotiation
- √ Token
- √ Beaconing
- √ Hierarchical star topology
- √ Fiber Distributed Data Interface (FDDI)

Techniques you'll need to master:

- √ Identifying 802.x standards from the IEEE used in computer networks today
- √ Understanding basic design rules for networks using the IEEE 802.3 standard
- √ Explaining the differences in design, access procedures, connectivity devices, and transmission media for IEEE 802.3u
- √ Understanding basic design rules for networks using the IEEE 802.5 standard, along with the media access procedures, transmission media, and connectivity devices used
- √ Understanding the basic design rules for FDDI networks, including the media access procedures, transmission media, and connectivity devices used

The world of networking owes its success to the development of standards, particularly those of the Institute of Electrical and Electronics Engineers (IEEE). The IEEE first shouldered the task of defining LAN standards for the Physical and Data Link layers of the Open Systems Interconnection (OSI) model in February 1980.

In this chapter, you'll learn about the lower-layer networking protocols, their various design rules, access procedures, connectivity devices, and transmission media.

IEEE 802.x Series

Originally, there was to be a single local area network (LAN) standard, ranging from 1 to 20MHz. Divided into a Physical layer (PHY), Media Access Control (MAC), and Higher Level interface (HILI), the standard was to support Ethernet (developed in 1973) as well as bus topologies. A token access method was added by the end of that year. At the end of 1981, there were three MACs defined: Carrier Sense Multiple Access with Collision Detection (CSMA/CD; 802.3), Token Passing Bus (802.4), and Token Ring (802.5). In this chapter, you'll learn about CSMA/CD and Token Ring.

The goal has always been to provide a common upper interface to the Logical Link Control (LLC) sublayer, common media interfaces, and common data framing elements. Increased data rates are now part of the standard. LANs have now grown to metropolitan area networks (MANs), and the IEEE standards process covers all. During your research, you may see references to the IEEE 802/LMSC, which is a newer name for the LAN/MAN Standards Committee.

Standards were added to support different, new upper-layer protocols used on different types of networks. One standard, 802.10, adds a framework for security and encryption. Figure 3.1 takes the seven-layer OSI model and matches it to the various 802.x standards.

This section concentrates primarily on 802.3 and 802.5, but you should have a general understanding of all the current IEEE 802.x protocols. The following list provides a quick overview of all relevant IEEE 802.x protocols:

➤ **IEEE 802.1** Defines the Physical and Data Link layer standards necessary for one network device to communicate with another IEEE 802 LAN device on a different LAN or wide area network (WAN).

➤ **IEEE 802.2** The LLC sublayer is used primarily with 802.3, 802.4, 802.5, and 802.6 networks. This protocol adds header fields to each frame to identify which upper-layer protocol is used inside the frame.

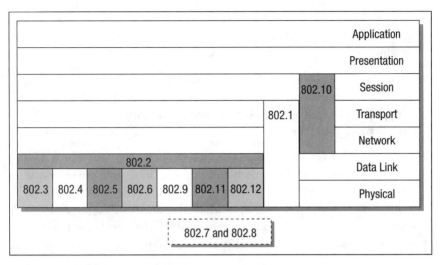

Figure 3.1   The 802.x protocols mapped to the OSI model.

➤ **IEEE 802.3** This is commonly called Ethernet, but in reality it describes the CSMA/CD protocol. 802.3 includes a variety of Physical layer options and signaling types. 802.3 covers baseband and broadband, multiple media types (for example, coax, unshielded twisted pair, and fiber), multiple physical topologies (bus or star), and data rates from 2Mbps to as high as 10Gbps.

➤ **IEEE 802.4** The Token Passing Bus protocol was designed for the special needs of factory automation but has never seen wide-scale implementation. This protocol defines a physical bus network carrying tokens similar to token ring. Physical media supported includes baseband, broadband, optical fiber, and even the same 75 ohm cable used by cable TV installations.

➤ **IEEE 802.5** Based on IBM's Token-Ring specifications, 802.5 employs a token-passing media access scheme in which a token is passed sequentially from one connected node to another at speeds of 1, 4, or 16Mbps. The IEEE 802.5 protocol supports a variety of media.

➤ **IEEE 802.6** Distributed Queue Dual Bus (DQDB) data transfer technology was designed to support both synchronous and asynchronous traffic for voice, video, and data communications.

➤ **IEEE 802.7** The broadband communications working group for IEEE 802.7 defined the design, installation, and test parameters for broadband use and is currently inactive.

➤ **IEEE 802.8** The Fiber Optic Technical Advisory Group (TAG) supports other 802 working groups on issues concerning fiber-optic technology and emerging standards.

➤ **IEEE 802.9** Isochronous Ethernet (IsoEnet) hopes to integrate voice and data transmissions over the same protocol. One difficulty involves supporting both sporadic and patterned traffic while maintaining voice quality and data transmission speed.

➤ **IEEE 802.10** Officially called the "Standards for Interoperable LAN/ MAN Security (SILS) Working Group," 802.10 defines a framework for secure data exchange with encryption across various services, protocols, data formats, and interfaces. Managing and distributing encryption key information is a critical component of 802.10. The key standard is separate from any particular encryption algorithm or transmission process.

➤ **IEEE 802.11** This protocol defines the standards for LANs over radio waves and light beams, supporting various spread-spectrum wireless and infrared devices.

➤ **IEEE 802.12** Demand contention is the label used by the IEEE for 802.12, which is a 100Mbps physical star topology first called 100VG-AnyLAN. Planned to support both Ethernet and token ring frame types, 802.12 hubs will grant transmission rights to the network after nodes make a request. Collisions are avoided by allowing the highest priority traffic through the network first.

Note: The IEEE Web site (www.ieee.org) also lists 802.13 as reserved, 802.14 for the cable modem working group, and two additional study groups on quality of service flow control and broadband wireless access.

IEEE 802.3 And Ethernet Network Design

Although many people assume 802.3 is Ethernet, this is technically inaccurate. Ethernet was developed first and designed to be a simple, low-overhead LAN architecture. IEEE 802.3 follows the same principles and specifies the standards for the Physical and Data Link layers of the OSI model, along with 802.2. Figure 3.2 shows where each protocol stacks up against the OSI model.

Physical Layer Standards

IEEE 802.3 has so many incarnations that there's a special 802.3 naming sequence that uses a three-part naming convention. First is a number representing

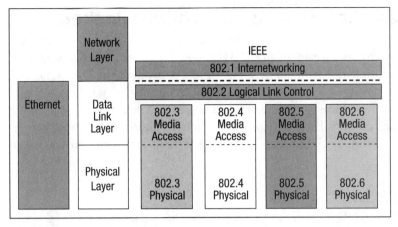

Figure 3.2 The combination of 802.2 and 802.3 matches well against the original Ethernet specification.

megabits per second. Next is *Base* for baseband or *Broad* for broadband. Last is either a distance indicator or some special designator used to cover unusual cases. The first three-part name to become truly popular was 10BaseT for unshielded twisted-pair (UTP) wiring. Table 3.1 shows the original Ethernet specifications along with the most popular 802.3 specifications.

This table stops at 10Mbps, but a variety of protocol enhancements are pushing the speed limit far into the gigabit range. Notice that 10Base5 matches up most closely to the earlier Ethernet standard; this is *thicknet* in popular parlance. 10Base2 uses coax cable, but it's the light coax referred to as *thinnet* in the industry. Thinnet allows the use of early wiring concentrators, which paved the way for the design changes made with 10BaseT. These physical differences are explained in the following sections. Only those who fought thicknet truly appreciate the advantages of twisted-pair Ethernet that appeared with 10BaseT.

Table 3.1 Popular 802.3 versions compared to Ethernet.					
Parameters	**Ethernet**	**10Base2**	**10Base5**	**10BaseF**	**10BaseT**
Topology	Bus	Bus	Bus	Star	Star
Media	50 ohm thick coax	50 ohm thin coax	50 ohm thick coax	Fiber	UTP
Data rate (Mbps)	10	10	10	10	10
Meters per segment	500	185	500	500-2,000	100

Media Access And Controlling Packets

The acronym CSMA/CD looks formidable, but it describes exactly what happens on the physical cable of an 802.3 (Ethernet) network. Network developers knew multiple nodes would be accessing the network at the same time, and they provided no mechanism to tell nodes when the network was clear. CSMA/CD is philosophically opposite of token ring, which does tell the nodes when they can transmit. Breaking down the acronym into its three parts, Carrier Sense, Multiple Access, and Collision Detection, makes the process much clearer.

Carrier Sense

Nodes on an 802.3 network that need to transmit a packet "listen" to the network cabling, monitoring the network for a carrier signal. This signal is nothing more than electrical impulses that build a series of 1s and 0s to form a packet. If a transmit-ready node "senses" another transmission on the network, it delays for a random number of milliseconds and listens again. This is where *carrier sense* comes from.

Multiple Access

If no signals are detected on the cable, the node transmits. However, it's common for two or more nodes to start transmitting at the same time, or one node to start transmitting before the signal from an earlier transmission reaches the second sending node. CSMA/CD allows multiple nodes to access the cable simultaneously, hence *multiple access*.

Collision Detection

Although *collision* sounds like physical packets are banging into each other like cars on a freeway, it actually refers to two or more electrical signals interfering with each other, garbling both. When a sending node detects this condition, it transmits a series of packets in a pattern called a *jam signal* to ensure that all nodes on the network are aware of the collision. Once the *collision detection* algorithm is activated, all competing nodes defer and wait a random number of milliseconds before repeating their transmission.

Ethernet is not loaded down with collisions that choke bandwidth. These packet collisions and retries happen in fractions of a second and the lower-level protocols handle the details of collision detection and retransmission. The higher-level protocols and applications do not get involved or delayed by the relatively few collisions that occur, even on large Ethernet networks.

Physical Topologies

Ethernet specifies a linear bus topology, using thick or thin coax cable. Each end of the coax cable is terminated with a 50 ohm resistor. Nodes attach by connecting directly to the coax cable. Different methods are used to connect to thick coax and thin coax.

Also within the IEEE 802.3 specifications is support for physical topologies based on connected hubs with nodes attached directly to the hubs. This *hierarchical star* physical topology is most commonly implemented with the 10BaseT products using UTP wiring.

Logical Topologies

IEEE 802.3 Ethernet always specifies a logical bus topology. Even the physical star topologies are electrically a bus inside the wiring concentrators and hubs.

 Remember that the logical topology refers to the pattern of the data movement (path) across the media, whereas physical topology refers to the physical layout of the network media.

Ethernet Rules For Coaxial Cable

Ethernet and the IEEE 802.3 specifications were developed using coaxial cable for transmission. Although coax is well shielded and allows fairly lengthy networks, there are some disadvantages to coax networks, which is why UTP has become the cabling of choice for most networks.

10Base5

The original network backbone, 10Base5, uses thick coax (RG-8) cable. It's commonly called *Thick Ethernet* or just *thicknet*. The cable is often bright yellow and looks like a water hose. A 50 ohm resistor must terminate each end of the coax.

Devices connect to the thick coax cable by way of large external Ethernet transceivers clamped directly to the coax cable. The transceiver uses a *vampire tap*, so named for the two sharp points that pierce the thick coax layers of insulation to reach the copper conductor at the center of the cable. A thick drop cable connects Attachment Unit Interface (AUI) 15-pin sockets on the transceiver and network board. Figure 3.3 shows the tap, transceiver, AUI plug, and drop cable. The network board must be set to use the external transceiver, so the 15-pin AUI plug is activated.

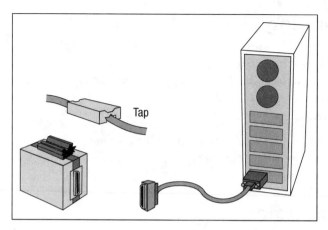

Figure 3.3 Thick coax Ethernet components.

Here are the critical thick Ethernet numbers to remember:

➤ **1** The number of grounds required per segment

➤ **2.5 meters (8 feet)** Minimum distance between taps on the thick coax

➤ **3** Maximum number of populated segments (with devices attached)

➤ **5 meters (16 feet)** Maximum drop cable length between tap and node

➤ **50** The number of ohms of the resistors at each end of the cable

➤ **100** The number of devices per segment, including repeaters

➤ **500 meters (1,640 feet)** The maximum segment length

➤ **1,500 meters (4,920 feet)** Maximum length of the trunk segment

Thicknet was the media choice for many large networks in the early days of LANs; however, thicknet has several disadvantages:

➤ It has distance restrictions, especially between the backbone and the nodes.

➤ Cable is stiff, inflexible, hard to use, and expensive.

➤ It's difficult to move, change, and add to it.

10Base2

Because thin Ethernet, or just thinnet, uses much thinner and less expensive RG-58 A/U or C/U cabling, it's easier to work with than thicknet. However, thinnet is still not as convenient as UTP wiring, and coax of any kind is rarely used in new installations.

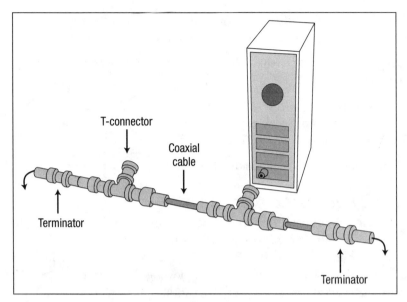

Figure 3.4 Thin Ethernet components.

Figure 3.4 shows the differences between thinnet and the thicknet shown in Figure 3.3. Notice the need for the cable to connect directly to the network board through a T-connector rather than a drop cable. The transceiver is included on the network board, so it must be configured to use the internal transceiver.

Thinnet is much more office friendly than thicknet. It helped ignite the growth of PC LANs. Here are the numbers for 10Base2:

➤ **.5 meters (1.5 feet)** Minimum distance between T-connectors

➤ **1** The number of necessary electrical grounds per segment

➤ **3** Maximum number of populated segments (segments with nodes attached)

➤ **30** Maximum number of nodes per segment

➤ **50** The number of ohms for the terminator required on each end of the cable

➤ **185 meters (1,000 feet)** Maximum segment length

➤ **555 meters (1,818 feet)** Maximum length of a trunk segment

Thinnet is a big improvement over thicknet, but there are still problems. Many customers have thinnet networks, and this cabling system causes problems in the following areas:

➤ Bringing the cable both to and from every connection requires two connectors in each wall, or at best a loop of cable to every system.

➤ Drop cables are not allowed. The T-connector must be attached directly to every node.

➤ Cables twist, bend, and loosen connectors, causing shorts that stop all network traffic. Any break or short in the cable anywhere on the network stops all traffic on that segment.

➤ Thinnet makes it difficult to add, move, and change network nodes.

The 5-4-3 Rule For Coax Ethernet

The CSMA/CD protocol operates on the assumption that all nodes on the network receive noise-free transmissions from any sending node almost simultaneously. This means that a sending station will always detect a collision if one occurs during the carrier sense period following the transmission, even if the collision occurs at the far end of the network. In reality, because both distance and signal regeneration through repeaters introduce signal latencies, restrictions must be placed on the size of the network to ensure that collisions do not go undetected. In addition, each connection to the media introduces some signal noise due to reflection of part of the signal back onto the media when the impedance boundary at the point of attachment is encountered.

You can think of each T-connector as producing a slight echo that alone is not significant, but in large enough numbers makes a signal too noisy to be read. The 5-4-3 rule defines the media limits that ensure proper operation of 802.3 CSMA/CD on coaxial cable. The rule limits a single network to:

➤ 5 Maximum cable segments per network

➤ 4 Maximum number of repeaters between the segments

➤ 3 Maximum number of segments that can be fully populated

Ethernet Rules For UTP Cable

10BaseT is the most common UTP Ethernet implementation. 1Base5 is an earlier version of UTP Ethernet, with speeds of 1Mbps running up to 250 meters per segment. 10BaseT has a shorter segment distance (100 meters) but runs at the Ethernet standard 10Mbps.

UTP cabling looks like, and is modeled after, telephone wire. Unlike home telephone jacks that use four-wire RJ-11 connectors, 10BaseT uses eight-wire (four pairs) RJ-45 connectors. The size is the only major difference; both plug into wall jacks and release in the same manner.

UTP Ethernet's physical topology is the hierarchical star, often called simply *star*. A powered wiring hub (concentrator) has a series of RJ-45 connectors. One or more patch-cable connections link this hub to other hubs, resulting in the string-of-stars hierarchical topology. End nodes are connected directly to the hubs.

Small networks may have an eight-port hub with UTP patch cables running to several workstations. Large networks will have a continuous network of hubs, patch panels, punch-down blocks, and wall jacks to connect all the network devices. Figure 3.5 shows the components of a large network.

Smaller networks may not need a separate patch panel and will connect from the punch-down block directly to the hub. Adding, moving, and removing connections with 10BaseT is as simple as plugging in a patch cable between the computer and wall jack, and from the punch-down block to the hub.

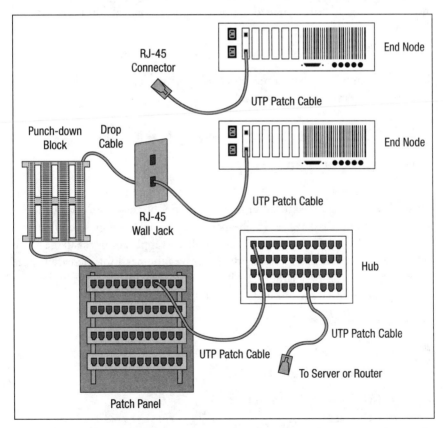

Figure 3.5   End node to wall jack to punch-down block to patch panel to hub is a common scenario for 10BaseT networks.

10BaseT

10BaseT uses the same 10Mbps Ethernet speed as coax-based Ethernet. The decreased distance per 100-meter segment is less of a problem in most office situations than the difficulties that arise from insufficient speed.

Here are the numbers for 10BaseT:

➤ **4** Maximum number of repeaters between communicating stations

➤ **100 meters (328 feet)** Maximum segment length

➤ **1,024** Maximum number of nodes attached

The 5-4-3 Rule For 10BaseT

The 5-4-3 rule can be applied in a modified form to the 10BaseT world. Because the wiring hub replaces the linear bus physical topology with a star, there's no basis for the "three populated segments" part of the 5-4-3 rule. What's left is sometimes called the 5-4 rule:

➤ **5** Maximum number of cable segments used per network

➤ **4** Maximum number of hubs (or multiport repeaters) allowed between any two communicating nodes

IEEE 802.3u And Fast Ethernet Network Design

In the late 1970s and early 1980s, 10Mbps was a killer bandwidth. Today, only small networks are forced to suffer such indignities because 100Mbps Ethernet is affordable and easy to use. High-speed PC bus technologies coupled with ever-faster CPU performance curves and high-end applications eat all the bandwidth available. IEEE 802.3u standards answer the need for increased speed with help from the Fast Ethernet Alliance. The 802.3u standards build upon the foundation of 802.3 and include the following:

➤ Physical topologies

➤ Logical topologies

➤ MAC (Media Access Control)

➤ MII (Media Independent Interface)

➤ AUTONEG (AutoNegotiation)

Physical Fast Ethernet Topologies

The physical bus composed of a long backbone cable with attached devices effectively died when 10BaseT became popular. Fast Ethernet follows 10BaseT Ethernet in using a hierarchical star topology. Repeaters, switches, and hubs are the network connection points for network nodes. These connection points can be joined to create an enterprise-sized network serving large companies and campuses.

Logical Fast Ethernet Topologies

Based on IEEE 802.3, Fast Ethernet follows the same logical bus topology supported by all 802.3 versions.

Media Access Control (MAC)

During the development of Fast Ethernet and some competing technologies, discussions often centered on defining Ethernet. The consensus was that Ethernet meant a core of strong CSMA/CD-based media access. Therefore, the Fast Ethernet Alliance wisely stayed with CSMA/CD for the new version. Existing investments in network analysis tools and design techniques were preserved.

Media Independent Interface (MII) Details

Higher transmission speeds require new connection methods and network media. Adding MII allows Fast Ethernet to work with a variety of transmission media. Three Physical Layer Devices (PLDs), new versions of transceivers, work with Fast Ethernet to connect nodes to the network. Extensions to the names indicate which network transmission media are supported—TX and T4 for twisted pair and FX for fiber.

100BaseTX

100BaseTX is modeled on 10BaseT and uses two pairs of UTP as one option. The difference is that the UTP cable must be Category 5 to support the high transmission rate. 10BaseT can use lower-grade cable, normally Category 3.

Here are the numbers for 100BaseTX:

➤ **1** Pair of STP (shielded twisted-pair) cabling (no longer common)

➤ **2** Pairs of Category 5 UTP cabling

➤ **100Mbps** Data transmission speed (10 times faster than 802.3)

➤ **100 meters (328 feet)** Maximum segment length between powered devices (node and hub, for example)

➤ **DB-9** Connectors used for STP cabling (small serial port connectors)

➤ **RJ-45** Modular connectors and jacks

100BaseT4

Similar to 100BaseTX, 100BaseT4 was designed to utilize existing lower-grade UTP wiring already installed in many locations. Using four UTP wire pairs of Category 3, 4, or 5 in place of the two pairs of higher-grade Category 5 UTP wires allows network equipment designers to control electrical cross-talk and interference well enough to maintain the 100-meter segment length.

Here are the numbers for 100BaseT4:

➤ **4** Pairs of Category 3, 4, or 5 UTP wire needed

➤ **100Mbps** Data transmission rate

➤ **100 meters (328 feet)** Maximum segment length between powered nodes

➤ **RJ-45** Standard RJ connector used

100BaseFX

High speed means fiber to many people, and Fast Ethernet included fiber support from the beginning. The dropping cost of fiber cabling and the ease of newer connector technology make fiber affordable for running to many desktops. Realistically, however, 100BaseFX is still more commonly used to cover long distances or to support servers rather than linking every desktop.

Some companies are beginning to install fiber for new network connections, regardless of the extra cost, to be prepared for future higher-bandwidth requirements. The increasing push of streaming audio and video guarantees the appetite for bandwidth will not abate soon. Connectors for Fast Ethernet/fiber follow the American National Standards Institute (ANSI) Fiber Distributed Data Interface (FDDI) standard, using Media Internet Connectors (MIC) or Subscriber Connectors (SC).

Here are the numbers for 100BaseFX:

➤ **2** Strands of 62.5/125 micron multimode or single-mode fiber

➤ **412 meters (1,352 feet)** Maximum segment length using half-duplex, multimode fiber

➤ **10,000 meters (32,808 feet)** Maximum distance for full-duplex, single-mode fiber

Fast Ethernet Repeaters

All the 100Base systems are compatible, but a Fast Ethernet repeater is required to interconnect segments using different protocols. The same is true for concentrators or switches that connect Fast Ethernet to traditional Ethernet segments.

There are two types of 100Mbps repeaters: Class I and Class II. The IEEE 802.3u standard specifies that only one Class I repeater or two Class II repeaters may be used in a single collision domain. A *collision domain* is a segment connected to one port of a switch or repeater where devices compete for bandwidth only with devices on the same segment. If an "Acme Ethernet Switch" has eight ports, and each port provides full bandwidth access to the rest of the network, each port is a single collision domain.

Here are the numbers for Fast Ethernet repeaters:

➤ **25MHz** Signal frequency for 100BaseT4 repeaters

➤ **41.6MHz** Signal frequency for 100BaseTX and 100BaseFX protocols

Obviously, any repeater connecting dissimilar frequencies must provide frequency translation. This extra work takes time. Frequency-converting repeaters add more latency to network transmission than single-frequency repeaters. The IEEE 802.3u standard dictates a maximum of two repeaters per collision domain. Five meters is the maximum inter-repeater cable-link length. The formula for calculating signal latency delay is as follows:

```
2(network board delay + cable delay + repeater delay)
```

To avoid collisions, the result must be less than or equal to 5.12 milliseconds.

AutoNegotiation Of Data Rate

Fast Ethernet, especially the 100BaseTX protocol, uses the same number of wiring pairs as 10BaseT. Because Category 5 cable came out before the 100BaseTX protocol, many companies have developed a mixed population of Ethernet and Fast Ethernet network nodes.

Most Fast Ethernet adapters support both 10Mbps and 100Mbps. Each is clearly marked and both are often labeled "dual speed adapters." Luckily, the hardware vendors, especially those dealing with wiring hubs and switches, introduced a feature called *AutoNegotiation of Data Rate*. The adapter tries to perform at the highest possible speed, and if the switch has AutoNegotiation, the switch senses the speed of the adapter and connects the adapter at 100Mbps.

The Ring That IBM Built: IEEE 802.5

IEEE 802.5 can be called "the ring that IBM built," because the standard deviates from IBM's Token Ring network only in minor ways. The IEEE approved the draft standard 802.5 on December 13, 1984. IEEE 802.5 Token Ring specifies the Physical layer and MAC sublayer standards.

Token ring started with a 4Mbps data transmission rate. An enhanced version bumped the speed up to 16Mbps. A token ring network consists of stations connected serially, each receiving information sequentially around a closed network ring. Each station receives packets and repeats them bit by bit, regenerating the packet. Figure 3.6 shows a basic token ring network diagram.

Physical Token Ring Topologies

The physical appearance of a token ring network overlays a physical star topology linked by a ring topology. Hardware devices called Multistation Access

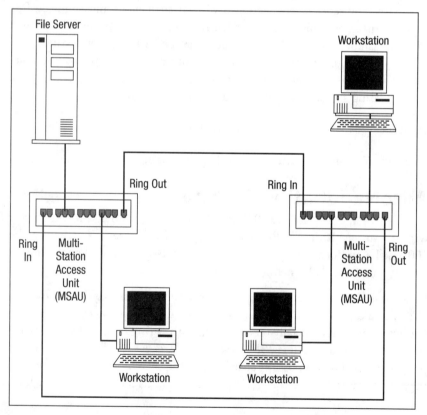

Figure 3.6   Basic token ring network diagram.

Units (MSAUs or MAUs) are linked in a ring, but the network nodes spread out physically from the MSAUs in a star pattern.

> *Note:*   *Token Ring Access Method and Physical Layer Specifications IEEE Std. 802.5, published by the IEEE in 1985, specifies shielded twisted-pair (STP) cabling.*

The thick, black cables used in a token ring network serve two functions:

➤ Adapter cables that connect the MSAUs.

➤ Patch cables that are used for short runs between devices and MSAUs.

Patch panels are sometimes used to help arrange the network cabling. Although they're expensive because of the connectors, token ring patch panels are less expensive than MSAUs.

Token Ring Rules

Although each station on the network regenerates the signal, there are still limits on distance and number of nodes. Node separation must be 2.5 meters (8 feet) or more. The numbers for token ring fall into two sections. The first is ring length, the distance between MSAUs on the main ring path. The second is lobe length, which is the distance between a node (called a *lobe* in token ring parlance) and an MSAU.

Ring length, again based on cable types, is as follows:

➤ **1 kilometer (0.6 miles)** Maximum length for fiber-optic segments

➤ **120 meters (400 feet)** Maximum length for Type 3 cable

➤ **200 meters (660 feet)** Maximum length for Types 1 and 2 cable

Lobe length based on cable types is as follows:

➤ **45 meters (150 feet)** Maximum length for Type 3 UTP cable

➤ **66 meters (220 feet)** Maximum length for Types 6 and 9 cable

➤ **100 meters (330 feet)** Maximum length for Types 1 and 2 cable

Other Token Ring Rules

The maximum number of nodes depends on the specification and cable type:

➤ **72 nodes** IBM UTP

➤ **250 nodes** IEEE 802.5 standard

➤ **260 nodes** IBM STP (shielded twisted pair)

The maximum number of MSAUs per network is 33, which brings us to the question of bridges. There are 4Mbps and 16Mbps token ring bridges, which provide the only way the two different speed networks can communicate. A 4Mbps network cannot become part of a 16Mbps network without a bridge to connect the networks. Cable type and quality always determine speed. 16Mbps token ring networks must use Type 4 cable as the minimum.

Logical Token Ring Topologies

Unlike Ethernet topology, token ring topology is a true, never-ending ring. The electrical path visits every node on the network in a giant loop.

Media Access Control

The token is a control signal circulating on the network, indicating the network is available for transmissions. Any station can "capture" the token by modifying the packet to indicate who is in control and to whom the information is addressed. When the addressee receives the packet, it copies the information. The original sending station takes the information off the network and issues a new, clear token.

A token-holding time algorithm controls how long any single station can monopolize the token. Special fields offer ways to assign priorities to token control, allowing time-sensitive traffic, such as realtime voice, to receive the necessary bandwidth.

One station in every token ring is the active monitor (AM). This station (or lobe) provides ring maintenance and keeps the token in good shape while it circulates around the network. The active monitor maintains the network clock, purges noise on the ring, creates a new token when necessary, and maintains the proper delay in the ring for proper receipt and forwarding of the token.

Any station can become the active monitor. Multiple stations can function as standby monitors (SMs), ready to take over in case the active monitor drops the ball (token). There are a number of situations that initiate the "token-claiming procedure," giving token ring networks more tools to maintain a healthy network than Ethernet.

The Early Token Release (ETR) feature allows a station to generate a new token immediately after finishing data transmission of the last frame on the previous token. ETR can be found on newer network boards, and increases network bandwidth. Multiple frames can be in transit around the network, even though there's still only one token.

Error Recovery

Token ring's physical topology (a ring of stars) allows network recovery when some stations drop off because of station failure or problems with network cabling. Network-management routines built into token ring help the network recover through a series of processes involving the active monitor and the token-claiming procedure. When network problems are serious, a process called *beaconing* comes into play. Stations detecting a ring failure send special beacon frames onto the network. These stations continue sending the beacon frame until they receive a beacon frame from their nearest upstream neighbor. This verifies that the network is sound between the first station and the next.

Eventually, only one station continues to send beacon frames. Once the ring error monitor routine deciphers the network problem location, a specialized beacon MAC frame is sent that explains the reason for the beacon. The MAC frame includes the fault domain, the station reporting the break's address, the Nearest Active Upstream Neighbor (NAUN), and the address of every station that may have failed.

Auto reconfiguration begins automatically, rebuilding the table of NAUNs for each device. In many, but not all, cases, the majority of the network will continue functioning. Stations attached to a malfunctioning MSAU (a common problem) will remain off the network until the network problem is resolved. Once they come back online, they appear as new stations and join in the token-circulation chores once again.

Fading Token Ring Fortunes

IBM developed and pushed token ring and convinced many industry heavyweights to go along. Today, however, token ring is losing market share to the increasingly popular Ethernet family. Part of the problem with token ring comes from the expensive network boards and MSAU hardware required. Additional problems arise when trying to extend the token ring architecture over WANs, limiting usefulness in today's Internet-friendly networking world.

FDDI

FDDI is an ANSI standard (X3T9.5) designed for fiber-optic network media, providing high speeds over medium distances. Using fiber-optic cabling adds to the physical security of the network because fiber is immune to electromagnetic interference (EMI) and eavesdropping. FDDI relies on the IEEE 802.2 LLC sublayer specifications and does not assume or rely on any upper-layer protocols. Figure 3.7 shows how FDDI stacks up against the bottom two layers of the OSI model.

Data Link	Connects to LLC (Logical Link Control) above MAC in Data Link layer
	MAC (Media Access Control)—Access to network media for data
Physical	PHY—Physical medium independent
	PMD—Physical medium dependent

Figure 3.7   FDDI splits the Physical layer and defines only the MAC portion of the Data Link layer.

The ANSI standard specifies the Physical layer, MAC sublayer, and Station Management (SMT) details. SMT monitors network health, allocates bandwidth, and troubleshoots the network as necessary.

FDDI and Token Ring IEEE 802.5 share the same media access method— tokens circulating on the network. FDDI operates at 100Mbps and is effective over greater distances than 802.5 because of the fiber-optic cable. Token ring has a fiber option, but the distance restrictions are far short of those for FDDI. FDDI data frame size is 4,500 data bytes. Eight or more extra bytes are used for a frame preamble.

Common FDDI uses include the following:

➤ **Backbone networks** Other networks link to this backbone for fast internetwork traffic.

➤ **Computer room networks** High speed and security make FDDI popular for mainframes, minicomputers, and high-end peripheral devices inside large data processing shops.

➤ **High-speed LANs** Engineering workstations, video production networks, and minicomputer-based LANs benefit from the high speed of FDDI.

Physical FDDI Topologies

It would not be out of line to call FDDI "fiber ring" to illustrate its relationship to token ring. FDDI's physical topology owes a lot to token ring. Both FDDI and token ring networks use a physical star topology, include strong troubleshooting capabilities, and have numerous built-in network management features.

FDDI networks appear to be a string of stars, because concentrators offer ways to link subnetworks. Often called a *hybrid network*, a star or tree network arrangement can link into the FDDI ring at a concentrator.

Here are the physical FDDI ring numbers:

➤ **2 kilometers (1.2 miles)** Maximum distance between repeaters

➤ **62.5 micrometers** Core diameter specified for FDDI multimode, fiber-optic cable

➤ **200 kilometers (124 miles)** Maximum length of the total FDDI ring

➤ **1,000 stations** Maximum number on one FDDI ring

Although the physical numbers state there can be 1,000 stations stretched over 200 kilometers, the practice is to halve both those figures. In case of a primary ring failure, FDDI tokens reroute through the counter-rotating ring architecture so they visit each node twice. Also, 500 stations and 100 kilometers are the numbers used for planning a network design.

Logical FDDI Topologies

Logical FDDI network design brings numerous improvements and differences to the token ring design topologies discussed in previous sections.

Counter-Rotating Rings

FDDI networks consist of two rings, each supporting traffic flows in opposite directions. One ring is the primary, and the other is the secondary ring. The dual-ring architecture provides fault tolerance when necessary, and out-of-band management capabilities when both rings are in operation (referred to as *counter-rotating rings*). Figure 3.8 shows the rings in normal operation, and after a failure.

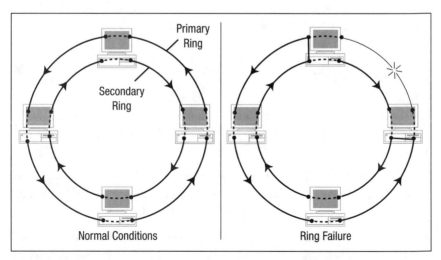

Figure 3.8 Counter-rotating rings for redundancy and management.

Normally, the primary ring is used for data and the secondary ring supports out-of-band management chores. If the primary ring fails, FDDI reroutes all traffic to the secondary ring, through the dual attached stations on either side of the point of failure, to reach stations on the other side of the failure. Traffic remains rerouted until the primary ring is once again functional.

Ring Configuration

Figure 3.8 shows a simple FDDI network in a ring configuration, a design often used for larger host nodes sharing information. Each device includes dual-fiber adapters so they're full members of the FDDI ring. This example illustrates an FDDI backbone. Many companies utilize a dual bypass switch to make it easier for the network to continue after a single node fails.

Star Configuration

Networks don't stay simple for long, and the strict FDDI ring eventually changes into a ring of stars. Adding concentrators to an FDDI ring and using them as wiring hubs for other devices connected in a star configuration leverages the speed and resiliency of the FDDI ring while somewhat moderating the cost.

There are two types of stations on FDDI: dual-attachment stations (DAS) and single-attachment stations (SAS). A DAS has two transceivers: one connected to the primary ring, and one connected to the secondary ring. These are also known as *Class A stations*. Single-attachment stations have a single transceiver, which reduces the cost but also eliminates fault tolerance. These are known as *Class B stations* and must connect to a concentrator.

There's no impact on the main FDDI ring if an SAS fails. The concentrator isolates the failed station and sends data packets around the problem. These concentrators and SASs are popular for workgroups as a star subnetwork attached to the FDDI ring.

FDDI Station Classes

There are two station classes for FDDI: Class A stations and Class B stations. One optimizes uptime (Class A), whereas the other defrays costs (Class B). Eliminating the second transceiver saves money because tranceivers are relatively expensive.

Class A stations connect to both the primary and secondary rings through their dual-attachment hardware. Concentrators are almost always Class A devices, because they must remain up to support their Class B clients.

Class B stations connect only to the primary ring (or a concentrator) through a single transceiver. Less expensive than Class A, the Class B stations must rely on their single network to keep them active, with no redundancy available.

Small FDDI networks may scrimp and use a single workgroup concentrator populated entirely with Class B single-attachment devices. Although this approach eliminates some of the expense of FDDI, the network is dependent on the state of the concentrator's health. Using a small network of Class B devices connected to a workgroup provides high-speed, large packet sizes as well as easier troubleshooting. Generally, the station with the problem is automatically bypassed and does not interfere with the working network.

Media Access Control In FDDI

FDDI uses a token-passing scheme, but it adds a bandwidth-expanding trick. Stations don't have to wait for an empty token to transmit frames. Every token-frame combination ends with the token, awaiting more frames if necessary. Many frames from many stations can be on the network at one time. The frames are all followed by the token inviting other frames to be added to the transmission.

Figure 3.9 shows another simple ring network, this time emphasizing token utilization. Notice that a token is always available at the end of the frames.

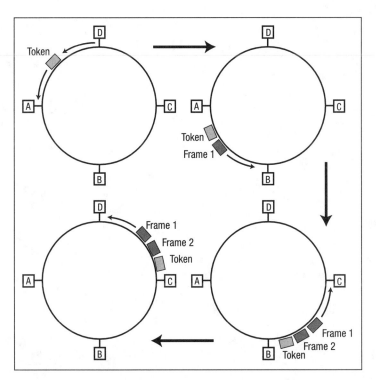

Figure 3.9   FDDI's constantly ready for more frames.

Just like token ring, FDDI uses beaconing when a network fault appears. Other FDDI functions include network monitoring to ensure the token is not corrupted, lost, or trapped by a node going offline. In the event of a token problem, beaconing starts until working nodes are accounted for; then a claim token procedure is started to put the network back on track.

Practice Questions

Question 1

Which of the OSI model layers match up with the IEEE 802.x map?

○ a. Physical and Network

○ b. Network and Transport

○ c. Physical and Transport

○ d. Physical and Data Link

○ e. Data Link and Transport

The correct answer is d. All IEEE 802.x committee standards cover all or parts of the Physical and Data Link layers. All other answers are incorrect.

Question 2

Which of the following statements are true about IEEE 802.3 and 10BaseT? [Choose the two best answers]

❏ a. Both use the same type of cabling.

❏ b. Both use CSMA/CD.

❏ c. Both transmit data at 10Mbps.

❏ d. Both are limited to 100 meters per segment.

❏ e. Both use fiber-optic cable as an option.

The correct answers are b and c. UTP cabling is defined for the 10BaseT specification but not for the earlier 802.3. Therefore, answer a is incorrect. Coax cable transmits data farther than UTP. Therefore, answer d is incorrect. The fiber-optic cable is not an option in the 10BaseT specifications. Therefore, answer e is incorrect.

Question 3

> Which of the following is an option *only* for Fast Ethernet (IEEE 802.3u)?
>
> O a. UTP, STP, and fiber cabling can be used.
>
> O b. Collisions are detected and packets are retransmitted automatically.
>
> O c. The logical network topology is a shared bus.
>
> O d. Network boards are available for all types of computer systems.
>
> O e. Concentrators adjust the speed rating to support the network board.

The correct answer is e. All the other answers are true of Ethernet of all types. Only Fast Ethernet needs AutoNegotiation for speed differences between 10Mbps and 100Mbps, because only Fast Ethernet (802.3u) offers a choice of speeds.

Question 4

> Which of the following cable types does *not* support IEEE 802.3u?
>
> O a. Shielded twisted pair
>
> O b. Thin coax
>
> O c. Unshielded twisted pair
>
> O d. Fiber optic

The correct answer is b. All other cabling types support Fast Ethernet (IEEE 802.3u), although the distances supported for each vary greatly. Therefore, answers a, c, and d are incorrect.

Question 5

> Which of the following are characteristics of both token ring and FDDI? [Choose the two best answers]
>
> ❑ a. Tokens are used.
> ❑ b. Beaconing is used when the network suffers certain problems.
> ❑ c. Specifications call for STP.
> ❑ d. One token can support traffic from multiple nodes.
> ❑ e. Network consists of counter-rotating rings.

The correct answers are a and b. FDDI specifications call for fiber cabling, although extensions from some vendors allow some copper cabling types. Therefore, answer c is incorrect. Token ring provides early release tokens (ERT), but they don't support frames from multiple nodes. Therefore, answer d is incorrect. Only FDDI has dual-ring architecture. Therefore, answer e is incorrect.

Question 6

> Which IEEE 802.x protocol uses active monitor and standby monitor?
>
> ○ a. 100BaseTX
> ○ b. FDDI
> ○ c. Token ring
> ○ d. 10BaseT

The correct answer is c. Only token-passing protocols require any type of active or standby monitor, so the choice is between token ring and FDDI. Therefore, answers a and d are incorrect. However, FDDI is more advanced and uses a set of specifications called SMT (Station Management) to provide the active monitor plus several other features. Therefore, answer b is incorrect.

Need To Know More?

 Miller, Mark. *LAN Protocol Handbook*. M&T Books. Redwood City, CA, 1990. ISBN 1-55851-099-0. This entire book focuses on LAN protocols.

 www.computer.org/standard/index.htm provides information about historical standards developed by the IEEE as well as its current work in progress.

WAN Protocols And The OSI Model

Terms you'll need to understand:

√ Wide area networking (WAN) protocols

√ Basic Rate Interface (BRI)

√ Primary Rate Interface (PRI)

√ Packet switching

√ Permanent virtual circuit (PVC)

√ Switched virtual circuit (SVC)

√ Constant bit rate (CBR)

√ Variable bit rate (VBR)

Techniques you'll need to master:

√ Understanding how each WAN protocol maps to the OSI model

√ Learning each WAN protocol's method of operation

√ Understanding the difference between PVCs and SVCs

Wide area network (WAN) protocols make it possible for you to connect individual remote personal computers or even entire remote networks to your local network. In this chapter, you'll learn about some of the more common WAN protocols for networking and how those protocols relate to the Open Systems Interconnection (OSI) reference model, often referred to simply as the *OSI model*.

WAN Protocols And The OSI Model

Understanding how WAN protocols fit into the OSI model helps you understand their behavior and characteristics. Most of the protocols we discuss in this chapter specify network functions that operate at one or more of the three lower layers of the OSI model.

SLIP And PPP

Serial Line Internet Protocol (SLIP) and Point-to-Point Protocol (PPP) were designed to provide connections to Transport Control Protocol/Internet Protocol (TCP/IP) networks through the Public Switched Telephone Network (PSTN). Today, you'll find that SLIP and PPP are commonly used to dial up to Internet Service Provider (ISP) networks connected to the Internet.

Serial Line Internet Protocol (SLIP)

SLIP, the predecessor of PPP, operates at the Physical layer of the OSI model to support point-to-point communication (for IP only, as its name implies) over an asynchronous dial-up connection. This protocol is easy to implement and, because of its simplicity, incurs little additional overhead beyond that inherent in all asynchronous protocols; there is no frame header, error checking isn't performed, and upper-layer protocols do not have to be specified, because IP is assumed to be the upper-layer transport protocol.

Functional limitations are imposed, however, by the simplicity of SLIP. Among the shortcomings that make SLIP generally unsuitable for most current environments are the following:

➤ The lack of support for the simultaneous transfer of multiple protocols (because of its IP-only nature)

➤ The lack of support for authentication

➤ The lack of support for IP address negotiation

In addition, many SLIP implementations are incompatible because developers aren't required to adhere to a single strict standard. This means that two physically connected devices might not be able to establish communication because their individual "dialects" of SLIP are too different.

Point-To-Point Protocol (PPP)

Much of the functionality missing from SLIP has been incorporated into the more recently designed PPP. The Internet Engineering Task Force (IETF) developed PPP to provide a more comprehensive dial-up alternative to SLIP. It provides the specifications for processes operating at both the Physical and Data Link layers of the OSI model. Among the functions supported by PPP implementations are the following:

➤ Simultaneous transfer of multiple protocols on the same link

➤ Password login

➤ IP address negotiation through Dynamic Host Configuration Protocol (DHCP)

➤ Error control

The IETF does not require all PPP implementations to support the full range of functionality defined in the standard. To minimize compatibility issues, however, it does require that, during connection establishment, there's negotiation of and agreement upon the level of functionality to be mutually supported for the duration of the connection (referred to as *class of service*).

For dial-up Internet accounts, PPP implementations are currently the most popular because they support multiple protocols on the same link, dynamic IP address assignment, and user authentication. Many desktop operating systems come with built-in PPP support for remote connectivity.

The X.25 Standard

The X.25 standard, first defined in 1974 by the Consultative Committee for International Telephone and Telegraph (CCITT), is actually one in a series of "X" recommendations that describe the Physical, Data Link, and Network layer specifications for the interface between the data terminating equipment (DTE), such as a computer, and the data circuit-terminating equipment (DCE), such as a modem, that acts as the gateway to a packet-switched network.

X.25 Functions And The OSI Model

Although the X.25 series of recommendations predates the OSI model, the functions of the processes operating at the three X.25-defined functional levels map relatively well to the lower layers of the OSI model. The following list shows the relationship between the X.25 functional levels and the lower three layers of the OSI model:

➤ **Level 1** Connectivity rules for Physical layer and Media Access Control (MAC) sublayer processes defined by X.21, X.21 bis, V.32, and other protocols

➤ **Level 2** Connection-oriented service rules for Logical Link Control (LLC) sublayer processes defined by the Link Access Procedures-Balanced (LAPB) protocol

➤ **Level 3** Packet-level rules (size, format, sequence, transport, and so on) for Network layer processes contained within information fields of LAPB command frames

Typical implementations of the X.25 standard offer dedicated, continuous bandwidth over a WAN. For full compliance with the X.25 standard, carriers are required to offer two essential services:

➤ **Switched virtual circuits (SVCs)** SVCs represent "on demand" connections that are established by DTEs at the beginning of a conversation over a packet switched network, maintained for the conversation's duration, and terminated by DTEs at the end of the conversation. The connection is "virtual" in the sense that a fixed path does not exist for the duration of the conversation. Instead, the "intelligence" of the protocols sets up and maintains a *conversation address* by associating a logical channel number on each of the two DTEs to be used exclusively with a particular conversation for the duration of the connection.

➤ **Permanent virtual circuits (PVCs)** PVCs represent connections established, not by DTEs, but by a service provider in response to the written request of a customer. The connection is maintained by the service provider until a written request is received to have it terminated. As with the SVC, the PVC has no "hard-wired" path for packets to move across. The value of the PVC lies in the availability of the connection solely for data transfer between DTEs, without the overhead associated with requiring the DTEs to establish, maintain, and terminate a connection each time data is transferred.

X.25 implementations are commonly employed by organizations with branch or remote offices. In some countries, X.25 is the only way to connect remote offices.

Main Points

As the most widely used interface for WANs, the X.25 recommendations provide organizations with a standard interface for connecting to packet-switched networks and transmitting data over packet-switched networks.

The X.25 recommendations do not specify the details of the network transmission implementations, but the standard interface they specify provides developers with a target and guidelines for compatible implementations.

 X.25 implementations are only suitable for data transmissions.

Reliability And Error Control

X.25 service providers offer both SVC and PVC connections to packet-switched networks. The DTE-to-X.25 network interface is designed to easily accommodate multiple, concurrent connections that are unrestricted with regard to service type concurrency. This is because the only differences in the service offerings are in the way the circuits are established and terminated; while the circuits are open, they are managed by the same processes. X.25 error control, regardless of service type, depends on DTEs and DCEs to provide end-to-end flow control and error control. The packet-switched network protocols provide window flow control and error control for each virtual circuit operated by the DTEs.

X.25 connections are reliable because of the connection-oriented, acknowledged service they offer. This level of reliability was incorporated into the X.25 specifications to compensate for the lack of reliability and high error rates associated with then existent WAN infrastructures. As current technologies provide greater reliability and more high-quality transmission media options, and as upper-layer protocols (such as TCP) that perform error correction and flow control become more popular, the overhead associated with providing connection-oriented reliable service has become the main drawback to implementing X.25.

Frame Relay Networks

Frame Relay networks offer a cost-effective way for organizations to connect geographically dispersed networks. *Frame Relay* is a digital service that employs statistical time division multiplexing (STDM) to set up multiple virtual circuits (often referred to as *channels*) over the same physical link, and it dynamically allocates bandwidth among all users on the link. Frame Relay is similar to X.25 in many respects, but it operates faster because it isn't burdened with X.25's reliable connection services overhead. Instead, it assumes a lower network error rate and depends on applications communicating over the Frame Relay link to handle error recovery with an upper-layer protocol, such as TCP.

Frame Relay is designed to handle only data transmissions, but the dynamic allocation of bandwidth makes it ideal for organizations that typically need high-speed, intermittent connections. The premise under which STDM operates, which makes the solution attractive for those organizations, is that all subscribers will not require their full allocation of bandwidth simultaneously. This means that, statistically, there's a high likelihood that additional bandwidth will be available for allocation to any given transmission request.

Understanding The Committed Information Rate (CIR)

CIR is a minimum capacity that you negotiate with a public carrier for your PVC. This means that if your negotiated CIR is 64Kbps, you pay for a guaranteed minimum capacity of 64Kbps whether you use it or not. However, when peak traffic is low, you may be able to reach much higher data transfer rates. This on-demand additional bandwidth above your CIR may or may not be available; you're guaranteed only your negotiated CIR.

Frame Relay And The OSI Model

Frame Relay operates at the Physical and Data Link layers of the OSI model. The Frame Relay addressing scheme uses Data Link Connection Identifiers (DLCIs) to identify the end points that make up each virtual circuit.

Additional general information about Frame Relay of which you need to be aware includes the following:

➤ It can be implemented over 56Kbps, T1, and T3 links.

➤ It can provide Data Link layer functionality for X.25 and Integrated Services Digital Networks (ISDN).

➤ It's commonly used to connect X.25, Ethernet, and token ring networks.

➤ It typically offers data rates from 56Kbps to 1.544Mbps.

ISDN Standards

In 1984, the CCITT—now named the International Telecommunication Union (ITU)—designed the international standards for ISDN and Broadband-ISDN (B-ISDN) to combine voice and data communications over digital telephone lines. ISDN is a synchronous dial-up service, offered by most telephone companies, that employs a circuit-switched technology. It can transmit voice and other types of data, such as multimedia and video, and can connect with other types of networks, such as X.25, Frame Relay, and PPP.

You need special equipment to combine voice and data over the same lines, because voice uses analog signals that must be converted to be carried over the digital lines. You also need terminal adapters (TAs) to hook older non-ISDN telephone units to the ISDN lines. The local telephone company must come out and install a network termination device to connect a site with the company's local loop.

ISDN is split into six-bit pipes labeled channels A, B, C, D, E, and H. The bit pipes can be mixed and matched as follows to create some common implementations of ISDN, depending on bandwidth requirements:

➤ **Basic Rate Interface (BRI)** Circuit-switching technology using 2 64Kbps B channels for voice and data plus 1 16Kbps D channel for signaling. Total bandwidth is equal to 128Kbps.

➤ **Primary Rate Interface (PRI)** Circuit-switching technology using 23 64Kbps B channels for voice and data plus 1 64Kbps D channel for signaling. Total bandwidth is equivalent to a T1 circuit or 1.544Mbps.

➤ **B-ISDN (Broadband ISDN)** Cell-switching technology using fiber-optic technology that includes 1 53-byte Asynchronous Transfer Mode (ATM) cell. Bandwidth is for speeds over 1.55Mbps.

 The two most common channels for ISDN are the B and D channels. Channel B is a 64Kbps digital channel used to carry data, and channel D is a signaling channel used typically for out-of-band signals.

ISDN And The OSI Model

ISDN operates at the bottom three layers of the OSI model (Network, Data Link, and Physical). To convert the analog voice signals to digital signals, time-division multiplexing (TDM) is performed at the Physical layer, with addressing stamped at the MAC sublayer and framing occurring at the LLC sublayer.

Broadband ISDN (B-ISDN)

B-ISDN uses ATM cell-relay technologies over fiber-optic media and was developed with high bandwidth requirements of applications such as multimedia. It's not uncommon to find television stations using B-ISDN for interconnection.

ATM

ATM is a cell-relay technology. As we just mentioned in the ISDN section of this chapter, it's one of the B-ISDN standards. It's a connection-oriented (see Chapter 2) protocol that uses fixed-length packets (53 bytes) called *cells* on virtual circuits. Because it's connection oriented, the virtual channel must be set up prior to the transmission of data. The benefit to having fixed-length cells traverse the network is that timing can be set perfectly. In an environment that implements variable-length packet protocols, it's difficult to predict the actual arrival time of packets as they traverse the network.

Organizations switching over to ATM from a frame-based network must install a device (called an *ATM switch*) that converts frames to cells. This device can either reside on the organization's network (private ATM network) or it can reside at the carrier's site (public ATM network). Inside the ATM network, internetworking units (IWUs or bridges, routers, repeaters, and so on) are used to interconnect networks.

The ITU-Telecommunications Standards Sector (ITU-TSS) and the ATM Forum are both involved in the ATM standards process. The ITU-TSS is responsible for creating the standard, and the ATM Forum defines the ways the standard can be implemented.

One of the goals of the ATM standard is transmission media independence to allow for implementations that use unshielded twisted pair (UTP), shielded twisted pair (STP), fiber optics, and so on.

ATM And The OSI Model

ATM operates at the Network and Data Link layers of the OSI model while depending on protocols of the Physical layer, such as Synchronous Optical Network (SONET—the international equivalent is called *Synchronous Digital Hierarchy*, or *SDH*) and Fiber Distributed Data Interface (FDDI). There are three functional layers defined by the ATM protocol that map to the OSI model as follows:

➤ **Physical layer** This layer defines the electrical and physical properties. It was designed so it could be implemented on top of UTP, STP, and so on. Obviously, ATM is better suited to run on higher-bandwidth media, and the most recommended at this time are FDDI and SONET. This layer maps to the Physical layer of the OSI model.

➤ **ATM layer** This layer defines the ATM cell structure, such as how many bytes are used for header information, which bytes are used for the virtual channel information, and so on. It also defines the route information of the virtual channels plus error control information. Within an ATM cell, the header information contains 5 bytes. The header information can be inserted by the user (called the *user network interface*, or *UNI*) or by a switch or router (called the *network-to-network interface*, or *NNI*). This layer maps to the Data Link layer of the OSI model.

➤ **ATM Adaptation Layer (AAL)** This layer is responsible for converting information to cells. Therefore, in the case in which there's an ATM switch converting frames from a network to cells on an ATM network, this is the layer where that conversion takes place. This layer also determines which data needs continuous realtime streams (video and audio) and which data streams can be sent without a continuous, uninterrupted stream. This layer maps to the Network layer of the OSI model.

The I Series Service Classes

The Network layer of ATM, or the AAL, is defined by a set of standards called the I Series, which is subdivided into the following four classes:

➤ **Class 1** Constant bit rate (CBR) service along with the timing necessary to transmit video and audio in a steady stream of data. Examples include voice, fixed-rate video, and leased line service.

➤ **Class 2** Variable bit rate (VBR) service that requires fixed delays. Examples include compressed voice and compressed video.

➤ **Class 3** Available bit rate (ABR) connection-oriented service (CONS) for applications in which timing is not important, such as conventional data streams.

➤ **Class 4** Available bit rate (ABR) connectionless service (CLNP) for applications in which timing is not important, such as datagrams (on an X.25 network, for example).

Practice Questions

Question 1

> At which OSI model layers does ISDN operate? [Choose the three best answers]
>
> ❏ a. Physical
> ❏ b. Data Link
> ❏ c. Network
> ❏ d. Session

Answers a, b, and c are correct because ISDN operates at the Physical, Data Link, and Network layers. Answer d is incorrect.

Question 2

> Which of the following ISDN implementations has a bandwidth comparable to that of a T1 line?
>
> ○ a. Basic Rate Interface (BRI)
> ○ b. Primary Rate Interface (PRI)
> ○ c. B-ISDN
> ○ d. ATM

The correct answer is b. The ISDN PRI has 23 B channels (64Kbps) and 1 D channel (64Kbps) for signaling. Answer a is incorrect because ISDN BRI only has two B channels and one D channel. Answer c is incorrect because B-ISDN can achieve bandwidth greater than that of a T1 line. Answer d is incorrect because ATM is an outgrowth of B-ISDN, and although you can run it over T1 lines at T1 speeds (1.54Mbps), it's really rated at much higher speeds (1.55Mbps and above), which is why this is a trick question.

Question 3

Which of the I Series classes would you select for realtime video that requires continuous streaming without interruption or delay?

○ a. Class 1

○ b. Class 2

○ c. Class 3

○ d. Class 4

The correct answer is a. Class 1 is required for CBR data. Answer b is incorrect because that class allows for data that can experience some loss and has a fixed delay. Answers c and d are both incorrect because timing is not included in either of those classes.

Question 4

Which layers of the OSI model and ATM model convert data in frame format to cell format when connecting an ATM network to another network? [Choose the two best answers]

❑ a. Physical

❑ b. Data Link

❑ c. Network

❑ d. ATM adaptation layer (AAL)

The correct answers are c and d. The process of converting the frame formats of data from the upper layers to cell format in ATM occurs at the AAL layer of the ATM model, which maps to the Network Layer of the OSI model. Answers a and b are incorrect.

Question 5

> Which of the following WAN protocols was designed primarily for dial-up connections to IP networks, permits multiple protocols on the same link, and operates at the Physical and Data Link layers of the OSI model?
>
> ○ a. SLIP
>
> ○ b. PPP
>
> ○ c. SLIP and PPP
>
> ○ d. X.25

The correct answer is b. PPP was designed after SLIP and fixes some of SLIP's shortcomings. PPP permits more than one protocol on a link, whereas SLIP does not. PPP operates at the Data Link and Physical layers of the OSI model, whereas SLIP only operates at the Physical layer. Therefore, answers a and c are incorrect. X.25 fits most of the question, but it was not designed primarily for dial-up to IP networks and it operates at the Network layer. Therefore, answer d is incorrect.

Question 6

> Which of the following statements is incorrect for the X.25 WAN protocol?
>
> ○ a. It operates at the Network layer of the OSI model.
>
> ○ b. It's a packet-switching network.
>
> ○ c. It supports permanent virtual circuits (PVCs) and switched virtual circuits (SVCs).
>
> ○ d. Error checking is done on the receiving end, causing transmission rates to be much faster.

The correct answer is d. X.25 requires an acknowledgement at each point in the network because it was designed back when networks were not reliable. Answers a, b, and c are all true of X.25 networks and are therefore incorrect answers for this question.

Question 7

> Which of the following WAN protocols relies on time-division
> multiplexing (TDM) at the Physical layer of the OSI model to con-
> vert analog signals to digital signals?
>
> O a. PPP
>
> O b. ISDN
>
> O c. X.25
>
> O d. ATM

The correct answer is b. ISDN combines both voice and data but must convert
the analog data to digital prior to transmitting across the digital lines. Answers
a and c are incorrect because they do not include voice data. Answer d is incorrect because it does not use TDM at the Physical layer.

Need To Know More?

 Clarke, David J. *Novell's CNE Study Guide for Core Technologies*. Novell Press. San Jose, CA, 1996. ISBN 0-7645-4501-9. Chapter 10 discusses WAN protocols in good detail as they relate to the OSI model.

 Sheldon, Tom. *Encyclopedia of Networking: Electronic Edition*. Osborne/McGraw Hill. Berkeley, CA, 1998. ISBN 0-07-882333-1. This book defines networking terms in alphabetical order. Good definitions for terms used in this chapter can be found in this book.

 info.internet.isi.edu/in-notes/rfc/files/rfc1994.txt is an RFC that includes information regarding PPP.

 www.incoma.ru/protocols/ppp.htm is a PPP FAQ.

Repeaters, Bridges, And Switches

5

Terms you'll need to understand:

√ Repeater

√ Attenuation

√ Bridge

√ Switch

√ Propagation delay

Techniques you'll need to master:

√ Understanding how the 5-4-3 rule applies to Ethernet networks

√ Understanding how the 80/20 rule should be applied when using bridges

√ Deciding when to use repeaters, bridges, and switches

As you learned in previous chapters, the Data Link layer of the Open Systems Interconnection (OSI) model is responsible for managing the physical addresses assigned to packets. You also learned that each networking standard has its limitations as to the number of devices that can reside on one network segment. In this chapter, you'll learn the basic functions of repeaters, bridges, and switches, and how they can be used to increase the length of a network cable segment as well as limit and direct traffic based on information in the physical address fields of a packet. You'll also learn how bridges and switches are designed.

Repeaters

Each networking standard includes a specification that limits the maximum length of a cable segment. For example, 10Base2 segments can be no longer than 185 meters. To overcome this type of media distance limitation, a Physical layer device called a *repeater* can be implemented.

The protocol-defined standards that place restrictions on cable segment length are included to combat a phenomenon known as *attenuation*. As a signal, either electrical or optical, travels through a medium, the strength of the signal fades as a function of the distance the signal has traveled. At distances beyond the protocol specifications, the signal becomes too weak for reliability to be ensured. The loss of signal strength over distance is called attenuation. Repeaters fight attenuation by either boosting or regenerating the signals they receive, pumping them back up to full strength, and sending them on down the line. Figure 5.1 illustrates this process. By placing a repeater at the end of the maximum cable length, you can effectively double the length of any cable segment.

Not only does the local area network (LAN) protocol define the maximum cable segment length, but it also defines the maximum number of repeaters that can exist on any single network segment. Each repeater adds a slight delay (known as *propagation delay*) to the signal. If the propagation delay is too long, the processes operating under the rules defined by that particular networking protocol may not function correctly. A good example of this is on a Carrier Sense Multiple Access/Collision Detection (CSMA/CD) network when two devices at opposite ends of the cable segment sense the media to see if it's available. If the segment is too long and has too many repeaters, they will both sense that the media is free and begin transmitting, thus causing a collision.

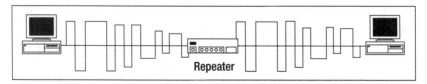

Figure 5.1   A repeater is used to regenerate the signals it receives.

There are two basic types of repeaters: amplifier and signal-regenerating. *Amplifiers* boost all signals exactly as they are received, including any aberrations in the signal that may have been caused by noise or interference on the line. This, of course, does not ensure that the amplified signal can be correctly interpreted by the intended recipient; it only ensures that it's stronger. As the number of amplifier repeaters that a signal must pass through on the network increases, the quality of the signal decreases. Although this is fine for voice networks, it can cause major problems with data networks.

Signal-regenerating repeaters, on the other hand, read the actual signal data to reconstruct the signals from scratch and send them down the line. The new signal that's created retains only the data from the original signal. The re-created signal is then passed on as a clean, full-strength copy of the original. The signal-regenerating repeater provides superior performance but incurs a higher cost than the amplifier repeater, because it requires more intricate and, therefore, more expensive internal logic to perform its function.

Note that many hubs are, in essence, repeaters. Hubs are used to connect networking media segments together to provide interconnectivity. An *active hub* regenerates a signal it receives and sends the signal down every port except the one on which the signal was received, thus making it a *multiport repeater*. Because they can regenerate the signals, active hubs can be used to increase the length of a network segment. This means that any rules that apply to repeaters apply also to active hubs.

Passive hubs, on the other hand, do not regenerate or amplify the signals they receive. They merely pass the received signal down multiple ports. This means that the distance limitations for each segment connected by a passive hub must conform to the total length specifications of a non-extended cable segment.

Ethernet

Some Ethernet networks use the 5-4-3 rule to define the maximum number of segments on the network (5), the maximum number of repeaters on the network (4), and the maximum number of populated segments on the network (3). This rule applies to all coaxial Ethernet networks, and a variation applies to twisted-pair networks. The rule for 10BaseT and other twisted-pair Ethernet networks—5 total segments and 4 repeaters—reflects the nature of the star-wired topology.

 Know the 5-4-3 rule for coaxial Ethernet and the 5-4 rule for twisted-pair Ethernet. These two rules are very important when considering network design and troubleshooting network problems.

Token Ring

On token ring networks, repeaters play a slightly different role. First, each computer in the ring acts as a repeater because it receives and re-creates each packet transmitted. Also, the central connection point—the Multistation Access Unit (MSAU)—also operates as a repeater. The 802.5 standard governs the number of repeaters on each ring, the maximum length of an adapter cable, and the maximum ring length.

Bridges

A step up in intelligence from repeaters, *bridges* are capable of selectively dropping or forwarding packets based on the physical addresses of the packets. To illustrate how repeaters and bridges differ, let's take a look at a repeater and a bridge that each have two ports. In Figure 5.2, the repeater regenerates and forwards the packet it receives, regardless of the destination. In this process, all stations on the network, including the intended recipient, receive the packet. In Figure 5.3, the bridge reads the packet header to determine whether to drop the packet or forward it to the other port.

How does a bridge perform its function? Unlike a repeater, which operates at the Physical layer of the OSI model, a bridge operates at the Data Link layer. Specifically, a bridge is able to read the Media Access Control (MAC) sublayer addressing information contained in the packet header. You'll recall that the MAC sublayer is responsible for handling physical addressing for packets, both source and destination. As the bridge reads the destination address of the packet, it determines whether to send the packet to the next segment based on the information contained in the bridging table it has constructed.

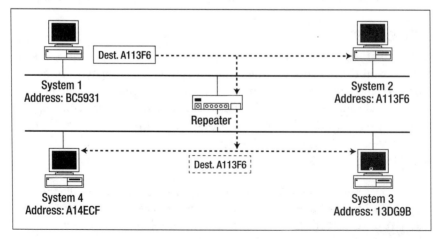

Figure 5.2   A repeater resends the signal, regardless of its destination.

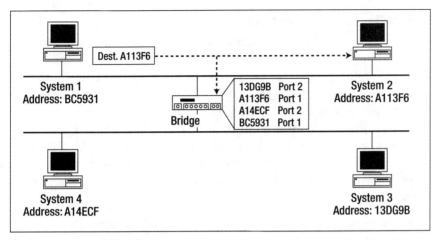

Figure 5.3   A bridge makes a determination on forwarding the packet.

Bridging tables are built and updated in one of two ways, depending on the type of bridge used. Bridges can be source routing, transparent, or a combination of the two—source-routing transparent. Each of these types of bridges is discussed in detail in Chapter 6 . If you look at Figure 5.3, you'll notice that the bridging table states that physical address A14ECF, which belongs to System 4, is located down Port 2. Because the packet is destined for System 2 (address A113F6), the packet is not transmitted down Port 2. If another packet were sent with the destination address of A14ECF, the bridge would recognize that the destination is located on Port 2 and would forward the packet.

Benefits

Because bridges are capable of determining whether traffic is destined for a specific segment, they can be used to confine local traffic to a segment and restrict traffic between segments to the sending and receiving (and possibly intermediate) segments. This effectively increases the available bandwidth on the network and ensures smoother operation. In addition, repeaters (bridges) work only up to the MAC sublayer of the Data Link layer; their function is totally independent of the upper layers involved in communication. This means that bridges can forward frames from different upper-layer protocols. In addition, bridges include the functionality of regenerating repeaters to increase the length of a network and the number of stations that are connected. The repeater function of the bridge requires adherence to the Physical layer specifications regarding the maximum number of repeaters (bridges) that can be attached to a particular network and the maximum number of segments on a network.

Using The 80/20 Rule

Although bridges are intended to limit traffic between network segments, some care must be taken in their placement on the network. The 80/20 rule that applies to bridging states that for latencies involved in the bridging process to be acceptable, at least 80 percent of the traffic on a segment should be local to the segment, and 20 percent or less intended for a remote destination. For example, in Figure 5.3, the majority of the traffic on Port 1 should be destined for other systems on Port 1, while no more than 20 percent should be destined for Port 2. When remote traffic is above 20 percent, bridging becomes counterproductive due to the time cost of sorting and directing the traffic between segments.

When networks have segments meeting the 80/20 criterion, bridging between the segments can allow two conversations to occur simultaneously on the two segments most of the time (refer to Figure 5.3).

Note: If there's no way to follow the 80/20 rule with an existing network configuration, some systems should be moved between segments.

Switches

Switches have a combination of the functionality of repeaters and bridges. As mentioned earlier, many bridges use only two ports to separate network segments. Although this works well for thicknet and thinnet networks, it does not readily apply to twisted-pair networks. Also, although multiport repeaters are very useful for connecting multiple systems to a central point, they're not equipped to limit network traffic.

A *switch* is a multiport device that includes bridging functionality. As Figure 5.4 shows, the switch will use its bridging capabilities to direct the packet down only the port to which the destination computer is connected.

Note that switches are limited by the same restrictions as repeaters and bridges. In addition, although switches are most often seen in twisted-pair environments, they're able to operate on virtually any type of network.

As you can imagine, because switches utilize bridging algorithms, they can also be used to limit the traffic on the network and free up additional bandwidth. In fact, because each port generally has very few systems attached, a switch is the most efficient networking device to use when limiting traffic. Of course, these benefits come at a higher price. Switches are significantly more expensive than both repeaters and single-port bridges.

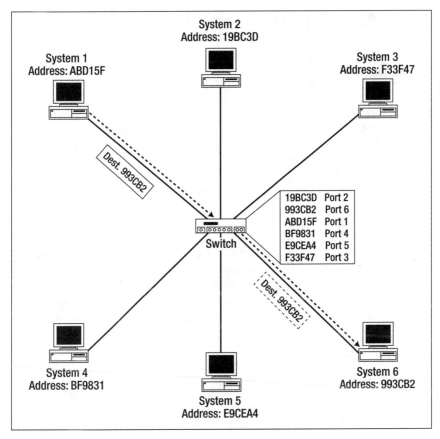

Figure 5.4 The switch directs the packet down the appropriate port.

Which One To Use?

Whether you use a repeater, bridge, or switch depends on the structure of your network and the goal you're trying to accomplish. A repeater is a wonderful connectivity device that provides for longer networks and centralized connections, but it has no beneficial effect on traffic. Although a bridge also provides nearly twice the maximum network segment length, it increases the available bandwidth on the network by limiting traffic. Generally, however, bridges only provide this type of service for two ports. If you need the traffic-limiting benefits of a bridge and the centralized connection point of a multiport repeater, then a switch is the way to go. Remember, however, that as the devices become more complex, their cost increases: A bridge is more expensive than a repeater, and a switch is more expensive than a bridge.

Practice Questions

Question 1

Which of the following types of repeaters uses more intricate internal functionality to ensure that the signal that's repeated is the most accurate possible?

○ a. Signal regenerating

○ b. Amplifying

○ c. Switching

Answer a is correct. A signal-regenerating repeater strips the data from the signal it receives and re-creates the signal from scratch, thus ensuring that the signal is as accurate as possible. Amplifying repeaters, on the other hand, regenerate the signals exactly as they are received, including noise and interference. Therefore, answer b is incorrect. There's no networking device called a switching repeater. Therefore, answer c is incorrect.

Question 2

At which layer or sublayer of the OSI model do switches operate?

○ a. Physical

○ b. Data Link

○ c. Media Access Control (MAC)

○ d. Logical Link Control (LLC)

Answer c is correct. Because switches use bridging algorithms to make decisions on the port down which to send a packet, they operate at the MAC sublayer of the Data Link layer. Other networking devices operate at the Physical layer, but not switches. Therefore, answer a is incorrect. Although the MAC sublayer is part of the Data Link layer, switches specifically operate at the MAC sublayer, which is why this is a trick question. Therefore, answer b is incorrect. The LLC sublayer of the Data Link layer is responsible for other networking functions, but not physical addressing. Therefore, answer d is incorrect.

Question 3

> Which of the following statements accurately describes the rea-
> son for limiting the number of repeaters on a network?
>
> ○ a. The propagation delay introduced by each repeater
>   increases the chance a repeater will lose the packet.
>
> ○ b. The propagation delay introduced by each repeater
>   increases the chance the packet will be lost due to
>   collision.
>
> ○ c. The propagation delay introduced by each repeater
>   decreases the amount of data that can be sent during any
>   transmission.
>
> ○ d. Too many repeaters makes wiring closets look cluttered.

Answer b is correct. Because each repeater on the network introduces a slight delay, called propagation delay, there's a chance that two devices will sense at the same time that the media is available and begin transmitting. This causes a collision, rendering the data useless. The other answers, particularly answer d, do not apply to limiting the number of repeaters on a network.

Question 4

> Which of the following rules applies to the percentage of local
> traffic that should be maintained when implementing a bridge?
>
> ○ a. 5-4-3 rule
> ○ b. 5-4 rule
> ○ c. Rule #1
> ○ d. The 80/20 rule

Answer d is correct. The 80/20 rule applies to implementing bridges and dictates that, when a bridge is installed, 80 percent of the traffic on each segment should be local and only 20 percent should be destined for the other segment. The 5-4-3 rule applies to Ethernet networks and defines the number of segments, repeaters, and populated segments that can be used to comprise a network. Therefore, answer a is incorrect. The 5-4 rule applies to twisted-pair Ethernet. Therefore, answer b is incorrect. Rule #1 varies from person to person and situation to situation. Therefore, answer c is incorrect.

Question 5

Which of the following are generally associated with multiport devices? [Choose the two best answers]

❑ a. Active hubs

❑ b. Switches

❑ c. Repeaters

❑ d. Bridges

Answers a and b are correct. Both active hubs and switches are multiport versions of other networking devices—repeaters and bridges, respectively. Because repeaters and bridges are generally considered to only have one input and one output port, they're not multiport devices. Therefore, answers c and d are incorrect.

Question 6

Which of the following is not a benefit of implementing a bridge on a network?

○ a. Bridges effectively increase the available bandwidth on a network.

○ b. Bridges are not restricted to the same limitations as repeaters, thus increasing the overall size of the network.

○ c. Bridges have no concern for the upper-layer protocols involved in a conversation.

○ d. Bridges use physical destination addresses to limit the traffic on the network.

Answer b is correct. Bridges are restricted by the same rules as repeaters in regard to the number of bridges allowed on the network. The statement listed in answer b is not a benefit of implementing a bridge. All other answer are benefits of implementing bridges. Therefore, answers a, c, and d are incorrect.

Question 7

> Which of the following terms is used to describe signal degrada-
> tion over distance?
>
> ○ a. Attenuation
>
> ○ b. Synchronization
>
> ○ c. Signal regeneration.

Answer a is correct. Attenuation refers to the loss of a signal's strength as it travels through the network. Synchronization deals with other areas of network communication, but not signal strength. Therefore, answer b is incorrect. Signal regeneration is used to fight attenuation. Therefore, answer c is incorrect.

Need To Know More?

 Clarke, David James IV. *Novell's CNE Study Guide for Core Technologies*. Novell Press. San Jose, CA, 1996. ISBN: 0-7645-4501-9. Chapter 9 is dedicated to the communications aspects of the OSI model and discusses repeaters and bridges.

 Niedermiller-Chaffins, Debra and Drew Haywood. *CNE Training Guide: Networking Technologies, 3rd Edition*. New Riders Publishing. Indianapolis, IN, 1994. ISBN: 1-56205-363-9. Chapter 22 includes descriptions of bridges and repeaters and how they're used on NetWare networks.

Bridging And Switching Techniques

6

Terms you'll need to understand:

√ Transparent bridge

√ Learning bridge

√ Bridge port

√ Bridge protocol data unit (BPDU)

√ Hello frame

√ Virtual LAN

Techniques you'll need to master:

√ Understanding transparent bridging

√ Understanding spanning tree and network reconfiguration

√ Identifying the ideal spanning tree environment

√ Understanding the five bridge states and the bridges' operations in each state

√ Understanding source-route bridging and its use

√ Understanding the benefits of implementing switches

√ Understanding the performance increase realized with full-duplex operation

Bridges and switches provide an important function in today's networks. To fully understand the various types of bridges and how they're used on today's networks, we'll examine both transparent and source-route bridging, as well as Ethernet and token ring switches.

Transparent Bridges

You might be surprised to learn that a transparent bridge is not a networking device encased in clear plastic that allows you to see its innards. Instead, a bridge is called *transparent* because the sending device doesn't know that the receiving device is on a physical network segment, or that there may be multiple bridges between them. These types of bridges are very popular because they don't require a significant amount of configuration. In fact, most transparent bridges require no configuration at all. As you learned in Chapter 5, bridges forward frames based on the physical (MAC) destination address of the packet. On a network using transparent bridges, the sending device simply transmits the packet, assuming the receiving device is on the same segment. In fact, there may or may not be a bridge in the middle that's used to filter traffic.

> *Note: Transparent bridging was defined as part of Project 802; specifically, the 802.1d standard applies.*

As you also learned in Chapter 5, a bridge determines whether to forward a frame based on information in its bridging table. When a transparent bridge is first initialized, it forwards all the frames it receives to all physical network segments except the one from which the frame was received. As it does this, the bridge records the source address of each frame and the port on which the frame was received, thus slowly building its database. Because transparent bridges are able to "learn" the MAC addresses on the network in this fashion, they're called *learning bridges*. However, this is not the only way a bridge's database can be populated. Entries in the transparent bridge's filtering database can also be made manually (using bridge management software) by the administrator for the network. In addition, some filtering database entries, such as broadcast addresses, are static and are added by the bridge manufacturer based on the protocol's specifications. Once the bridge's filtering database is in place, it will only forward those frames that require forwarding.

 If a transparent bridge encounters a destination address that isn't in its filtering database, it automatically forwards the frame down all ports except the port on which the frame was received. This is very important to know because it's very different than what routers do—routers drop packets destined for unknown networks.

The bridge's filtering database uses what is known as a *flat addressing scheme*. An address entry for each device on the network must exist in the database along with every broadcast address and multicast address to be forwarded between physical network segments. Because there's no hierarchy to the structure, as there is with network addresses, this addressing scheme is *flat*.

Understanding Port States

A bridge is actually connected to the physical network segments via at least two bridge ports. If you like, consider these ports as individual network boards for the bridge's separate network segments. Along these lines, a four-port bridge could be considered to have four network boards. Each of the bridge ports operates in one of five states: disabled, blocking, listening, learning, or forwarding. Here's a description of each state:

> *Note: When a bridge is operating using the spanning tree protocol (which is discussed later in this chapter), the ports step through the various states in order when the network is being reconfigured. However, bridges that are disabled do not participate in network reconfiguration.*

➤ **State 1—Disabled** Disabled ports do not share in other stages of the spanning tree operation, such as forwarding or learning. Consider this an "off" switch for the port configured through bridge management.

➤ **State 2—Blocking** The blocking state, also called *standby mode*, is the initial configuration state of all bridges and the constant state of backup bridges in a bridge pair. Nearly all frames received by a port in the blocking state are ignored. Only those frames addressed to the bridge's multicast address are processed.

> *Note: The multicast address is used to manage the bridge.*

➤ **State 3—Listening** When a port is in the listening state, it's getting ready for the learning and forwarding states. A timer is associated with the listening state that's set to allow the network to stabilize during a topology change. While a topology change is occurring, learning and forwarding are disabled to ensure that incorrect information is not added to the filtering database to prevent bridging loops (which we'll discuss at the end of this section).

➤ **State 4—Learning** When a port is in the learning state, it's temporarily unable to forward frames. A timer is also applied to this state to allow the network to stabilize before forwarding to avoid bridging loops.

During this time, the bridge is able to populate its database to the greatest extent before forwarding frames to reduce the number of frames forwarded unnecessarily.

➤ **State 5—Forwarding** The forwarding state is the normal operating state for a bridge. When in this state, the port is able to forward packets, to learn about the network to populate the bridge's filtering table, and to continue in its learning state to maintain the bridge's filtering table. A port is only allowed to transmit frames when it's in the forwarding state.

Understanding The Bridge Relay Entity

When a bridge has two or more ports in forwarding mode, the *relay entity* provides the actual forwarding and filtering services of the bridge. The forwarding entity uses the information in the filtering database to determine whether a particular frame is to be forwarded to another port. The relay entity uses four criteria to determine whether a frame should be forwarded. If a particular frame meets all four criteria, it's sent to the appropriate port; if not, it's discarded. First, the frame must be destined for a remote segment based on the information in the filtering database. Second, the frame must have some upper-layer data. (Because the bridge operates at the Media Access Control, or MAC, sublayer of the Data Link layer of the Open Systems Interconnection (OSI) model, any information from the Logical Link Control, or LLC, sublayer up is considered *upper-layer data*.) Third, the frame must have a valid cyclic redundancy check (CRC). Finally, the frame must not be addressed to the bridge itself. If, and only if, all of these criteria are met, the frame is forwarded to its destination.

For example, using the network shown in Figure 6.1, when Port A of the bridge receives a packet destined for Station 6, the relay agent forwards the frame to Port B based on the information in its filtering database. However, if Port A receives a packet whose destination address is the bridge itself, the frame is processed but not forwarded.

Understanding Store-And-Forward

By default, transparent bridges operate in what is known as *store-and-forward mode*. This means that when a bridge receives a frame, it reads the entire message, stores it temporarily while the frame's CRC is verified, and then forwards the frame if it meets all four of the criteria mentioned earlier. As you know, the CRC is a checksum that's calculated for the frame. When the frame is sent, the sending device calculates a CRC number based on the length of the frame. When the bridge receives the frame, it calculates its own CRC based on the frame it received and compares the new CRC with the original sent with the frame. If they match, the bridge considers the frame to be valid and can forward it. If not, the frame is discarded.

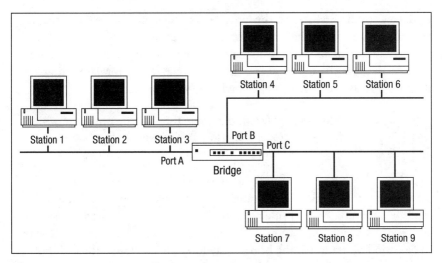

Figure 6.1   A sample network configuration with a bridge.

Because the bridge stores the frame for even a small amount of time, latency (or *delay*) is added to the network transmission by the bridge. As the size of the frame increases, the latency increases. For example, a token ring frame is larger than an Ethernet frame. Therefore, token ring bridges introduce more latency than Ethernet bridges. Of course, by reading the entire frame and calculating its CRC, you can easily remove bad frames from the network.

It's important to note that store-and-forward bridging is not the same as store-and-forward networking. The latter is another term for *message switching*, which is used by applications such as email for message delivery. This is only one of a number of instances in which similar terms are used to describe different networking functions. It's very, very important that you know which function is being discussed.

One other note should be made regarding bridges. They are generally rated by their filtering and forwarding rate, expressed in *packets per second*. Local area network (LAN) bridges can generally filter 10,000 to 12,000 packets per second and forward 6,000 to 8,000 packets per second. As the number of packets per second increases, the bridge becomes more intricate and therefore more expensive.

Understanding The Filtering Database

Using the network discussed earlier and shown in Figure 6.1, let's examine the process of populating the bridge's filtering database. On the network shown in Figure 6.1, the central bridge has been reset and needs to completely populate its database. The first step in this process occurs when Station 3 sends a message to Station 8. As the bridge receives the packet, it stores the packet in memory and adds to notes in its database that Station 3 is located through Port A. Because the database is empty, the relay agent forwards the packet through Port B and Port C, both of which are in forwarding mode.

 A bridge will not forward a frame through the port from which the frame was received. Also, a bridge will not forward a frame through a port that's in any state except forwarding.

As with most network conversations, Station 8 has a reply for Station 3 and sends its response. As the bridge receives this frame, it reads the source address and records Station 8's location on Port C. In addition, because it already knows the location of Station 3, the bridge only forwards the frame through Port A. At this point, any remaining conversation between Station 3 and Station 8 will be correctly forwarded by the bridge, thus eliminating any extraneous traffic on the segment attached to Port B.

As you can imagine, the same process takes place when Station 5 and Station 7 communicate. The bridge receives the first frame from Station 5, records its location on Port B, and forwards the frame through both Port A and Port C. Then, when Station 7 responds, it records its location on Port C and forwards the frame through Port B. Table 6.1 shows an example of the filtering database built by the bridge so far.

The bridge is able to further populate its filtering database when Station 6 converses with Station 5. As the bridge receives the frame from Station 6 on Port B, it stores the frame and records Station 6's location on Port B. However, because the bridge already knows the location of Station 5 and realizes that it's on the same segment as the frame that was received, it does not forward the frame, but instead discards it. This process repeats as the various stations communicate amongst themselves. Eventually, the bridge knows the location of all devices on all segments and is able to accurately filter all traffic.

Table 6.1   The filtering database for the sample network.

Port/Segment	Station
A	3
B	5
C	7,8

Understanding Bridging Loops

Of course, a network with a single bridge includes a single point of failure—the bridge itself. For this reason, many networks are designed with redundant bridges for fault tolerance. This can, however, lead to rather large problems in the form of bridging loops. A *bridging loop* is created when data packets circle in an endless loop between two bridges and never reach their proper destination. The term bridging loop is also applied to broadcast storms that occur when the spanning tree algorithm is not used on a bridged network. A *broadcast storm* is actually a variation of a typical bridging loop in that new packets are continuously transmitted by redundant bridges. Both of these occurrences can prove catastrophic for a LAN.

In the first scenario, shown in Figure 6.2, two network segments are connected to two bridges. As Station 1 transmits a frame destined for Station 6, both bridges receive the frame, note its location on Segment A, and then forward it on to Segment B. However, because each bridge is different and a small distance apart from the other bridges on the network, one bridge is able to transmit the frame slightly before the other—in this case, Bridge B. When Bridge A receives the frame, it has no indication that the frame was forwarded by another bridge, but thinks that Station 1, which it had noted was on Segment A, is now on Segment B and updates its bridging table. Table 6.2 shows the bridging tables for Bridge A and Bridge B at this moment.

Bridge A, acting as all good bridges would, then forwards the frame noting that Station 1 is on Segment B. Bridge B then receives the frame that was

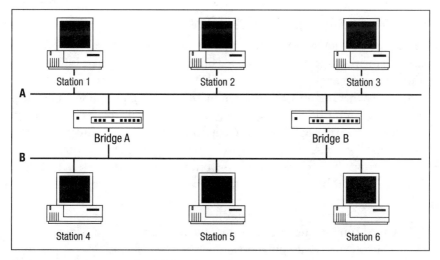

Figure 6.2   A network with bridging loop potential.

Table 6.2	The bridging tables' databases.	
Bridge	**Port/Segment**	**Station**
A	Segment A	
A	Segment B	Station 1
B	Segment A	Station 1
B	Segment B	

forwarded from Bridge A. The source address for this notes that Station 1 is on Segment B, and Bridge B updates its database accordingly. To recap, at this point, Bridges A and B both think that Station 1 is located on Segment B, which is, of course, not the case. This process could go on indefinitely with each bridge updating its tables continuously, switching between the correct segment and the incorrect segment—and all this from only one frame and two bridges. If more stations were to attempt to send data in this environment or more bridges were involved, the problem would be compounded by traffic congestion and a slow down would occur.

Eliminating Bridging Loops

The spanning tree protocol was designed to eliminate bridging loops on networks. It's a bridging hierarchy protocol that defines routes between network segments with redundant paths. Like transparent bridging in general, the spanning tree protocol is part of the IEEE 802.1d standard.

Benefits Of Spanning Tree

To eliminate bridging loops, the spanning tree protocol assigns one bridge in each pair of bridges to be the designated bridge—the other bridge is the backup bridge. In this manner, each bridge can dynamically discover a segment of the bridged tree that is loop-free. In addition, the spanning tree protocol provides mechanisms for the bridges to communicate among themselves and to be aware of each other's existence. This is different from other bridging situations in that bridges that do not use the spanning tree protocol are not aware of other bridges on the network. This capability lets the bridges automatically detect a bridge or segment failure and reconfigure themselves to correct for the problem.

 Spanning tree eliminates bridging loops, provides dynamic path configuration between redundant bridges, and provides dynamic reconfiguration in the event of a failure.

As with all hierarchies, something has to be in charge. In a spanning tree network, it's the root bridge. The *root bridge* is primarily responsible for periodically sending configuration messages that are forwarded by the designated bridges. These configuration messages are the means by which a spanning tree network recognizes an error in the network and reconfigures the bridges accordingly. Figure 6.3 shows a sample network with a root bridge, designated bridges, and backup bridges.

Spanning Tree Configuration

To configure the spanning tree, the protocol includes a specialized packet called the *bridge protocol data unit (BPDU)*. By using the BPDU, bridges are able to communicate with each other to establish the root bridge and the designated and backup bridges.

Understanding Bridge Identification Numbers (Bridge IDs)

The bridge identification number (bridge ID) plays a key role in the spanning tree network. The bridge with the lowest bridge ID automatically becomes the root bridge. Fortunately, bridge IDs can often be set by the administrator, which gives the administrator control over how the network is reconfigured in the

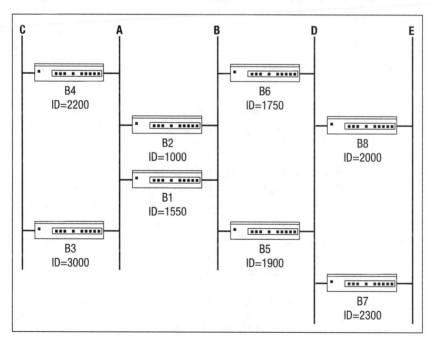

Figure 6.3   A sample spanning tree network.

event of a failure. (We'll examine this process more closely later in this chapter.) The lowest bridge ID should be assigned to the bridge closest to the center of the network. This speeds up the time required to reconfigure the bridges in the event of a failure.

 Each spanning tree network can have only one root bridge.

A bridge ID is an 8-byte number in which only two of the bytes (the first two) can be configured by the administrator. The last 6 bytes are actually the remainder of the universally assigned MAC address for the port adapter. You need to consider a bridge's configuration options when designing your network and purchasing bridges. The ability to configure bridge and port IDs is very important and generally involves some type of management software, which is often based on the Simple Network Management Protocol (SNMP).

Choosing The Root Bridge

To initiate the process of setting up a spanning tree network, the bridges must first select the root bridge. To do this, every bridge on the network broadcasts a frame down all ports containing, in addition to normal fields for the network type, the BPDU. The BPDU itself is divided into six sections:

➤ **Bridge ID** The 8-byte ID of the bridge sending the message.

➤ **Constants** The constants field includes a 2-byte protocol identifier entry, a 1-byte version entry, and a 1-byte message type entry.

➤ **Flag** This 1-byte field indicates whether the frame is for topology change notification (TC) or topology change notification acknowledgement (TCA).

➤ **Miscellaneous** The miscellaneous fields include the port ID (used to determine the root bridge if two bridges have the same bridge ID), the message age (the amount of time since the last configuration message), the max age (the amount of time before the message is deleted), the hello time (the amount of time since the last configuration message from the root bridge), and the forward delay (the delay before proceeding to the next state during reconfiguration).

➤ **Port Cost** The 4-byte cost assignment of the path to the root bridge.

➤ **Root ID** The 8-byte ID of the root bridge.

To fully examine this process, let's use a hypothetical (though slightly unrealistic) network environment in which all bridges are powered on at the same time. As this happens, each bridge broadcasts itself as the root bridge by populating both the Root ID and Bridge ID fields of the BPDU with its ID. The frame's LLC control field contains a message that tells each bridge to copy all BPDUs it receives. If a bridge receives a frame containing a lower bridge ID than its own in the Root ID field, it stops broadcasting itself as the root bridge and inserts the lower bridge ID into the Root ID field for all subsequent broadcasts. Use the information in Table 6.3 as a reference for the following example.

Let's say that all the bridges are powered on at the same time. Bridge B4 begins by broadcasting a frame with the Bridge ID equal to 2200 and the root ID equal to 2200. As the various frames traverse the network, Bridge B4 receives a frame from Bridge B5. At this point, B4 changes its broadcast frame to the following:

➤ Bridge ID=2200

➤ Root ID=1900

As this process continues and B4 receives a frame from B3, it does not change the Root ID in its broadcast frame, but rather ignores the information because it already knows that Bridge ID 1900 (B5) is the root. However, as B4 receives a broadcast frame from B2, or another bridge that has already determined that B2 is the correct root, B4 again changes its broadcast frame to Bridge ID=2200, Root ID=1000. This continues until all bridges recognize B2 as the valid root bridge. At this point, Bridge B2 uses the spanning tree protocol to transmit BPDU frames down all its ports every two seconds, which is the Institute of Electrical and Electronics Engineers (IEEE) recommended default.

Table 6.3 Sample network bridge ID configurations.	
Bridge	**Bridge ID**
B1	1550
B2	1000
B3	3000
B4	2200
B5	1900
B6	1750
B7	2300
B8	2000

Designated Bridges

Once the root bridge has been determined, each pair of redundant bridges must specify the designated bridge for that pair before they can forward frames. The BPDUs sent on the network are copied from the bridge's root ports—the ports closest to the root bridge. Each BPDU includes a field for port cost. The root bridge sets the port cost for its BPDU to 0. All other bridges have port costs assigned by the administrator. As a bridge receives the BPDU from the root bridge, it includes its port cost in the new BPDU that it broadcasts down its other ports. As the bridges on a given network segment receive the BPDUs from the other bridges, they examine the port costs assigned to the other bridges. For a given redundant bridge pair, the bridge with the lowest port cost becomes the designated bridge. The other bridge places the involved port into the blocking state and becomes the backup bridge for the pair.

Using the sample network discussed earlier, shown again in Figure 6.4, with port costs added, let's take a look at how the various pairs of bridges determine the designated bridge.

As B5 receives the BPDU from the root bridge (B2), its port cost is 0. It then adds its port cost to the existing port cost and broadcasts the BPDU with a port cost of 25. At the same time, B6 receives the BPDU and resends it with a

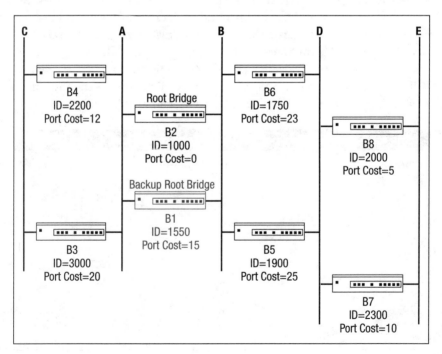

Figure 6.4 The sample bridging network.

port cost of 23. As each bridge receives the other's BPDU on network segment D, it determines that B6 should be the designated bridge because it has the lower port cost. At that point, B5 goes into blocking state, thus becoming the backup bridge, and B6 rebroadcasts the BPDU on segment D. Bridges B7 and B8 receive the BPDU from B6 and go through the same process, adding their respective port costs to the BPDU and sending them down segment E. The BPDU from B7 has a port cost of 33, whereas the BPDU from B8 has a port cost of 28, making B8 the designated bridge for that pair. While all this has been going on, bridges B3 and B4 have gone through the same process and determined that B4 is the designated bridge for the pair.

The Topology Change Process

In the previous example, B2 is the root bridge, and bridges B4, B6, and B8 are the designated bridges for their segments. So what happens when the topology of the network changes, such as when bridge B6 fails? In this case, before the failure, B5 is the backup bridge and is in the blocking state. While in this state, it monitors BPDUs on the network but no other traffic. When B5 does not receive a BPDU from the designated bridge within a certain amount of time, it determines that B6 is not longer functioning and sends a topology change notification (TC) BPDU on its root port. The only time a bridge in the blocking state will send a frame is when it finds it necessary to send a TC.

The bridge that detected the failure (B5) will continue to broadcast TC frames until the upstream designated bridge acknowledges receipt. This continues until the root bridge acknowledges the receipt. When this occurs, the root bridge begins transmitting BPDUs with the topology change notification acknowledgement (TCA) bit set every two seconds. Eventually, all bridges receive the TCA BPDUs. When a bridge receives a BPDU with the TCA bit set, it stops forwarding frames (switches to the blocking state) and clears its database of all dynamically configured records; permanent records are not deleted.

Once all bridges are in the blocking state, they wait a specific amount of time as designated in the BPDU from the root bridge. Once this timeout has passed, all bridges repeat the process of determining the designated bridge for a particular network segment based on port cost. At this point, bridges B4 and B8 remain the designated bridges, and bridge B5 becomes the new designated bridge for its pair. Once the reconfiguration is complete, normal BPDUs (without the TCA bit set) will be sent by the root bridge.

Configuring An Ideal Spanning Tree

When designing a spanning tree network, you need to take into account the network reconfiguration process in the event of a failure. The more spread out

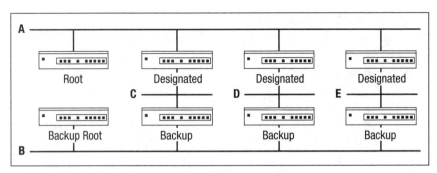

Figure 6.5 The ideal spanning tree network.

the network design, the longer the reconfiguration process. Figure 6.5 shows an ideal spanning tree network configuration.

In the configuration shown in Figure 6.5, there's a redundant route to every segment, providing access for all devices in the event of a failure. In addition, no frame will have to travel through more than two bridges between source and destination during normal operation, and no more than three bridges in the event of a failure. This decreases travel time and increases network performance. Finally, this network configuration provides for fast reconfiguration in the event of a failure because all BPDUs are forwarded only one level to and from the root bridge, because each bridge's root port is located on the same segment as the root bridge.

Source-Routing Bridges

Source-routing bridges, which are most often used on token ring networks, are very different from transparent bridges. Source-routing bridges do not maintain a filtering database; instead, each device in a source-routing network maintains its own table of routes for the devices with which it communicates. *Source routing* means that the frame's source determines the route the frame will take through the network.

The routing information for source-routing networks is included in the MAC header of the frame. The bridges then forward or filter the frame based on the information contained in this header. Also, unlike transparent bridges, source-routing bridges only copy frames that include source-routing information in the header, whereas transparent bridges copy all frames.

Although the header information for a source-routing frame contains a specific route through the network, the process is still technically bridging because it pertains to physical addresses rather than network addresses.

The Route Discovery Process

Each device on a source-routing network maintains its own list of routes to devices with which it communicates. Source-routing devices do this through a process called *route discovery*. When performing route discovery, a device sends a hello frame to the destination device. As the packet passes through each intermediate device on the network, the various bridges append new route information to the information already carried on the frame.

In doing this, by the time the frame reaches the destination device, it contains a complete route from the source to the destination. At that point, the receiving device returns the hello frame with the complete route included. When the hello frame is received by the original sender, it records the route information in its table.

Most source-routing network environments, including IBM Token Ring, use a form of the Logical Link Control (LLC) Exchange Identification (XID) packet as the hello packet. However, any protocol that uses a hello packet that requires a handshake between the two devices will work in a source-routing network.

In a typical token ring environment, devices attempt to reduce network traffic by first sending a frame without source-routing information. The sending system knows that the destination device is on the local ring if the frame returns with the Address Recognized Indicator (ARI) bit set. If not, it will send a new frame that includes the source-routing information. As the routing table is populated, it's typically stored in RAM and is dynamic. Entries are maintained as long as the system is powered on or until a particular entry is reset or written over when the time limit is exceeded.

Ethernet Switches

Historically, as Ethernet networks grew and were slowly bogged down by excessive traffic, there were relatively few options available to improve performance. The network's administrator could choose to either segment the network with bridges or replace Ethernet with a network architecture that provided higher throughput. Neither of these solutions was ideal. Segmenting the network with bridges introduced a number of limitations and caveats, including bridging loops, a lack of redundancy, and message flooding or broadcast storms. Implementing a higher-performance network architecture often required replacing nearly all components in the network, including network boards in the computers, hubs, routers, bridges, networked printer adapters, and sometimes even the network wiring. This could be very costly both in time and money.

Types Of Switches

Nowadays, however, a third option is available—switching hubs. As you learned in Chapter 5, a switching hub allows you to increase usable network bandwidth by combining the functions of a multiport repeater and a high-speed bridge that operates more quickly than a standard hub. Implementing a switching hub allows you to use existing hardware, except for the hubs being replaced.

To perform its function, a switching hub builds a table containing the MAC addresses of all devices connected to each port, rather than broadcasting an incoming frame down all ports of the bridge. As with a bridge, a switch will only pass an incoming frame down the port to which the destination device is connected. Typically, a switch can monitor traffic on every port and switch among multiple ports. Each port on the switch can be connected to a single station or even to a smaller 10BaseT hub. On a switch, each port represents an independent collision domain in which devices only compete for bandwidth with other devices in the domain. For example, if a 100-port switch has one port attached to a 12-port Ethernet hub, only those 12 computers attached to the hub must compete for it rather than compete with 100 or more stations. This significantly reduces congestion and collisions on the network as a whole.

By connecting a single computer to each port on the switch, you're in effect dedicating bandwidth to that computer. For example, if 12 computers are connected to a 10BaseT hub, all 12 computers share 10Mbps. However, if the network uses a switch, each computer is able to use a full 10Mbps pipe.

Perhaps the biggest problem with switches today is the lack of available management tools. Most conventional network analyzers see only what is transmitted on the cable to which the analyzer is attached. In this environment, the analyzer will not paint an accurate picture of the network traffic. Some switch vendors have created proprietary solutions that solve this monitoring problem. Other vendors provide a management port or the ability to configure a port to monitor network traffic.

There are typically two basic types of Ethernet switches available—10Mbps and 100Mbps. Many network boards are available that will automatically detect the speed of the network to ease configuration and transition between 10Mbps and 100Mbps Ethernet. Most often, available switches can include both 10Mbps and 100Mbps ports. What's more, some switches are able to alternate between various MAC-layer protocols, such as Ethernet and Fiber Distributed Data Interface (FDDI).

In addition to the speed of the network, a switch can operate as either a store-and-forward switch or a cut-through switch. A switch that receives the entire frame and verifies its integrity before forwarding is a store-and-forward switch.

This switch operates in the same way as a transparent bridge. The latency introduced through store-and-forward switching varies from switch to switch, but it generally averages around 1,200 microseconds. The latency increases as the size of the frame increases.

A cut-through switch, on the other hand, reduces the latency to around 40 microseconds by reading only the destination address in the header of the frame and immediately forwarding the frame to its destination before receiving the entire frame. In addition, a cut-through switch's latency does not vary depending on frame size but stays at a constant 40 microseconds. This yields a much higher throughput on the network but increases the risk of propagating bad packets.

There are some switches that can be configured to operate in either store-and-forward or cut-through mode. In addition, many switches include a monitoring port to track network performance and, when operating in cut-through mode, revert to store-and-forward mode if the number of errors on the port exceeds a specific threshold.

Switch Ports In Full-Duplex Mode

In those networks where a dedicated link can be made between a switch port and a server or workstation, the workstation no longer needs to listen for collisions. This means that the link can operate in full-duplex mode. In this configuration, if the inbound and outbound traffic are balanced, throughput on this type of link can reach 20Mbps (10Mbps inbound and 10Mbps outbound). This type of configuration is seen most often with high-traffic servers, such as those hosting video conferencing, because the traffic tends to be the same in both directions. If the inbound and outbound traffic are not symmetrical, the benefits of operating in full-duplex mode are minimal.

Multiple Connections Between Switch And Server

One option available with NetWare servers is to connect more than one server network board to a switch. For example, if a server includes four network boards, each board can be connected to its own port on the switch, thus providing up to 400Mbps in the correct circumstances. This type of configuration requires a special NetWare Loadable Module (NLM) on the server that balances the traffic between the various network boards.

Switches And Virtual Local Area Networks (LANs)

Whereas a standard Ethernet switch provides evident improvements over bridges or repeaters in many situations, a switch is still limited in that it creates a flat Data Link layer architecture. This setup does not scale well beyond more than a few dozen network segments because restrictions, such as excessive broad-cast propagation, limit all bridge topologies. Many Ethernet switches, therefore, can be configured to support multiple broadcast domains called virtual LANs (VLANs), as shown in Figure 6.6.

A *VLAN* is, in essence, a group of LAN segments combined to create a sepa-rate network. The effect is the same as dedicating one switch to a particular set of segments. In a VLAN, broadcasts travel to all end stations in the group, rather than to all stations connected to the switch. A switch can create VLANs at either the OSI Data Link layer or the Network layer.

Data Link Layer

The administrator usually configures switches that utilize the Data Link layer to create VLANs. The configuration software allows you to specify a group of switch ports as a low-latency switched workgroup. Traffic within the workgroup is switched using the MAC addresses of the end stations. However, for VLANs on the same switch to communicate, some type of router is generally required. The router can be either a separate box or a Network layer-aware card in the switch itself.

 Except in special configurations, VLANs on a switch are not allowed to communicate with each other. If a switch is divided into three VLANs, a device on VLAN 1 will not be able to commu-nicate with a device on VLAN 3 without the intervention of a router.

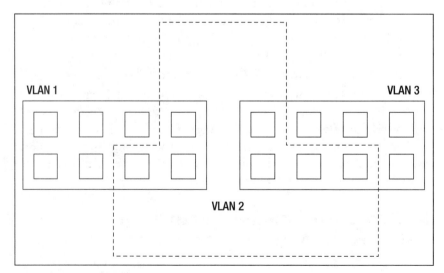

Figure 6.6 VLANs can be configured on many switches.

Network Layer

Some newer switches include Network layer technology that's used to create VLANs. These Layer-3 (Network) switches are protocol-aware and understand the subnet fields of IP and other protocols. Like Data Link layer VLANs, Network layer VLANs are created by configuring specific ports as subnets using specific protocols. Traffic within the virtual subnet is switched at the Data Link layer, whereas traffic between the virtual subnets is routed at the Network layer. Ethernet switches that include Network layer functionality are generally powerful enough only to handle routing within a local departmental setting. They generally do not have the extended capabilities to handle enterprise routing.

It should be noted that many Network layer switches are able to configure separate VLANs for each protocol, and that each port on a particular switch can support as many different VLANs as there are protocols. For example, in Figure 6.7, Port 1 is configured for Internetwork Packet Exchange (IPX) VLAN1 and Internet Protocol (IP) VLAN2, Port 2 is configured for IPX VLAN1 and IP VLAN1, Port 3 is configured for IPX VLAN2 and IP VLAN1, and Port 4 is configured for IPX VLAN2 and IP VLAN1. When you're dealing with this type of switch, detailed diagrams are often necessary to keep track of the various VLANs, their protocols, and their addresses.

Switches On Token Ring Networks

Although many token ring advocates have not, until recently, seen the need for token ring switches, these switches are slowly becoming more and more prevalent in today's networks. Most token ring administrators have been content with

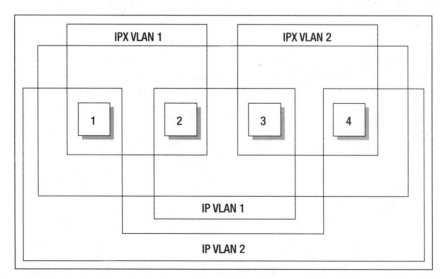

Figure 6.7   A switch with separate VLANs for each protocol.

the 16Mbps throughput and high utilization realized with standard token ring installations. However, as the need for bandwidth grows, token ring switches are taking their place in networking.

Like Ethernet switches, token ring switches can operate in either cut-through or store-and-forward mode, offer many of the same advantages, and suffer the same disadvantages. Token ring switches are easy to install and offer a simple plug-and-play solution for over-taxed token ring backbones. Installation is as easy as removing the cables from the existing dual-port bridges and plugging them into the switch ports. On networks using dual-port source-routing bridges, the switch can replace the physical backbone ring and most of the bridges attached to the ring.

Token ring switches offer performance benefits similar to Ethernet switches. The most recognized of these is that by implementing a switch, you provide the network the capability to provide full 16Mbps connections between any two ring segments at any time. This is similar to the dedicated 10Mbps or 100Mbps afforded to Ethernet switch ports. In this manner, token ring switches eliminate campus-wide bottlenecks created by backbone rings. In addition, implementing a switch can ease the design restrictions imposed on token ring networks by reducing the number of hops in campus networks. All segments attached to the switch see the switch as a single hop. By reducing the number of hops, you reduce the latency in the network, thereby increasing the throughput on the network.

Also like Ethernet switches, token ring switches can increase available server bandwidth by dedicating a full 16Mbps to the server's connection and, when using NetWare, dynamically balance the load between multiple server network boards. Of course, this also requires a specialized NLM running on the server. In a typical token ring network, half-duplex communication is standard. Token ring switches, like Ethernet switches, are able to utilize full-duplex mode to provide up to 32Mbps communication paths.

The single biggest drawback to token ring switches is also shared by Ethernet switches: the lack of analysis tools. However, again like Ethernet switches, token ring switches are now appearing on the market with the capability to remotely monitor their communication through a monitoring port.

Practice Questions

Question 1

During a topology change in a spanning tree network, which bridge is responsible for transmitting the TCA frame?

○ a. Root bridge

○ b. Designated bridge

○ c. Backup root bridge

○ d. Backup bridge

Answer a is correct. Once the root bridge receives the TCN frame, it transmits the TCA frame, notifying all bridges on the network that a reconfiguration is necessary. The designated bridge receives and retransmits the TCA frame, but does not initiate transmission of the TCA frame. Therefore, answer b is incorrect. The backup root bridge and backup bridge are most often in the blocking state and will not initiate a TCA frame. Therefore, answers c and d are incorrect.

Question 2

In the event that two bridges have been assigned the same bridge ID and are both eligible to be the root bridge, which of the following fields is used to determine which bridge will become the root?

○ a. Port cost

○ b. Port state

○ c. Port name

○ d. Port ID

Answer d is correct. When two bridges have the same ID, the port ID is used to determine which bridge will become the root. The port cost, on the other hand, is used to determine which bridge will be the designated bridge. Therefore, answer a is incorrect. Port state and port name are not fields that are included in the BPDU. Therefore, answers b and c are incorrect.

Question 3

During the source route discovery process, which device is responsible for sending a hello frame?

- ○ a. The transparent bridge attempting to populate its filtering database
- ○ b. The destination device
- ○ c. The source device
- ○ d. The intermediate bridge between the source and destination

Answer c is correct. During route discovery, the source device sends a hello frame to determine the route to the destination device. A transparent bridge does not deal with hello packets. Therefore, answer a is incorrect. The destination device responds to the source with a complete route but does not transmit a hello frame. Therefore, answer b is incorrect. During route discovery, the intermediate bridge includes its information in the packet as part of the route, but it does not initiate sending the hello frame. Therefore, answer d is incorrect.

Question 4

Which of the following bridge operating modes introduces the least amount of latency in an Ethernet network?

- ○ a. Cut-through mode
- ○ b. Forwarding mode
- ○ c. Store-and-forward mode
- ○ d. Blocking mode

Answer a is correct. A bridge operating in cut-through mode introduces less delay than a bridge operating in store-and-forward mode. The forwarding and blocking states have no effect on latency. Therefore, answers b and d are incorrect. As mentioned, store-and-forward introduces greater latency than cut-through mode. Therefore, answer c is incorrect.

Question 5

> Which of the following statements correctly describes the con-
> figuration of the root bridge?
>
> ○ a. The root bridge has the lowest bridge ID and is assigned
>   a port cost of 0.
>
> ○ b. The root bridge has the lowest bridge ID and is assigned
>   a port cost manually.
>
> ○ c. The root bridge has the highest bridge ID and is assigned
>   a port cost of 0.
>
> ○ d. The root bridge has the highest bridge ID and is assigned
>   a port cost manually.

Answer a is correct. The root bridge is the bridge on the network with the lowest bridge ID. After the root bridge has been determined, it overrides its manually configured port cost and broadcasts its port cost as 0. The other configurations listed in the question do not accurately describe the root bridge. Therefore, answers b, c, and d are incorrect.

Question 6

> During normal bridge operation, in which of the following states
> are transparent bridges able to transmit frames?
>
> ○ a. Blocking
>
> ○ b. Forwarding
>
> ○ c. Learning
>
> ○ d. Listening

Answer b is correct. Bridges are only able to forward frames when they are in the forwarding state. When a backup bridge senses an error on the network, it's able to transmit a TCN frame from the blocking state, but this is not part of normal bridge operation. Therefore, answer a is incorrect. During the learning and listening states, the bridge is not able to transmit frames at all. Therefore, answers c and d are incorrect.

Question 7

> What is the maximum throughput in megabits per second for a single token ring switch port?
>
> O a. 16Mbps
>
> O b. 10Mbps
>
> O c. 32Mbps
>
> O d. 20Mbps

Answer c is correct. A token ring bridge port operating in full-duplex mode can achieve up to 32Mbps transfer rate. 16Mbps is one of the standard operating speeds for a token ring network, but it does not represent the maximum throughput available through a token ring switch. Therefore, answer a is incorrect—and the reason why this is a trick question. 10Mbps and 20Mbps represent Ethernet transmission speeds, not token ring. Therefore, answers b and d are incorrect.

Question 8

> Which of the following statements accurately describes the role of the relay entity?
>
> O a. The relay entity transmits the hello packet to determine the route from source to destination.
>
> O b. The relay entity identifies the designated bridge.
>
> O c. The relay entity provides the forwarding and filtering services of the bridge.
>
> O d. The relay entity is responsible for VLAN creation and maintenance.

Answer c is correct. The relay entity is responsible for the forwarding and filtering services of the bridge. The other roles mentioned are performed by portions of the bridge other than the relay entity. Therefore, answers a, b, and d are incorrect.

Question 9

> At which two layers of the OSI model are switches able to establish VLANs? [Choose the two best answers]
>
> ❏ a. Physical
>
> ❏ b. Data Link
>
> ❏ c. Network
>
> ❏ d. Transport

Answers b and c are correct. Depending on the type of switch used, VLANs can be established at either the Data Link or Network layer. The Physical and Transport layers are not involved in VLAN creation. Therefore, answers a and d are incorrect.

Question 10

> Which of the following are eliminated by implementing the spanning tree protocol? [Choose the two best answers]
>
> ❏ a. Faulty packets
>
> ❏ b. Bridging loops
>
> ❏ c. Broadcast storms
>
> ❏ d. Extraneous traffic

Answers b and c are correct. Although the spanning tree protocol was initially designed to eliminate bridging loops, it also serves to remove broadcast storms from networks. Removal of both faulty packets and extraneous traffic are benefits realized by implementing bridges in general, not just those using the spanning tree protocol. Therefore, answers a and d are incorrect—and the reason why this is a trick question.

Need To Know More?

 Niedermiller-Chaffins, Debra and Drew Haywood. *CNE Training Guide: Networking Technologies, 3rd Edition*. New Riders Publishing. Indianapolis, IN, 1994. ISBN 1-56205-363-9. Chapter 3 discusses both transparent and source-routing bridges.

 Perlman, Radia. *Interconnections: Bridges and Routers*. Addison-Wesley. Reading, MA, 1992. ISBN 0-201-56332-0. Chapter 3 is dedicated to transparent bridges and the spanning tree protocol, and Chapter 4 deals with source-route bridging. Radia Perlman played a pivotal role in the creation of the spanning tree algorithm and presents this section from the perspective of one of its key designers.

Routers And Routing Protocols

7

Terms you'll need to understand:

√ Logical or software address

√ Hop

√ Routing information table

√ Distance vector algorithms

√ Link-state algorithms

√ Convergence

√ Count-to-infinity problem

√ Split horizon and split horizon with poison reverse

√ Link State Packet (LSP)

Techniques you'll need to master:

√ Understanding the basic routing process and the roles of the Open Systems Interconnection (OSI) layers involved

√ Understanding how distance vector routers populate their routing information tables

√ Understanding the count-to-infinity problem and how it can be reduced on distance vector networks

√ Understanding how link-state routing algorithms work

√ Understanding how load balancing can increase available network bandwidth

As networks grow to incorporate more devices, the various networking limitations come into play. Each networking architecture limits the maximum length of a network segment and the maximum number of devices attached to that segment. To alleviate this potential problem, complex networking devices called *routers* were developed. With the implementation of routers comes routing techniques to determine paths between the networks.

Understanding Routing

Before we examine the process of routing information between devices on an internetwork, let's recap the process of communicating between devices on the same subnet. As data on the sending device is passed from the Application layer through to the Physical layer of the Open Systems Interconnection (OSI) model, each layer adds header information that's used by its peer layer on the receiving device. Upon receipt, these headers are stripped off and acted upon until, at the Application layer, the final header is removed and only the pure data remains. Figure 7.1 shows an example of the headers added to the source data. Note that the Application layer's header is closest to the data, then the Presentation layer's header, the Session layer's header, and so on until the header information on the outside of the packet belongs to the Physical layer.

It should be noted that at each layer of the OSI model, the lower layer treats the entire data block, including existing headers and trailers, as "data." For example, at the Transport layer, the data section of the packet includes the original data message and the Application, Presentation, and Session headers. (We should also mention that the Data Link layer header information includes physical source and destination fields, whereas the Network layer header includes logical source and destination fields.)

During communication between devices on the same subnet, only the Data Link layer header information is involved. As a packet traverses the network, the Physical layer on each device reads the packet and passes it to the Data Link layer. The Data Link layer then reads the destination physical address from the packet and determines whether it's the packet's destination. If it's not, the Data Link layer discards the packet and waits for the next transmission. If it is, the Data Link layer passes the information on to the upper layers involved in the conversation.

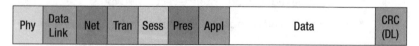

Figure 7.1   A sample packet structure with each layer's information attached.

An additional dynamic is introduced when routing information on an internetwork. The source device must be able to recognize that the destination device is not on the local subnet and forward the packet to the appropriate intermediary device, such as a router. To route packets through an internetwork, routers need to know a path to the destination network. This process is independent of the underlying media and uses logical software addresses assigned to the networks. Remember that software (logical) addresses differ from hardware (physical) addresses. A *physical address* defines a specific device, whereas a *software address* defines both the device and the network. The network part of the software address can be configured to mirror a hierarchical network topology.

The software address used by the Network layer can be either purely logical or partially based on the physical address of the device. The Internet Protocol (IP), whose addressing scheme you'll learn about in Chapter 9, is an example of a purely logical Network layer protocol. The logical address comprises both the network and device addresses. With this type of protocol, an association must be made between the software address and the hardware address. Internetwork Packet Exchange (IPX), on the other hand, uses a logical network address and the physical address of the device to create the Network layer addresses. (IPX is covered in detail in Chapters 15, 16, and 17.)

The Routing Process

At first glance, routing is a daunting process. However, when examined at its most basic level, it can be a simple and elegant solution for getting from point A to point B or, as in the example shown in Figure 7.2, from Station 1 to Station 8. To make understanding this whole process much easier, we'll assign addresses based on the device or network's name. For example, Station 1's physical address is 111, Router 2's physical address is RT2, and Network D's logical address is DDD.

In the network shown in Figure 7.2, Station 1 has a physical address of 111 and is on Network A, whose network address is AAA. Rather than discuss an existing protocol in this example, we'll use the example DWJ (Data Without Jumbles) protocol, whose structure is similar to IPX. DWJ uses a logical network address and the physical address of the devices to create the Network layer source and destination addresses. In our sample network, all devices are able to communicate using DWJ. Networks A, B, C, and D are all Ethernet networks, whereas Network F is Fiber Distributed Data Interface (FDDI). (You'll learn more about the various types of networks in later chapters in this book.) This is important to note because routing takes place above the Physical and Data Link layers and can be used to send information across different types of networks.

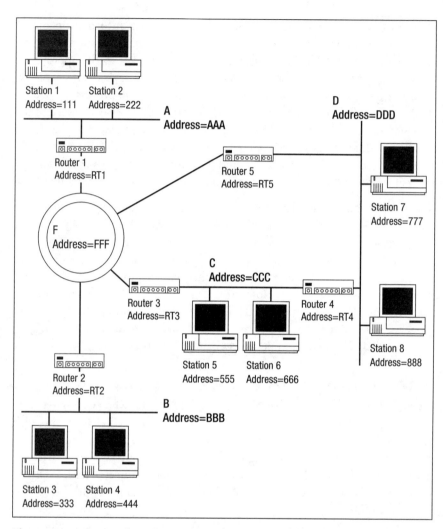

Figure 7.2 A sample routing network.

When a process on Station 1 determines that it has information to send to Station 8, it acquires its software address and queues the data to be transmitted. In the DWJ protocol format, this is *network.physical address*, or DDD.888. As the information is passed through the layers of the OSI model on the workstation, the Network layer header is added with the following information: source=AAA.111, destination=DDD.888. When building this header, the DWJ protocol recognizes that the destination device is not on the local network; therefore, it must send the information to an intermediary device, such as Router 1. At this point, the protocol instructs the Data Link layer to transmit the packet in a Media Access Control (MAC) frame with a physical destination

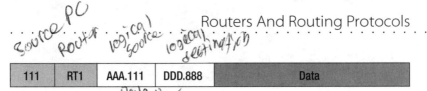

[handwritten annotations: Source PC, Router, logical source, logical destination]

| 111 | RT1 | AAA.111 | DDD.888 | Data |

[handwritten annotations: Data link, Physical]

Figure 7.3 A data packet ready to be transmitted from Station 1 to Station 8, via Router 1.

address of RT1. Figure 7.3 shows what this packet might look like at the Data Link layer. This packet is then passed to the Physical layer for transmission over the network.

When Router 1 receives the packet, it strips the Physical layer header and passes the information to the Data Link layer. At this point, the Data Link layer verifies the validity of the packet by checking its cyclic redundancy check (CRC) and then strips its headers and passes the packet to the Network layer. The routing table for Router 1 is shown in Table 7.1.

The Network layer on Router 1 immediately recognizes that it's not connected directly to Network D and references its routing table to determine which router is the next step in reaching the packet's destination—in this case, Router 5. In the routing table, Router 1 notices that Network D is only one hop, or router, away. This means that Router 5 is directly connected to the destination network. Once the DWJ protocol has determined where to send the packet, it sends the data to the Data Link layer with instructions to send the data to Router 5. The new packet that's created is shown in Figure 7.4. This packet is then sent to the Physical layer for transmission over Network F.

Similarly, when Router 5 copies the packet from the network, it strips the Physical layer header and sends it to the Data Link layer, which verifies the CRC, strips its own headers, and sends the data to the Network layer. When the Network layer on Router 5 reads the destination field, it knows that it's connected directly to the destination network. The DWJ protocol on Router 5

Table 7.1	Router 1's routing table.	
Network	**Hops**	**Next Hop**
FFF	0	None
BBB	1	RT2
CCC	1	RT3
DDD	1	RT5

| RT1 | RT5 | AAA.111 | DDD.888 | Data |

Figure 7.4 The packet with the new physical source and destination information.

RT5	888	AAA.111	DDD.888	Data

Figure 7.5 The last packet with the new physical source and destination addresses.

then sends the information back to the Data Link layer with instructions to send the packet with Station 8's address as the physical destination address. This last packet is shown in Figure 7.5.

Now, on Station 8, the DWJ protocol copies the packet off the network and determines that the physical destination is itself. It then sends the information to the Network layer, which reviews the software address and makes the same determination. At this point, it strips the Network layer header and sends the information up the OSI model to the upper layers.

The Routing Database

As you saw in the previous example, a router uses the information in its *routing information table*, also called a *routing database* or *routing table*, to determine the packet's path through the network. These tables describe the location of all the networks that make up the internetwork with respect to each router's position in the internetwork. As you also saw earlier, each router will examine a packet it receives and either forward it to the destination device or to the next step on the road to the destination—another router. As the next router receives the packet, it performs the same function until the packet is received by the destination device.

The process of passing the packet from one router to another is referred to as a *hop*. Many routing protocols limit the number of hops a packet can take to ensure that packets are not continuously routed through the internetwork. In a router's database, each route to a network is assigned a cost, often based on the number of hops between the router and the destination. Some protocols, however, are able to use other variables, such as the speed of the line connecting the routers, to determine the cost for a particular route. When multiple routes exist between a router and a destination network, the router will generally only keep the route with the lowest cost in its routing information table. Routing protocols, sometimes called *route discovery protocols*, are used to populate and maintain a router's routing information table.

In many ways, a routing protocol is like an upper-layer process. The routing protocol is included as part of the Network layer packet and reserves its own service address. However, unlike most upper-layer processes, the routing protocol defines the Network layer functionality used. Using routing protocols, routers communicate directly over dedicated links and operate independently of the Physical or Data Link layer processes involved. Routing protocols only focus on how the internetworks are connected. Because they operate independently of the Physical and Data Link layers, routers (and routing protocols) can be used to interconnect different network types. One router can support Ethernet, token ring, FDDI, and various wide area network (WAN) technologies, all from the same box.

A routing protocol allows the router to discover routes and services, maintain route and service information, alert other routers of network problems, such as failures or congestion and advertise the path cost for each route. Most dynamically configured routing protocols are based on either distance vector or link-state routing algorithms. These algorithms are used to build and maintain routing tables and to determine which route should be used to forward packets. All of the most common routing protocols are based on one of these two algorithms.

Understanding Distance Vector Routing

Routers that use distance vector routing utilize the most basic routing algorithm. A distance vector router builds it routing database based on information received from other routers on the internetwork. For example, if a particular router indicates that Network 123 is four hops away, the next router in the path will note that Network 123 is five hops away in its routing table. In the event that a router learns of a particular network from different routers, it will assign the route with the lowest cost to its routing database.

Figure 7.6 shows a sample network using distance vector routing to determine the best path between networks. In this case, Router 1's routing table indicates that the best path to Network B is through Router 4. Along this path there are three hops, whereas the path through Router 2 requires four hops.

For all purposes, a distance vector router relies on second-hand information from other routers. A router's information table is populated based on the

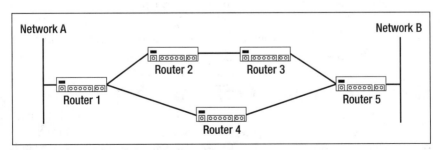

Figure 7.6   A distance vector network.

information it receives from its neighbors. First, a router calculates its own routing table. After it finishes the calculation, it shares the information with the other routers with which it shares a connection to enable them to create their own routing information tables. Finally, the router receives the updated information from a neighbor, recalculates its routes, and passes the new routing table on to the other routers.

All routing table entries share a timeout period. During normal operation, a router will receive an update from its neighbor within a specific amount of time. If this update is not received within the timeout, the router considers the routing table entry suspect. Eventually, if no update is received, the router considers the entry invalid and deletes it from its table. Generally, the update time on distance vector routers is fairly short—between 10 seconds and 2 minutes.

 The most common distance vector routing protocols are AppleTalk's Routing Table Maintenance Protocol (RTMP), the IPX Routing Information Protocol (RIP), and IP RIP.

Disadvantages

Unfortunately, distance vector networks take quite a bit of time to spread updated routing information to all routers on the internetwork. This large convergence time is perhaps the biggest disadvantage of distance vector networks. During the convergence process, the network routing mechanism is interrupted, which increases the chance that packets are misrouted or lost. Convergence on these networks is slow because each router recalculates its entire routing database based on the new information before passing the information on to its neighbor. In addition, distance vector routers are prone to the count-to-infinity problem (discussed in the following section).

Aside from the convergence issues involved with distance vector routing, the overhead required by routers using distance vector algorithms is a hindrance. Distance vector routers require more bandwidth to update their neighbors because they generally send their entire routing information tables to other routers to ensure that all routers in the network know all possible routes. This limitation means that distance vector routers are poorly suited for complex LANs or internetworks using WAN technologies.

Count-To-Infinity Problem

One of the drawbacks to using a distance vector routing algorithm is its propensity to succumb to the count-to-infinity problem. For example, in the internetwork shown in Figure 7.7, Router 4 knows that Network A is four

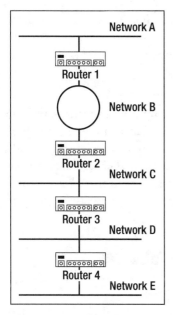

Figure 7.7   A network susceptible to the count-to-infinity problem.

hops away, Router 3 knows that it's three hops away, Router 2, two hops, and Router 1, one hop.

If, at some point, Router 1 fails or a failure occurs on Network B, Router 2 must update its routing table. However, Router 2 does not understand that Network A is not available; instead, it updates its information based on the message from Router 3 and records that Network A is now four hops away (three, plus one for itself). After Router 2 recalculates its routing information, it sends its entire routing table to Router 3, which now thinks that Network A is five hops away. Router 3 then sends this information to Router 4 *and* Router 2. When Router 2 receives the updated information, it recalculates its routing information table again, and the whole process starts all over, to infinity. Of course, the hop count cannot actually reach infinity because there's a maximum limit to the number of hops a particular route can have—usually 16.

To reduce the count-to-infinity problem on distance vector networks, two algorithms have been devised. The first of these is called *split horizon* or *best information*. This algorithm does not allow a router to readvertise a route to the router from which it was received. This is similar to how a repeater operates, in that it will send the new information to all routers other than the one from which it was received. Second is the *split horizon with poison reverse algorithm*, or simply *poison reverse algorithm*. This algorithm advertises the cost for any path on the network from which it was received as infinity (actually 16). The effect of this is the same as split horizon's effect, but it occurs in less time. However, this method uses larger update messages because two separate routing tables must be advertised to each network to which a router is connected.

Advantages

The single biggest advantage of distance vector routing implementations is their ease of installation. They are robust and can easily be installed in typical local area network (LAN) environments where router processor usage and bandwidth requirements are fairly insignificant. In addition, because the distance vector algorithm is the original distributed routing algorithm, it's been around for a while, which means that it's stable and supported by the vast majority of router manufacturers.

Understanding Link-State Routing

Link-state routing is a more recent development designed to eliminate the problems associated with distance vector routing, including the count-to-infinity problem. Link-state routers use special packets called *Link State Packets (LSPs)* to transmit information about a router's directly connected links and their costs. An LSP is flooded, or sent to all networks except the one on which it was received, to other routers to ensure that all routers have accurate information on the structure of the network. Because each router's LSP only contains information about those links attached directly to the router, when a router receives an LSP from all routers on the internetwork, it has a complete firsthand map of the network. This is unlike distance vector networks, which rely on second-hand information passed from router to router.

As a link-state router receives an LSP from its neighboring router, it recalculates its routing tables based on the information it receives. When choosing the appropriate route with which to populate its table, a link-state router will choose the router with the lowest cost. However, unlike distance vector routes, the cost metrics involved in link-state routing are a bit more flexible. Instead of a simple hop count, link-state routers are able to use metrics such as line speed and network congestion. In addition, a separate cost can be assigned to outbound data in each direction, and special costs can be calculated to provide load balancing.

Figure 7.8 shows the same network described earlier, but it includes line speed. If this network uses a link-state routing protocol, which bases its cost on line speed, Router 1 will now choose the path to Network B through Router 2, because the three T1 lines indicated are significantly faster than the two 56Kbps lines attached to Router 4.

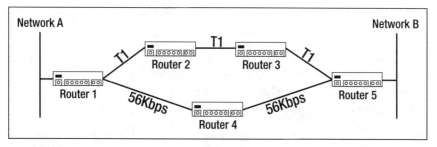

Figure 7.8 A link-state routing network.

 The most common distance vector routing protocols are the OSI protocol Intermediate System to Intermediate System (IS-IS), IPX NetWare Link Services Protocol (NLSP), and IP Open Shortest Path First (OSPF).

Disadvantages

Link-state routing sees its biggest disadvantage in small LAN environments. In the most simple configurations, the overhead and bandwidth required for link-state operations may be slightly more than that required for distance vector operations. However, this is a minor disadvantage because simple network configurations don't require much information.

Advantages

The advantages of link-state routing over distance vector routing are numerous and significant. First is the convergence time associated with link-state routing. Link-state routers require less convergence time because they do not have the count-to-infinity problem to contend with. Link-state networks also take less time to converge because the routers do not have to recalculate their route databases before forwarding route change information. In addition, because link-state routers do not use second-hand information, fewer route determination errors are likely. Finally, accurate, first-hand information about the network's status can be obtained by querying a single router because all routers save a copy of all LSPs they receive.

Understanding Load Balancing

As mentioned, routers can be configured to balance the network load between multiple routes from source to destination. *Load balancing* (or *splitting*) traffic is used to more efficiently utilize multiple links between networks. Both distance vector and link-state networks are able to keep alternate routes in their routing information tables. These routes can be configured to distribute the traffic load over the network. The type of load balancing used depends on the network implementation and routing protocols in place.

The load can be balanced among various links in a couple of ways. First, the router can select all routes sequentially in a continuous loop, sometimes called *round-robin load balancing*. Also, the router can select the routes randomly, choosing the routes with higher costs or congestion less frequently.

Load balancing provides for the efficient use of available network bandwidth. In many networking situations, a backup route must be operational at all times and is often only used in the event of a network failure. Load balancing more easily justifies the added expense of maintaining a separate route. When load balancing is implemented, packets can be routed over slower links, but the distribution of the load over various links increases the overall network bandwidth.

Practice Questions

Question 1

Which of the following networking difficulties and resolutions are realized with distance vector networks?

○ a. Broadcast storms are reduced by using split horizon.

○ b. The count-to-infinity problem is reduced by using poison reverse.

○ c. Broadcast storms are reduced by implementing bridging.

○ d. The count-to-infinity problem is reduced by implementing bridging.

Answer b is correct. The count-to-infinity problem is reduced by using poison reverse or split horizon. Answer c is also a true statement in that broadcast storms can be reduced by implementing bridging. However, broadcast storms are not a consequence of implementing distance vector networks. Therefore, answer c is incorrect. Answers a and d are intended for misdirection in that they mix the other two true statements. Therefore, answers a and d are incorrect, and are the reason why this is a trick question.

Question 2

Which of the following routing algorithms are able to use load balancing? [Choose the two best answers]

❑ a. Distance vector

❑ b. Store-and-forward

❑ c. Link state

❑ d. Cut-through

Answers a and c are correct. Both distance vector and link-state routing algorithms can be configured to support load balancing, although it's a bit easier to configure on link-state routers. Store-and-forward and cut-through are both types of switching operations, not routing. Therefore, answers b and d are incorrect.

Question 3

On distance vector networks, which metric is generally used to calculate the cost of a route?

○ a. Line speed

○ b. Congestion

○ c. Hop count

○ d. Manual configuration

Answer c is correct. For distance vector routing networks, the hop count is the basis for the cost of a particular route. Other metrics, such as line speed and congestion, are used by link-state routing networks to calculate a route's cost. In addition, some link-state routing configurations allow for manual cost configuration. Therefore, answers a, b, and d are incorrect.

Question 4

Which of the following statements accurately describes the reason routers are able to interconnect networks with varied architectures?

○ a. Routers utilize split horizon algorithms to provide connectivity options between varied network architectures.

○ b. Routers include networking algorithms that provide the capability to translate between differing networking architectures.

○ c. Routers are cognizant of the physical addresses of the networking devices and operate without regard for the upper-layer protocols involved.

○ d. Routers operate above the Physical and Data Link layers and are therefore able to translate between various network architectures.

Answer d is correct. Because routers operate above the Physical and Data Link layers, they are able to translate between different network architectures, such as Ethernet, token ring, and FDDI. None of the remaining answers accurately describe this capability. Therefore, answers a, b, and c are incorrect.

Question 5

> Which of the following statements correctly describes an advantage of distance vector routing?
>
> ○ a. Distance vector routing networks provide faster convergence than link-state routing networks.
>
> ○ b. Distance vector routing networks are easy to implement.
>
> ○ c. Distance vector routing networks utilize first-hand information.
>
> ○ d. Distance vector routing networks' statuses can be obtained by querying a single router.

Answer b is correct. The biggest advantage of distance vector routing networks is their ease of implementation. The other advantages listed apply not to distance vector networks but rather to link-state networks. Therefore, answers a, c, and d are incorrect.

Question 6

> Which of the following types of addresses can be either purely logical or based in part on the device's address?
>
> ○ a. Physical
>
> ○ b. Hardware
>
> ○ c. Software
>
> ○ d. MAC

Answer c is correct. Depending on the networking protocol used, the software address can be either purely logical or based in part on the physical address of the networking device. The other addresses listed describe the Data Link layer MAC address. Therefore, answers a, b, and d are incorrect.

Question 7

> When traversing an internetwork, which of the following fields
> change with each pass through a router? [Choose the two best
> answers]
>
> ❑ a. Physical source
>
> ❑ b. Logical source
>
> ❑ c. Logical destination
>
> ❑ d. Physical destination

Answers a and d are correct. The physical source and destination fields can be
changed to reflect the routers involved in the transmission. Conversely, because the logical source and destination addresses are part of the Network layer,
they generally remain the same throughout the transmission across the
internetwork. Therefore, answers b and c are incorrect.

Need To Know More?

 Clarke, David James IV. *CNE Study Guide for Core Technologies.* Novell Press. San Jose, CA, 1996. ISBN 0-7645-4501-9. The routing section of Chapter 10 tackles general routing techniques and route discovery.

 Perlman, Radia. *Interconnections: Bridges and Routers.* Addison-Wesley. Reading, MA, 1992. ISBN 0-201-56332-0. Chapter 9 deals with routing algorithm issues, including a comparison between distance vector and link-state routing.

Connectivity Issues And Options

8

Terms you'll need to understand:

√ Nonroutable

√ Brouter

√ Level 3 switch

Techniques you'll need to master:

√ Understanding nonroutable protocols and their structure

√ Transmitting nonroutable protocols over an internetwork

√ Understanding the various combination networking devices available today

√ Understanding the differences between switches, bridges, and routers and when each networking device should be used

As you learned in Chapter 7, routers move information through an internetwork. However, protocols that do not include Network layer information cannot be routed. In this chapter, you'll learn about "nonroutable" protocols and how they're transmitted through a network. In addition, you'll learn about combination devices, such as bridging routers (brouters) and switching hubs and routers.

Nonroutable Protocols

Although routers can manipulate the majority of today's protocols, many popular protocols were designed for environments that do not include multiple networks and were not designed to be routed.

What Are Nonroutable Protocols?

Protocols that do not contain the necessary Network layer information headers cannot be handled by routers. These protocols are considered *nonroutable* (or *unroutable*). Three common protocols fall into this category: Network Basic Input/Output System (NetBIOS), NetBIOS Extended (or Enhanced) User Interface (NetBEUI), and Digital Equipment Corp's Local Area Transport (DEC LAT).

NetBIOS operates at the Session layer and establishes communication sessions between applications on different computers across a local area network (LAN). Microsoft and IBM designed NetBIOS for use only within LANs, based on the premise that PCs on a LAN only need to talk to other PCs on the same LAN. For this reason, NetBIOS does not have a Network layer and is nonroutable.

IBM designed NetBEUI for its LAN Manager product. NetBEUI acts as a transport protocol for NetBIOS in much the same way IP acts as a transport for TCP. NetBEUI's primary difference from NetBIOS is formalization of the frame format, which was not specified in NetBIOS. Like NetBIOS, NetBEUI is designed only for small-to-medium-sized LANs and contains no Network layer information.

> *Note: Although NetBEUI acts as a transport protocol for NetBIOS, recent NetBIOS implementations are able to use other protocols for transport. The newest Microsoft operating systems are able to use IPX/SPX or TCP/IP as the transport for NetBIOS.*

Finally, DEC LAT is designed to connect terminals to host systems via a network using DECnet. Like the other nonroutable protocols, LAT does not include Network layer information because it's intended for use on a single network segment only.

Another form of nonroutable protocols uses static routes that cannot be updated to traverse an internetwork. These protocols use a simple table lookup for "route discovery." This function is actually route lookup rather than route discovery. The most common protocol of this type is IBM's Systems Network Architecture (SNA). SNA routes are predefined in the routing table and are not automatically updated. SNA front-end devices route information by looking up the destination address in the routing table and converting the destination address format into a local format. It should be noted, however, that SNA is being replaced by IBM's newer Advanced Peer-to-Peer Networking (APPN) architecture, which includes a dynamically routable protocol.

Transporting Nonroutable Data

There are generally two ways in which nonroutable data can be transmitted across an internetwork. The first and simplest solution is *bridging*. Bridging nonroutable protocols is no different than bridging any other protocol because the Data Link layer information exists in any case. The second solution is *encapsulation*, or *tunneling*. Tunneling is the process of encapsulating one protocol within another. It's most often used to transmit LAN protocols (such as NetBEUI and SNA) across links that do not support the particular protocol. For example, suppose two networks on a wide area network (WAN) are using NetBEUI locally. Normally, NetBEUI cannot be sent across the WAN link because it isn't routable. However, when NetBEUI data is encapsulated in a routable protocol such as IP, communication between the two networks is possible. Encapsulating is more efficient than bridging over the WAN link because routable protocols were designed with internetwork connectivity in mind.

Combination Connectivity Devices

It's rare to find a completely homogeneous networking environment. Most networks contain a mixture of technologies and protocols, using many different networking devices. Another way of transmitting unroutable protocols is to combine the functionality of two or more devices. These types of devices are more common in modern networks than "pure" bridges, routers, and switches. (See Chapter 6 for more information on bridging and switching techniques.)

Understanding Switching Hubs/Routers

The switching hub that includes routing functionality is another popular combination device. Also called *layer 3 switches*, these devices take routing to a new level by including switches' high-speed functionality and virtual LANs with full routing capabilities. However, these devices are relatively new, there are a few implementation issues, and product choices are limited at present. Layer 3 switches should be considered only for the most advanced networks.

Understanding Brouters

A *brouter*, or *bridging router*, is a device that combines the functionality of both a bridge and a router. For those protocols that can be routed, the brouter is configured as a router to transmit the data across the internetwork. However, for protocols that cannot be routed, a brouter can be configured to operate as a bridge, making path determinations based on physical addresses, rather than logical network addresses. These devices are perfect for today's heterogeneous networks because they reduce the number of devices on the network. Brouters generally cost less than purchasing both a bridge and a router. On the other hand, they can be more expensive than an individual "pure" device, so brouters should only be purchased for those networks on which both bridging and routing are required.

Comparing Connectivity Devices

How do you decide which device is best to use? The answer depends on your network requirements and the amount of money available. For this part of the discussion, we consider bridges and (layer 2) switches interchangeable because they perform the same function based on the physical destination address contained in the packet.

Remember that the difference between bridges and routers is the OSI layer at which they operate. Bridges operate at the Data Link layer, whereas routers operate at the Network layer. Therefore, the difference between bridges and routers is the difference between the services offered by the Data Link layer and the services offered by the Network layer. One of the biggest differences between the two layers is that the Network layer is able to break down and reassemble packets, whereas the Data Link layer is not.

In their simplest form, bridges are designed to bridge network segments and provide more bandwidth by limiting the traffic on the network. Routers, on the other hand, are designed to connect network segments to create *internetworks*. In addition, routers are able to limit broadcast traffic as well as provide security, control, and some level of redundancy between network segments.

Only routers are able to limit broadcast traffic; because broadcasts are directed to all connected devices, bridges and switches allow broadcast traffic to pass through.

Remember that bridges and switches rely on physical addresses to make their path determinations; they are not aware of geographical information. In other words, a bridge does not know where a device resides; it only knows which port accesses the device. On the other hand, the network addresses used by routers include the geographical information. Of course, brouters are able to provide the functionality of both bridges and routers.

> *Note:* *All network segments connected to routers have the same Network layer address and are therefore members of the same broadcast domain. However, because bridges use a flat addressing scheme, there's no differentiation between bridges in broadcasts.*

Advantages Of Bridges And Switches

There are situations in which bridges or switches are preferable to routers. In general, these devices should be chosen based on price, functionality, or the configuration required.

Bridges are more cost-efficient than routers because they forward more frames per second for a lower price. Routers require more overhead to decode and forward packets and are therefore slower.

Bridges and switches operate independently of the upper-layer protocols. This means that they're ideal for networks using nonroutable protocols such as NetBEUI and SNA. Remember that routers are protocol-dependent; if a router does not recognize a packet's protocol, it cannot route the packet and discards it.

Finally, bridges and switches require very little configuration compared to routers, which often require extensive configuration. This means that a bridge or switch is preferable to a router in a networking environment in which the staff has little or no protocol-handling expertise.

 Basically, you want to use a switch to connect a workgroup and eliminate congestion. You want to use a bridge to connect network segments and workgroups, and to provide fault tolerance.

Advantages Of Routers

There are also a number of situations in which a router should be installed rather than a bridge or switch. The majority of these situations deal with connecting multiple networks and the functionality provided by the Network layer. As mentioned earlier, routers are generally able to break down and reassemble packets that are too large to forward on to the next network; bridges discard packets that are too large. Unlike bridges or switches, routers can be used to interconnect dissimilar network types, such as LAN and WAN technologies.

A router builds its routing tables based on the entire structure of the internetwork, so it can determine the best path for packets between the source and destination devices. Bridges, on the other hand, work within a limited network topology—generally a single network. Some switches support virtual LANs, in essence providing access to multiple networks through the switch. In addition, routers using dynamic routing reconfigure themselves more quickly than spanning tree networks using bridges. During the convergence, routers are able to route packets while they notify other routers of the change in the status of the network. Bridge networks are reconfigured more slowly and must stop forwarding frames for a specific period of time, which is designated by the root bridge. After that time, they must relearn the location of all network devices before they can resume forwarding frames.

When networks become overloaded, many routers can use TCP/IP's Internet Control Message Protocol (ICMP), which you'll learn about in Chapter 14, to notify stations of congestion. Bridges do not have this kind of functionality. Routers are also able to filter packets and forward them directly to the destination network, thus providing protection against broadcast storms. Bridges forward any frame that contains valid information, including broadcasts, thus opening the network to potentially debilitating broadcast storms and other maladies. Finally, routers operate independently of the underlying media access methods used; an Ethernet packet can be routed between an Ethernet network and a token ring network as easily as between two Ethernet networks. Adding this type of functionality to a bridge or switch involves greatly increasing its internal logic, slowing it down, and making it more expensive.

Use a router when you need to increase security, connect individual networks to create an internetwork, and provide fault tolerance and rapid reconfiguration of the network.

So when do you use a particular device? Let's look at a couple sample scenarios and determine which type of device best suits a given situation.

Scenario 1: Amalgamated Millworks, Inc.

Amalgamated Millworks, Inc. (AMI) is a small but rapidly growing company. Its paper-printing business has taken off, and it's adding three to five employees each month. Until recently, all the computers were connected through a repeater. However, the systems are operating slowly and a new solution is needed. There are currently 50 PCs connected to the network using NetBIOS, and more are being added weekly.

What type of networking device is required in this situation? First, there's no reason to use a router because there's no connectivity to other networks. The network uses NetBIOS, so a bridging solution is in order. Whether to use a bridge or a switch depends on the network infrastructure in place. If the existing network uses coaxial cable, such as 10Base2, a bridge can increase available bandwidth and provide better client response. However, if the network is currently using twisted-pair cabling, such as 10BaseT, a switch may be in order. In addition, because AMI is growing so rapidly, a switch might be the best solution because it allows virtual LANs to be established.

Scenario 2: Megalopolis Enterprises

Megalopolis Enterprises is a large company that's currently involved in connecting its various networks throughout the country. In addition to its current install base, Megalopolis plans to purchase three other companies in the very near future. Although all of Megalopolis Enterprises' current holdings use TCP/IP for communication, two of the three new companies use IPX/SPX and one uses SNA to connect to its IBM mainframes. Megalopolis anticipates connecting up to 3,500 devices to its new network once the mergers are complete.

Which type of networking device is best suited to this situation? A pure bridging solution is out of the question because of the size of the network involved. It's possible to use a combination switch and router, but that's not a good solution given the amount of traffic involved. Although Megalopolis can currently use a pure router, the addition of the company requiring SNA connectivity poses a bit of a problem. For this reason, only a hybrid brouter would fulfill this company's requirements.

Practice Questions

Question 1

> Which of the following networking phenomena is best addressed
> by implementing a router?
>
> O a. Resolution storm
>
> O b. Link state convergence
>
> O c. Split horizon
>
> O d. Broadcast storm

Answer d is correct. Broadcast storms are a potential problem in bridged networks because bridges forward broadcasts. Routers do not forward broadcasts,
thus eliminating the potential for broadcast storms. There's no phenomenon
known as a resolution storm or a link state convergence. Therefore, answers a
and b are incorrect. Split horizon is a routing technique that prevents a router
from sending information it receives back down the link from which it was
received. Therefore, answer c is incorrect.

Question 2

> Which of the following protocols must be bridged to traverse an
> internetwork? [Choose the two best answers]
>
> ❏ a. IPX/SPX
>
> ❏ b. NetBEUI
>
> ❏ c. TCP/IP
>
> ❏ d. SNA

Answers b and d are correct. This question may be confusing at first because
you must remember that only *nonroutable* protocols have to be bridged.
NetBEUI and SNA are nonroutable and must be bridged. Both IPX/SPX and
TCP/IP are routable protocol suites and do not have to be bridged to be sent
through an internetwork. Therefore, answers a and c are incorrect.

Question 3

> Which of the following does not represent an advantage of a switch over a router?
>
> ○ a. Switches require less configuration than routers.
>
> ○ b. Switches are able to quickly reconfigure their network configuration in the event of a change.
>
> ○ c. Switches are more cost-effective than routers.
>
> ○ d. Switches operate independently of upper-layer protocols, thus allowing them to forward nonroutable protocols.

Answer b is correct. Routers are much faster in situations that require reconfiguration and are able to continue forwarding packets while the reconfiguration takes place. This is not the case for bridges and switches. All other statements represent advantages of switches over routers. Therefore, answers a, c, and d are incorrect.

Question 4

> Which of the following networking devices are able to notify workstations if network congestion occurs? [Choose the two best answers]
>
> ❏ a. Bridge
>
> ❏ b. Brouter
>
> ❏ c. Router
>
> ❏ d. Switch

Answers b and c are correct. By design, routers include the functionality required to use TCP/IP's ICMP protocol to notify workstations of network congestion. Brouters also have this ability because they combine the functionality of a router with a bridge. Pure bridges and (layer 2) switches are not designed to monitor traffic levels or to notify stations if certain conditions are present. Therefore, answers a and d are incorrect.

Question 5

> Which networking device easily translates data between different
> media access methods?
>
> O a. Router
> O b. Bridge
> O c. Switch

Answer a is correct. Because routers operate independently of the underlying
media access methods, they're able to translate between different network types,
such as Ethernet and token ring. Neither bridges nor switches provide this
ability. Therefore, answers b and c are incorrect.

Question 6

> Which of the following best describes the reason that some pro-
> tocols are nonroutable?
>
> O a. They do not contain the appropriate Data Link layer
>   information required by routers.
> O b. Their CRC data produces too much overhead to allow
>   routers to process them.
> O c. They do not contain the appropriate Network layer
>   information required by routers.
> O d. They consist only of broadcasts, which are discarded by
>   routers.

Answer c is correct. Nonroutable protocols do not contain Network layer information, which means that routers cannot interpret their addresses. Routers
are not concerned with Data Link layer information. Therefore, answer a is
incorrect. The checksum, or CRC, information is used at various layers of the
OSI model but has no effect on whether a protocol can be routed. Therefore,
answer b is incorrect. Although routers do discard broadcasts, this is not the
only means of communication used by nonroutable protocols. Therefore, answer d is incorrect.

Need To Know More?

 Clarke, David James IV. *CNE Study Guide for Core Technologies*. Novell Press. San Jose, CA, 1996. ISBN 0-7645-4501-9. Chapter 9 is dedicated to the communications aspects of the OSI model and discusses bridges and routers.

 Niedermiller-Chaffins, Debra and Drew Haywood. *CNE Training Guide: Networking Technologies, 3rd Edition*. New Riders Publishing. Indianapolis, IN, 1994. ISBN 1-56205-363-9. Chapter 22 includes descriptions of bridges and routers and how they're used on NetWare networks.

IP Addressing

Terms you'll need to understand:

√ Host

√ Network ID

√ Host ID

√ Dotted octet

√ Dotted decimal

√ IP registry

√ Registered address

√ Unregistered address

Techniques you'll need to master:

√ Explaining the IP address structure

√ Converting binary bits to decimal numbers to represent an IP address

√ Converting decimal numbers to binary bits to represent an IP address

√ Identifying the IP network class from dotted octet and dotted decimal address notations

√ Describing the format of the different address classes and how they are used

√ Listing the special and reserved IP addresses and their functions

√ Assigning host and private network addresses

Communication protocols define rules for the addressing schemes used at different layers of the OSI model. In this chapter, you're introduced to the addressing scheme defined by the Internet Protocol (IP) suite—TCP/IP—for processes and operations at the Network layer of the OSI model. Addresses at this layer are used by routers to move data to its destination through an internetwork.

In addition to learning about the IP address structure, you'll also learn about the key concepts and tools that are critical to mastering the topics covered in Chapters 10, 11, and 12.

The Structure Of An IP Address

The TCP/IP (Transport Control Protocol/Internet Protocol) protocol suite defines a 32-bit addressing scheme at the Internet layer of the Department of Defense (DoD) model. At this layer, all hosts must have a software address that identifies both the host and the network to which the host is attached. This software address is referred to as the *Internet address* or *IP address* of the host. Routers use the address to forward packets through the internetwork to the proper destination.

> *Note: Although the TCP/IP protocols can be mapped to the OSI model fairly well, they're actually based on an earlier, four-layer model of networking developed by the Department of Defense. The lower layer of the DoD model (called the Network Access layer) includes the functions associated with the Physical and Data Link layers of the OSI model. The Internet and Host-To-Host layers of the DoD model map well to the OSI Network and Transport layers, respectively. The upper layer (called the Process/Application layer) includes the functionality of the OSI Session, Presentation, and Application layers. Keep in mind that references to Internet and Host-To-Host layer processes, in this and other texts, are used to specify processes that are defined by TCP/IP protocols and operate at the Network and Transport layers of the OSI model. See Chapter 12 for more information on the DoD model.*

Dotted Decimal And Dotted Octet Notation

The IP address of a host occupies 4 sets of 8 bits (an *octet* of bits per set) for a total of 32 bits. Although the actual address is a stream of 32 bits, for convenience, the 4 sets of 8 bits are usually separated by a period between each set. The technique (called *dotted quad notation*) is routinely employed with binary, decimal, and hexadecimal representations of the octet values.

You need to be familiar with the two versions used here: the binary format (called *dotted octet notation*) and the decimal format (called *dotted decimal notation*). The binary format, as the name implies, uses a period to group zeroes and ones into octets, thus making it easier to visually distinguish the beginning and end of each octet. The decimal format replaces the binary octet with its decimal equivalent to produce a representation of the IP address that, for most tasks, is easier to work with. The result of applying the decimal format is the familiar host address number that network users are accustomed to seeing. Figure 9.1 illustrates the effects of applying the two formats to an unformatted binary bit stream for a single IP address.

Although working with decimal numbers simplifies most tasks, you'll find that representing IP addresses in dotted octet notation provides a number of time-saving visual shortcuts that are invaluable when determining network class and when working with network subnets and supernets (discussed in Chapter 11).

 When working with IP addresses, you need to be able to quickly convert IP addresses expressed in binary format to decimal format. Take the time to learn the decimal equivalent of each of the eight binary place values from 2^0 to 2^7.

Converting from dotted octet to dotted decimal notation is done on an octet-by-octet basis. Within each octet, the sum of the decimal equivalents for each of the binary place positions occupied by a 1 equals the decimal value of that octet. The process, illustrated in Figure 9.2, can also be used with partial octets to determine subnet addresses (explained in Chapter 11).

Unformatted Bit Stream

1100111001001101010001110011101

Dotted Octet Notation

1100|110.0100|101.0100|0111.0011|1101

Dotted Decimal Notation

206.77.71.61

Figure 9.1 The effect of applying dotted octet and dotted decimal formats to an unformatted bit stream representing an IP address.

Binary Position	2^7	2^6	2^5	2^4	2^3	2^2	2^1	2^0
Decimal Value	128	64	32	16	8	4	2	1
Octet	1	0	1	1	0	0	0	1

+128   +32 +16   +1 = 177

The sum of the decimal values of positions in the octet
occupied by 1 gives the decimal value of the octet.

Figure 9.2 Conversion of a binary octet to its decimal equivalent.

The decimal value of each octet in a node address falls in the
range of 0 to 255. Not all systems support 0 as a node address, and
255 is reserved for broadcast packets. Consequently, 0 and 255 are
not always available for use in assigning host addresses. Unless
specifically stated otherwise, it's safe to assume that the node
address range within the last octet of the node is 1 through 254.

Network And Host IDs

The four octet (or four byte) IP address of a host is divided into two parts. The
first part, the network ID, consists of between 1 and 3 bytes and uniquely
identifies a network on the internetwork. The second part of the address, the
host ID, is the remaining 1 to 3 bytes that uniquely identifies a particular node
on that network. For example, the IP address 132.133.42.26 uniquely identifies a host on the Internet as follows:

➤ The first 2 bytes of the address, 132.133, represent the network ID
   portion of the address and point to a specific network on the Internet.

➤ The last 2 bytes of the address, 42.26, represent the host ID and point to
   a specific node on the network (132.133).

Because the network ID is unique on the Internet, and the host ID is unique
on the network, the IP address of the host uniquely identifies its connection to
the Internet.

The number of bytes associated with each portion of the IP address is dependent on the network class or type (discussed in the following subsection).

Network Address Classes

Five address classes, A through E, exist in the IP addressing scheme. Addresses that can be assigned to hosts come from Classes A, B, and C. Classes D and E are reserved for special uses and are not assigned to hosts. The five address classes are illustrated in Figure 9.3.

Table 9.1 contains a brief description of the address types.

> *Note:*   *IPv6 (an IP addressing scheme that will allow an almost unlimited number of IP addresses) is expected to be available before all class C addresses are exhausted.*

 You can easily determine the network class when viewing dotted octet notation by associating the position of the first 0 from the left in the first byte of the network address with the network class. In addition, the decimal value of the ones to the left of that 0 give you the beginning value for the address range for that network class. Both relationships are illustrated in Figure 9.4.

Reserved Addresses

Certain addresses in the TCP/IP protocol suite have special meaning and should not be used when assigning host addresses. The following is a list of reserved addresses of which you need to be aware:

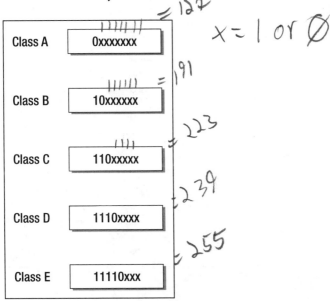

Figure 9.3   IP address Classes A through E.

Table 9.1   Class descriptions.

Class	Range	Networks Available	Hosts Available	High-Order Bits	Description
A	0-127	126	16,777,214	0	The value of the first byte is also the network ID; the remaining three bytes identify the node. Network IDs of all zeroes or all ones are not allowed, and the network ID 127 is reserved. Almost all of the Class A addresses have already been assigned.
B	128-191	16,384	65,534	1 and 0	The first two bytes identify the network. The last two bytes identify the node on the network. There are very few Class B addresses available.
C	192-223	2,097,152	254	1, 1, and 0	The first three bytes identify the network. The last byte identifies the node. There are still many Class C addresses available. Class C addresses are some times assigned to organizations that request a registered Class B address.
D	224-239	N/A	N/A	1, 1, 1, and 0	Used for IP multicast packets, which are used in communications between routers only.
E	240-255	N/A	N/A	1, 1, 1, 1, and 0	Reserved for experimental use. May be used for future addressing modes. Class E addresses are also used for broadcasts. The special Class E address 255.255.255.255 is used to identify a broadcast message that's transmitted to every host on the network from which the broadcast originates. This is necessary because routers don't usually forward broadcast messages to other networks.

Start of Address Range	Network Class	2^7 128	2^6 64	2^5 32	2^4 16	2^3 8	2^2 4	2^1 2	2^0 1
0	A	0	x	x	x	x	x	x	x
128	B	1	0	x	x	x	x	x	x
192	C	1	1	0	x	x	x	x	x
224	D	1	1	1	0	x	x	x	x
240	E	1	1	1	1	0	x	x	x

Figure 9.4 By carefully examining the first zero in the binary value of the first octet of an IP address, you can determine the address class.

➤ **Network 0.0.0.0** This address refers to the default route. It's used to simplify routing tables used by IP.

➤ **Network 127.0.0.1** This address is reserved for loopback. The address 127.0.0.1 is typically used to refer to the local host.

➤ **255.255.255.255** This address is used to broadcast a message meant for hosts on this network only.

➤ **A network or node address with all bits set to 1** This type of address is used to refer to all "hosts."

➤ **An address with all host bits set to 0** This address refers to the network itself, and this notation is used in routing tables. For example, the address 132.21.0.0 can be used to refer to the network 132.21.

➤ **An address with all network bits set to 0** This address is used to refer to a host on "this" network. For example, 0.0.21.2 would address node 21.2 on the local Class B network.

Registered IP Addresses

Internet routers are able to forward packets to a host on the Internet because the host IP address corresponds to a unique node attached to a unique network on the Internet. Duplication of IP addresses on the Internet would render this process impossible. The size and public nature of the Internet makes it necessary to register IP addresses to prevent duplication and ensure the uniqueness of each host connection.

IP Registries

Until recently, Network Solutions, Inc. (NSI), also called the InterNIC, was responsible for assigning IP addresses. Typically, IP addresses are assigned to Internet Service Providers (ISPs) in large blocks. The ISPs then assign or sub-allocate portions of the IP addresses to smaller, downstream ISPs, which, in turn, provide users with registered IP addresses for hosts on a network.

Now, a nonprofit organization called the American Registry for Internet Numbers (ARIN) has been established to administer the IP addresses. This organization is modeled after the organizations that administer IP addresses in Europe and the Asia-Pacific region: Reseaux IP Europeens (RIPE) and the Asia Pacific Network Information Center (APNIC). InterNIC and ARIN currently manage IP numbers in North America, South America, South Africa, and the Caribbean.

> *Note: Consult the following URLs for more information on the IP registry in your region:*

> ➤ *www.arin.net   American Registry for Internet Numbers (ARIN)*

> ➤ *www.ripe.net   Reseaux IP Europeens (RIPE)*

> ➤ *www.apnic.net   Asia Pacific Network Information Center (APNIC)*

Assigning IP Addresses To Hosts

The method used to assign IP addresses to hosts on a network depends on whether the network is public and connected to the Internet, or is maintained as a private network and isolated from the Internet.

Public Networks

InterNIC and ARIN currently manage IP numbers in North America, South America, South Africa, and the Caribbean. Hosts on a network connected to the Internet must use the registered network ID assigned to the network in conjunction with a locally assigned host ID. For example, if a network is assigned the Class C network ID of 202.33.4.0 (and assuming a default mask of 255.255.255.0), then any of the following addresses would be valid for hosts on that network:

➤ 202.33.4.7

➤ 202.33.4.25

➤ 202.33.4.221

➤ 202.33.4.252

Note that the fourth byte, which comprises the host portion of the IP address in this example, must be in the range 1 to 255 (the range for networks that support host addresses of 0 would be 0 to 255).

Private Networks

InterNIC has reserved blocks of IP addresses for Class A, Class B, and Class C networks that use TCP/IP on their intranet but have not been assigned registered network IDs. These addresses are normally filtered out by Internet routers and do not conflict with registered addresses. If your intranet connects to the Internet at any time, however, you must obtain registered IP addresses. Private network address blocks include the following:

➤ Class A 10.0.0.0 to 10.255.255.255

➤ Class B 172.16.0.0 to 172.31.255.255

➤ Class C 192.168.0.0 to 192.168.255.255

Practice Questions

Question 1

Which of the following IP addresses would be on a Class B network? [Choose the two best answers]

❑ a. 11011001.10011011.10101100.11110001

❑ b. 206.77.77.31

❑ c. 10011001.10011011.10101100.11110001

❑ d. 129.33.33.61

❑ e. 11110001.10011011.10101100.11110001

The correct answers are c and d. The value of the first byte of the IP address on Class B networks is in the range 128 to 191, and the first zero in the byte is in the second position from the left. Therefore, only answers c and d are correct.

Question 2

Which of the following IP addresses could not be assigned to a host on the Internet? [Choose the two best answers]

❑ a. 11011001.10011011.10101100.11110001

❑ b. 6.7.77.31

❑ c. 10011001.10011011.10101100.11110001

❑ d. 127.33.33.61

❑ e. 11110001.10011011.10101100.11110001

The correct answers are d and e. The network ID 127.0.0.0 is reserved and cannot be assigned to a host on the Internet. Therefore, answer d is correct. The address in answer e has four ones and then a zero in the fifth position, which represents a Class E network. Class E networks are reserved for experimental and future use and broadcast messages. Therefore, answer e is correct. Answers a, b, and c all represent valid Internet ID addresses and are incorrect.

Question 3

Which of the following IP addresses is the dotted decimal equivalent of 11001101.01001011.10101111.00000101?

○ a. 205.75.175.5

○ b. 206.77.177.41

○ c. 217.75.175.5

○ d. 128.33.33.61

○ e. 206.75.175.5

The correct answer is a. Adding the decimal values, within each octet, of the place positions occupied by a 1 yields the values 205, 75, 175, and 5 for the octets. Only answer a has these decimal values for the octets and is therefore the only correct answer.

Question 4

Which of the following registries should you contact when obtaining a registered IP address in South Africa?

○ a. IANA

○ b. RIPE

○ c. ARIN

○ d. SAIR

The correct answer is c. ARIN and InterNIC are responsible for assigning and managing registered IP addresses in North America, South America, South Africa, and the Caribbean. Therefore, answer c is correct. IANA does not handle IP address registrations, RIPE administers IP addresses in Europe, and SAIR does not exist. Therefore, answers b, c, and d are incorrect.

Question 5

> Which of the following IP addresses would likely be found on a private network? [Choose the three best answers]
>
> ❑ a. 10.0.0.1
>
> ❑ b. 206.77.77.31
>
> ❑ c. 172.16.0.1
>
> ❑ d. 192.168.255.33

The correct answers are a, c, and d. InterNIC has reserved blocks of IP addresses for private networks in the following ranges:

➤ 10.0.0.0 to 10.255.255.255

➤ 172.16.0.0 to 172.31.255.255

➤ 192.168.0.0 to 192.168.255.255

Answers a, c, and d have addresses that fall within one of the ranges. The address in answer b is not in the range of any of the reserved blocks and is therefore incorrect.

Question 6

> What does the IP address 0.0.0.45 refer to?
>
> ○ a. Node 45 on any network
>
> ○ b. Network 45
>
> ○ c. Node 45 on a non-IP network
>
> ○ d. Node 45 on the local network

The correct answer is d. An IP address with all network bits set to 0 refers to "this" (or the local) network. A node ID would represent that node on the local network. Therefore, answers a, b, and c are incorrect.

Question 7

Which network class is reserved for multicast addresses?

○ a. Class A

○ b. Class B

○ c. Class C

○ d. Class D

○ e. Class E

The correct answer is d. Class D networks are reserved for multicast addresses. Class A, B, and C networks contain assignable addresses, and Class E networks are reserved for future and experimental use as well as for broadcasts. Therefore, answers a, b, c, and e are incorrect.

Need To Know More?

 Clarke, David James IV. *CNE Study Guide for Core Technologies*. Novell Press. San Jose, CA, 1996. ISBN: 0-7645-4501-9. Chapter 10, "OSI Model: Networking," contains information on TCP/IP.

 Lewis, Chris. *Cisco TCP/IP Routing Professional Reference, 2nd Edition*. McGraw-Hill. New York, 1998. ISBN: 0-07-041130-1. Chapter 2 of this book provides a very good overview of the OSI reference model and the DoD networking model.

 Parker, Timothy. *Teach Yourself TCP/IP in 14 Days, 2nd Edition*. Sams Publishing. Indianapolis, IN, 1998. ISBN: 0-672-30885-1. Chapter 1 includes additional information on the topics of standards and protocols that is pertinent to this chapter.

 www.arin.net/aboutarin.html provides information about the American Registry for Internet Numbers and links to all registry information.

Hostnames, DNS, And IP Addressing

Terms you'll need to understand:

√ Hostnames

√ Host tables

√ Domain Name System (DNS)

√ DNS zones

√ Master name servers

√ Replica name servers

√ DNS resolvers

Techniques you'll need to master:

√ Creating a host table

√ Explaining the function of the Domain Name System (DNS)

√ Identifying the DNS zone types

√ Describing the role of master name servers and replica name servers

√ Describing the process of DNS name resolution

All hosts on the Internet have IP addresses that uniquely identify their connection to the Internet. As you learned in Chapter 9, referencing these unique addresses makes it possible to communicate with and route messages to any host on the Internet. Although the 32-bit IP address is required to send information to remote hosts, people find it easier to remember a name associated with an Internet resource or Internet host. Assigning a unique name to each network host and associating it with the host's IP address gives users a way to communicate with remote hosts without having to memorize or look up the IP address.

> *Note: The processes operating at each layer of the OSI model use different addressing schemes. For example, Data Link layer processes recognize and act upon hardware or MAC address information contained in the Data Link header of network packets. Because the Data Link header (and the hardware address information) is removed from the packets prior to delivery to the Network layer, the processes operating at the Network layer are not concerned with hardware address information. Instead, the Network layer processes read the Network layer header and route packets across the internetwork based on the network address information in the header. Packets are passed to the Transport layer where the only available address information is in the Transport layer header. The addresses at this layer are ports associated with connections and are independent of hardware and network addresses. The Application layer of the OSI model provides the user interface. At this layer of functionality, processes and applications recognize addresses that are in the form of symbolic names.*

In this chapter, you learn how to create and manage a locally stored directory (called a *host table*) that machines on your network can use to associate symbolic names with IP addresses. You also learn how the Domain Name System (DNS) works and when it's appropriate to use on your network.

Symbolic Names

Symbolic names provide the address information required by most upper-layer protocols and many TCP/IP applications for communication with remote hosts. A symbolic name (called a *hostname*) is associated with a single IP address to identify a specific connection to the network. The IP address association is required to provide Network layer processes with the information they need for internetwork routing. Network hosts are able to match hostnames to IP addresses by either referencing a local host table or using DNS.

In the following section, you'll learn about host tables. You need to pay special attention to the table format and how the table is commonly stored on the local host.

Defining Host Tables

A *host table* is a locally maintained ASCII text file that contains a list of known IP addresses and the hostname (or names) associated with each address. On Unix systems, for example, the host table is maintained in the text file /ETC/HOSTS.

The host table is arranged in two columns, as shown in Figure 10.1, with IP addresses to the left and hostnames on the same line to the right. Note that the hostname is separated from the IP address by at least one space. The list of addresses in the table can be in any order. Whenever a user or application specifies a hostname, the host table is searched for a matching name and the IP address is read from the line on which that the name is found.

> In a host table, any characters in a line to the right of a pound sign (#) are ignored by the system. Adding text to the right of the pound sign is a convenient way to document or add comments to the host table.

When more than one name is associated with an address, those names are separated from one another by spaces and listed on the same line as the IP

```
hosts - Notepad
File  Edit  Search  Help
#
# SYS:ETC\HOSTS
#
#        Mappings of host names and host aliases to IP address.
#
127.0.0.1        loopback lb localhost    # normal loopback address

#
# Local
#

133.47.4.2       toad tim
133.47.6.40      robin
133.47.6.144     hp4-prt # HP LJ4 Print Station
154.40.40.16     merlin
154.40.40.19     dan dj

#
# Remote
#

206.77.71.60     lanlord
206.77.71.61     lh-2j
```

Figure 10.1   A sample host table. Each IP address on the left is followed by a space and then, on the same line, its associated hostname.

address. Each additional name (called an *alias*) is recognized as a valid hostname for that address. For example, a user or application can address the host at IP address 154.40.40.19 (shown in Figure 10.1) as either "dan" or "dj".

Although there's no limit to the number of names that can be in a host table, there is a practical limit to the size and number of host tables that can be managed properly in a given environment. All host tables on the network must be continually updated to ensure that they accurately reflect the current network configuration. This means that seemingly minor network reconfigurations can result in considerable administrative overhead if hundreds of local host tables have to be updated. Although host tables are appropriate for small networks, you should not rely on them to meet the needs of large networks.

The growth of the Internet provided the impetus for the development of a system other than host tables to handle name-to-address resolution. In the following section, you'll learn about the DNS style of naming and the protocols and servers used to implement domain name services.

Domain Name System (DNS)

The DNS specifies a naming system based on the concept of a hierarchical namespace encompassing the entire Internet. The hierarchy is intended to correlate generally to the organizational structure of the Internet. The namespace is represented in Figure 10.2 as an inverted tree diagram, where the root of the

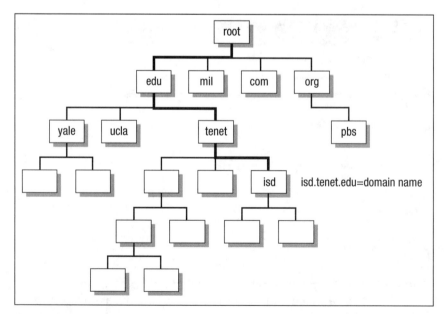

Figure 10.2 The inverted tree structure of the DNS namespace.

tree is at the top, representing the organizational top of the hierarchy, with multiple levels of branches below it.

The labeled squares on the tree represent domains within the namespace. The domain name of any domain in the tree is the list of labels, separated by periods, starting from the domain being named along the path to the root of the tree. In Figure 10.2, for example, the domain name for the square labeled "isd" is "isd.tenet.edu".

 You need to know the following characteristics of domain names:

➤ Domain names are not case sensitive.

➤ Labels at each hierarchical level can be up to 63 characters in length. (The "zero" length or "null" label is reserved for the "root" domain.)

➤ The total length of the domain name cannot exceed 255 characters.

A number of top-level domains have been set up in the United States for the Internet. The following list contains the names and organizational functions of some of the more familiar top-level domains:

➤ **COM** Commercial (business) entities

➤ **EDU** Educational institutions

➤ **GOV** U.S. government agencies

➤ **MIL** U.S. military

➤ **NET** Network service providers

➤ **ORG** Organizations that do not fit into other top-level domain categories

In addition, two-character country code domains have been set up as top-level domains for each country outside the U.S. A few of the top-level country code domains and countries are shown in the following list:

➤ **AU** Australia

➤ **BR** Brazil

➤ **CA** Canada

➤ **DE** Germany

➤ **FR** France

➤ IN India

➤ JP Japan

➤ NZ New Zealand

➤ UK Great Britain

Domain names can identify a specific host, service, Web server, email address, and so forth on the internetwork. On private networks, hostnames need to be unique within the network. If the network is connected to the Internet, however, hostnames with their accompanied domain name must be unique across the entire Internet, because a 1:1 correlation exists between each domain name and a registered IP address. Domain names must be officially registered to prevent accidental duplication of domain names and to ensure that each name-to-address association is unique on the Internet.

Registered Domain Names

Registered domain names are available in the U.S. by application through InterNIC. The application process involves the following steps:

1. Select a name and search InterNIC's Whois database to ensure that the name you want is not already registered.

2. Complete and submit the application template, available online from InterNIC, to the hostmaster at InterNIC.

3. Submit the registration fee upon notification from InterNIC that your application has been processed. You must pay renewal fees every two years to keep the registration active.

Your domain name information is added to InterNIC's Whois database and to the zone files used by DNS.

Registered domain names outside the U.S. are available by application to the manager of a country code top-level domain. A manager's status and authority to register domain names is obtained through application to and approval by the Internet Assigned Numbers Authority (IANA). The completed application template (the same template used to apply in the U.S.) is submitted to iana@iana.org instead of the hostmaster at InterNIC.

Understanding DNS Zones

The DNS namespace is partitioned into administrative sections called *zones* or *subdomains*. Zones are created by making logical divisions in the namespace between two adjacent nodes in a way that isolates a node or a group of connected nodes. An organization makes the divisions or cuts at points in the namespace where it wants to have administrative control over a subtree. The partition formed becomes an administrative zone, managed by the organization. It's authoritative for all names within that zone.

Because the divisions in the namespace are logical, the zones formed are not required to correlate to physical network segments. A single zone may span many networks, or a single network may contain more than one zone.

The tree structure of the namespace ensures that one node in the zone will be closer to the root than any other node. The name of the node that's closest to the root is typically used to name the zone (see Figure 10.3). The zone extends from the topmost domain downward through the tree until it either reaches a terminal node or the beginning of another subzone.

Standard DNS zones contain the information used by name servers to map names to IP addresses. The following two types of zones are also used in DNS:

➤ **IP6.INT zones** IPv6 is a new addressing scheme currently under development that defines a 16-octet or 128-bit IP address. The IPv6 zone type contains the information necessary for resolving domain names to IPv6 addresses. The scheme is designed to provide an almost limitless number of IP addresses to accommodate the ever-increasing use of the Internet and the limitations imposed by the current version (IPv4).

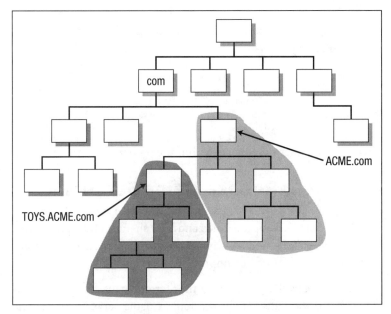

Figure 10.3 DNS zones and domain names.

➤ **IN-ADDR.ARPA zones** This zone type handles requests to find the IP address associated with a particular name. It contains information in a format that enables mapping IP addresses to names as opposed to the standard zone mapping of names to IP addresses. The IP addresses in an IN-ADDR.ARPA zone are defined with the order of the dotted octets reversed (hence the IN-ADDR, which means *Inverse Address*). For example, a domain that has an IP address of 132.77.71.24 in a standard zone will have the address 24.71.77.132.in-addr.arpa in an IN-ADDR. ARPA subzone.

DNS Name Servers

A single name server (called the *domain master name server*) within each zone is the repository for the portion of the DNS database that contains all namespace information for that zone. Backup name servers (called *replica name servers*) provide fault tolerance and load-sharing functions. You need to know the characteristics and functions of both name server types.

Understanding Master Name Servers

The portion of the DNS database stored on the domain master server is called the *authoritative database* for that zone. All changes and updates to the DNS information for the domain are made at this server. The information in the database includes:

➤ The addresses of name servers for domains that link the current domain to the DNS hierarchy

➤ The addresses of root domain name servers

➤ The addresses of the name servers for all subzones

➤ The names of all subzones

➤ IP addresses and names of all hosts within the domain

Understanding Replica Name Servers

Replica name servers hold a copy of the authoritative database for a domain. In addition to the functions of fault tolerance and load sharing, the replica name servers can be strategically located anywhere in the DNS namespace to reduce wide area network (WAN) traffic or improve host accessibility.

Periodic downloads of a fresh copy of the authoritative database from the master name server keep the database on the replica name server current. The process of replacing the replica name server database with a new copy from the master name server is called a *zone transfer*.

Understanding DNS Resolvers

A *resolver* is a DNS Server that queries itself or other name servers on behalf of the client. The name server tries to resolve the address from cache or its own domain databases, if the address exists within the local domain. If the requested address lies outside its domain, the server contacts a root name server, maintained by InterNIC, to start the resolving for the address. All of the following events occur as a typical address request is processed:

➤ A client requests the IP address of an Internet host from the local domain name server.

➤ The local domain name server tries to resolve the name to an IP address from cache or from its local databases, and returns the address to the client.

➤ If the local domain server cannot resolve the name to an IP address, it requests assistance from name servers outside the local domain, starting with the root domain name server.

For example, if the query is **www.novell.com** and the local DNS can't resolve the Web server, the DNS (now acting as a DNS resolver) queries one of the root servers maintained by InterNIC. (There are currently about 15 root servers.) The root server looks at the query (**www.novell.com**) and tells the DNS resolver where the .com server is located by giving it the IP address for the .com domain server. The DNS resolver will then query the .com server and ask it where the **www.novell.com** server is located, and the .com server will look for .novell.com in its database. When it finds .novell.com, it will refer the DNS resolver to the Novell DNS server. Finally, the DNS resolver queries the .novell.com DNS server to find out where **www.novell.com** is, and the Novell DNS server responds with the IP address of its Web server (www).

➤ The local domain server caches the address for future reference and returns the address to the requesting client.

Practice Questions

Question 1

How many hostnames are allowed in a host table?

○ a. One hostname per IP address with no limit on the total.

○ b. One hostname per IP address with no more than 255 per host table.

○ c. Four octets for IPv4 or 16 octets for IPv6.

○ d. The number of hostnames per table is unlimited.

○ e. No hostnames are allowed; the host table only contains IP addresses that are assigned to hostnames dynamically.

The correct answer is d. The number of hostnames in a host table is unlimited (although very large host tables are impractical in most environments). Answers a and b are incorrect because multiple hostnames can refer to a single IP address. Answer c is incorrect because the number of octets in an address has no bearing on the number of hostnames in a host table. Answer e is incorrect because host tables require hostnames by definition.

Question 2

Which answer shows the correct pairing of domain names from
the first list with the associations from the second list?

A COM

B GOV

C DE

D ORG

1 Government agencies

2 Common namespace

3 Denmark

4 U.S. military

5 Commercial entities

6 Germany

7 Miscellaneous organizations

○ a. A-2, B-1, C-6, D-7

○ b. A-5, B-4, C-3, D-1

○ c. A-5, B-1, C-6, D-7

○ d. A-2, B-4, C-2, D-1

The correct answer is c because the pairings correctly match the domain names
with their general functions. Answers a, b, and d are incorrect because at least
one of the pairings in each of those answers incorrectly matches a domain
name with a function.

Question 3

Where should you send a completed application template requesting a registered domain name under the country code domain for Germany?

○ a. iana@iana.org

○ b. hostmaster@internic.net

○ c. NIC.MASTER.DE

○ d. NIC.MASTER.GER

Answer a is correct. Requests for registered domain names outside the U.S. are submitted to **iana@iana.org**. Requests for registered domain names inside the U.S. are submitted to **hostmaster@internic.net**. Therefore, answer b is incorrect. Answers c and d are not valid email addresses and are therefore incorrect.

Question 4

How is a DNS name-to-address resolution initiated?

○ a. A name server searches its local database to start the process.

○ b. A client requests an IP address from a name server in the local domain.

○ c. A user addresses a network communication with a hostname.

○ d. A root domain name server broadcasts an update request to the Internet.

The correct answer is b. Clients will usually request IP addresses from name servers in their local domain. Answer a is incorrect because the name server searches its database after receiving a request for name resolution. Answer c is incorrect because the name-to-address resolution could be handled locally by referencing a host table. Answer d is incorrect because the event described is not part of the DNS protocol. This is a trick question because the events in answers b and c can both initiate DNS name resolution; however, answer c is not DNS specific.

Question 5

How do you add comments to a host table?

- ○ a. Enter the comment as text on any line to the right of a pound sign (#).
- ○ b. Type "rem" in front of the comment so it will be ignored by the system.
- ○ c. Create a comment section with a comment header.
- ○ d. Insert the text into the table as an image file.

The correct answer is a. When the system encounters a pound sign in a line, it ignores anything else on the line and moves to the start of the next line. You can enter comments as text to the right of a pound sign on any line. Answer b is incorrect because "rem" is not used to add comments to host tables. Answers c and d are incorrect because they are not included in the definition of a host table.

Question 6

Which DNS zone is able to resolve IP addresses to names?

- ○ a. IPv6 zones
- ○ b. Standard DNS zones
- ○ c. IN-ADDR.ARPA zones
- ○ d. IP6.INT zones

The correct answer is c. An IP address in an IN-ADDR.ARPA zone has the dotted octet order reversed and is used to resolve IP addresses to names. IPv6 is not a valid zone name. The zone for IPv6 is IP6.INT. Therefore, answer a is incorrect. Standard DNS zones resolve names to IP addresses. Therefore, answer b is incorrect. IP6.INT zones resolve domain names to IPv6 IP addresses. Therefore, answer d is incorrect.

Need To Know More?

 Albitz, Paul and Cricket Liu. *DNS & BIND, 3rd Edition.* O'Reilly & Associates, Inc. Sebastopol, CA, 1998. ISBN 1-56592-512-2. This entire book contains valuable information on DNS.

 Lewis, Chris. *Cisco TCP/IP Routing Professional Reference, 2nd Edition.* McGraw-Hill. New York, 1998. ISBN 0-07-041130-1. Chapter 7 includes information on managing hostnames and provides a general overview of DNS topics.

 Parker, Timothy. *Teach Yourself TCP/IP in 14 Days, 2nd Edition.* Sams Publishing. Indianapolis, IN, 1998. ISBN 0-672-30885-1. Chapter 11 of this book provides a very good overview of DNS, including setting up a DNS server.

 www.internic.net contains the Whois database of registered domain names. Forms, policies, payment information, and help are available if you're interested in applying for a registered domain name.

 www.garlic.com/~lynn/rfcidx3.htm#1034 contains RFC 1034, which explains the purpose of the Domain Name System and defines the key concepts.

Subnets And Supernets

Terms you'll need to understand:

√   Subnet

√   Supernet

√   Subnet mask

√   Classful subnet hierarchy

√   Classless subnet hierarchy

√   Classless InterDomain Routing (CIDR)

√   Address aggregation

Techniques you'll need to master:

√   Explaining the purpose of subnetting

√   Describing the subnet mask

√   Explaining how subnet masks are used

√   Planning and assigning subnet masks

√   Planning and assigning subnet addresses

√   Recommending and implementing a subnetting scheme based on a sample company scenario

√   Explaining the purpose of supernetting

√   Identifying IP address criteria for supernetting

√   Describing the routing considerations for supernetting

The rapid growth of the Internet has led to an enormous increase in the number of requests submitted for registered IP addresses. The result is a drastic reduction in available registered addresses. Virtually all Class A and Class B addresses have already been assigned. Although there are still many Class C addresses, their numbers are rapidly dropping. In addition, the relatively small number of available Class C hosts places unrealistic configuration constraints on intranet infrastructures that support heavily populated network segments.

By definition, any registered IP address must identify a unique connection to the Internet. The 32-bit address specifies both a unique network on the Internet and a unique host on that network. With the number of registered IP addresses limited, as it is in the current version of IP (IPv4), this requirement poses two commonly encountered dilemmas.

Suppose a corporation has a registered Class B network address and a corporate intranet that includes ten separate networks. Because the registered Class B network address must uniquely identify a single LAN attached to the Internet, only one of the corporate networks is able to connect to the Internet without additional networks within that single registered IP address needing to be defined. *Subnetting* addresses this problem.

A company that has a single network populated with 400 hosts illustrates another common dilemma. With the number of available Class B addresses in short supply, the company is unable to obtain a registered Class B address but instead is granted two Class C addresses. Without some way of defining its corporate network as a single network within the two registered IP addresses, the company will be forced to divide the network, possibly at considerable expense. *Supernetting* addresses this problem.

In this chapter, you learn how the technique of subnetting allows you to define multiple networks within a single IP address as well as how to plan and implement subnetting. You also learn how supernetting allows you to define contiguous network addresses as a single address to increase the number of hosts that can be supported on a single network segment. You also learn how to plan and implement a supernetting strategy.

Subnets

When necessary, a network administrator can divide a single IP network into multiple, connected networks, called *subnets*. Reasons for creating subnets include the following:

➤ **Network extension** You can extend a network by adding routers and creating subnetworks to support connecting additional hosts when the network needs to grow beyond its physical limits defined by the Physical layer protocols.

➤ **Reducing network congestion** Communication between hosts on a single network creates intranetwork traffic. Adding hosts to the network results in network congestion when the amount of traffic supporting interhost communication becomes excessive. By dividing the network into subnetworks and group hosts that share communications on the same subnets, most interhost communications are isolated to the individual subnets, and overall network congestion is reduced.

➤ **Reducing host CPU overhead** Subnetting to reduce network congestion also reduces CPU overhead. Because all hosts on a network monitor and act on all network communications by deciding whether to accept or discard the communication, CPU overhead increases as the amount of network traffic increases. Dividing the network into subnets to reduce congestion causes a decrease in the total number of communications processed by each host. This results in reduced CPU use per host across the network.

➤ **Using multiple network media types** When a network is divided into subnets, different physical media types can be used on each subnet.

➤ **Isolating network problems** Subnetting can reduce the overall impact of a network communication problem, such as a cable break on a 10Base2 Ethernet network, by isolating it to the subnet on which it occurs.

➤ **Improving network security** Subnetting allows you to restrict communications containing sensitive information to a specific subnet. In addition, because only registered IP addresses are visible from the Internet, the structure of a private corporate network, connected to the Internet through a single registered IP address, is invisible from the outside.

Subnet Masks

In Chapter 9, you learned that each IP address contains both a complete network address and a complete host address within its 32-bit address. The TCP/IP protocol uses a technique called *subnet masking* to indicate which of the bits in an IP address represent the network address, and which represent the host address. For this reason, each IP address must be assigned a subnet mask even if the network is not segmented into subnetworks.

The subnet mask is a 32-bit number commonly expressed in dotted octet (binary) or dotted decimal format. Binary *ones* indicate the corresponding bit positions in an IP address that are to be read as the *network* portion of the address. The binary *zeros* in a subnet mask indicate the corresponding bit positions in an IP address that are to be read as the host portion of the address.

A router identifies the network and host addresses of a host by logically ANDing the subnet mask with an IP address. You can use a truth table to predict the outcome when a binary or Boolean operation (AND, OR, XOR, and NOT) is performed on two operands, X and Y. Table 11.1 is a truth table for the AND operation used by routers with the IP address (X) against the subnet mask (Y) to determine whether the value of a bit position is to be read as part of the network address.

The router reads only the value of the bit position as part of the network address when X AND Y is true. This occurs only when both the IP address and subnet mask have 1 in corresponding bit positions.

Figure 11.1 illustrates the results of using the ANDing operation with the following IP address and subnet mask:

➤ **IP address** 00101101.00001101.00000110.10001001 (45.13.6.137)

➤ **Subnet mask** 11111111.00000000.00000000.00000000 (255.0.0.0)

In the example shown in Figure 11.1, the bit positions that identify the network portion of the IP address (reading from left to right) are in the first octet. The router reads the network address from bit positions that are true for both the IP address and the subnet mask. The mask hides the values at all other bit positions in the IP address from the router. This means that the router sees the value of only the network portion of the IP address. This is the portion necessary for routing a packet to the proper destination network. Default masks are assigned to Class A, B, and C networks, as illustrated in Figure 11.2.

The default Class A mask in Figure 11.2 has all 8 bits in the first octet set to 1, with the remaining 24 bits set to 0. The Class B mask has all 16 bits in the first two octets set to 1 with the remaining 16 bits set to 0. The Class C mask has all 24 bits in the first three octets set to 1 with the remaining 8 bits set to 0. Because a bit position value is read as part of the network address only if both

Table 11.1 Predicting the outcome of an AND operation.

X	Y	X AND Y
0	0	0
0	1	0
1	0	0
1	1	1

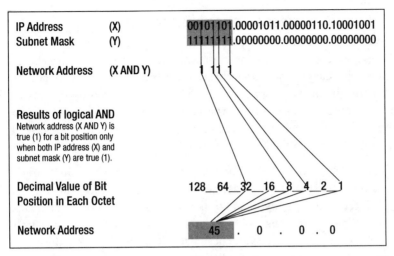

Figure 11.1 A logical AND operation performed by a router with the IP address against the subnet mask reveals the bit values used for the network address.

the IP address and the subnet mask have a 1 in the same position, Class A network addresses can be defined only in the first octet of an IP address. The same process applies for both Class B and C network addresses, which must be defined in the first two and first three octets of an IP address, respectively.

Note: Class A, B, and C network addresses are all specified in the first three bits of the first octet, as follows:

➤   *Class A networks 0xx (addresses 1 to 127)*

➤   *Class B networks 10x (addresses 128 to 191)*

➤   *Class C networks 110 (addresses 192 to 223)*

Network Class	Subnet Mask
A	**Network** 11111111.00000000.00000000.00000000 255.0.0.0
B	**Network Network** 11111111.11111111.00000000.00000000 255.255.0.0
C	**Network Network Network** 11111111.11111111.11111111.00000000 255.255.255.0

Figure 11.2 Default masks for Class A, B, and C networks.

Classful And Classless Subnet Hierarchies

IP addresses that conform to the default mask assignments for different network classes are recognized as members of a *classful subnet hierarchy*. In a classful subnet hierarchy, Class A networks always use 8 bits for the network address and 24 bits for the host address, and Class B networks always use 16 bits for the network address and 16 bits for the host address. Internet routers route packets in a classful subnet hierarchy using the default mask for the network class, as defined in the initial bits of the first octet.

Dividing a network into smaller subnetworks involves borrowing bits from the host portion of the IP address to define the additional subnet addresses. In Figure 11.3, the Class A network, 44.0.0.0, is divided into subnetworks via a subnet mask, 255.255.0.0, that "borrows" the 8 bits of the second octet from the host portion of the IP address and designates them as network address bits.

When you borrow bits from the host portion of the IP address to create subnets, you have IP addresses that use nonstandard numbers of bits to represent the network and host portions of the address. IP addresses that do not conform to the default mask assignments make up a *classless subnet hierarchy*. Routers inside a subnetted network are configured with subnet masks that recognize subnet addresses and route to subnets using classless addresses.

In Figure 11.3, an Internet router configured to route in a classful hierarchy applies the default Class A mask (255.0.0.0) and routes to the only network address it sees: network 44.0.0.0. A router within network 44.0.0.0, configured

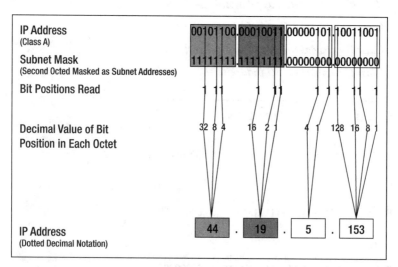

Figure 11.3 Borrowing the second octet of bits to define additional subnet addresses on a Class A network.

with the subnet mask 255.255.0.0, can read the classless address, thus allowing it to route to the subnet address 40.19.0.0.

Planning Subnet Numbers

The number of bits borrowed from the host address field determines the maximum number of possible subnets that can be created and the number of host addresses that will be available on each subnet. Figure 11.4 illustrates the effects of borrowing one and two octets to create subnets using a Class A network address.

The number of possible subnets made available by assigning a subnet mask is calculated as follows

```
Possible Subnets = 2ⁿ - 2
```

where n is the number of bits masked from the host portion of the IP address.

The two addresses subtracted out of the total are the "all 1s" and "all 0s" network addresses, because they are not supported by all routers.

The number of possible host addresses that can be assigned to each subnet is calculated as follows

```
Possible Hosts = 2ᵐ - 2
```

where m is the *number of unmasked bits* remaining in the host portion of the IP address after bits have been borrowed for subnetting.

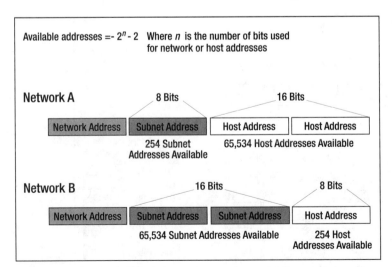

Figure 11.4   Number of subnets versus hosts when masking one and two octets.

Again, the two addresses subtracted out of the total are the all-1s and all-0s addresses.

 When calculating the number of available subnets or hosts, always assume that all 1s and all 0s are not supported unless specified otherwise.

You can use these methods when masking partial and complete octets. In the following section, you learn how partial octets can be used to define and create subnets.

Subnetting With Partial Octets

Creating subnets by masking a full octet may be inappropriate or even impossible in some cases. For example, you can mask the entire fourth octet of a Class C address, but doing so leaves no host bits available for assigning host addresses. It's common to mask part of the octet to provide subnet addresses while leaving unmasked bits available for assigning host addresses. This provides multiple networks within the constraints of a single Class C address.

Consider a situation in which a Class C address needs to support three subnets with less than 20 hosts per subnet. Masking the first three bits of the fourth octet easily accommodates this (see Figure 11.5).

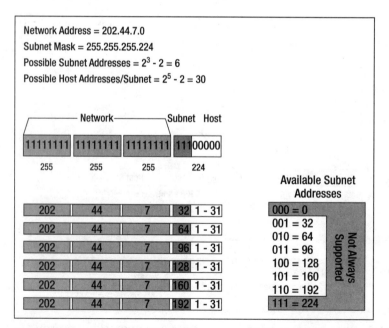

Figure 11.5   Masking a partial octet using the three high-order bits.

This solution allows you to assign up to 6 subnet addresses, with each subnet supporting up to 30 hosts. Figure 11.5 shows these three components for each IP address after the subnet mask is applied:

➤ **A network component** The first three octets. The network component reflects the network class—in this case, a Class C network. The network components for Class A and Class B networks would consist of one and two octets, respectively. This component is common to all hosts on the network. It's the *classful address* recognized by Internet routers as a unique network on the Internet. When IP addresses are assigned, every host on this network will use 202.44.7.0 for the network component.

➤ **A subnet component** The bits that are masked. In this case, it's the first three bits of the fourth octet. Each network segment or subnet is assigned a unique value for the subnet component from the list of available subnet addresses.

➤ **A host component** The bits that are unmasked. In this case, it's the last five bits of the fourth octet. Within each subnet, every host is assigned a unique host value from 1 to 31.

 You'll often see bits referred to as *high-order* bits when they're read starting from the left side of an octet and *low-order* bits when they're read starting from the right side of an octet.

Note that this solution physically segregates contiguous sets of IP addresses onto network segments based on the first three bits of the fourth octet. For instance, IP addresses that include 001 as the first three bits in the fourth octet are assigned only to hosts on subnet 202.44.7.32 (the masked bits are 001).

The range of host addresses that can be assigned on subnet 202.44.7.32 is 202.44.7.33 to 202.44.7.63 when expressed as classful addresses, which is how you normally view them. Note that the available host addresses are equal to 32 + 1 through 32 + 31, which is the subnet plus host portions of the classless address (refer to Figure 11.5). Table 11.2 shows a comparison of a few of the classless and classful addresses. A colon (:) is placed between the subnet and host portions of the classless address for clarity.

The hosts on the next subnet (subnet 202.44.7.64) have 010 as the first three bits in the fourth octet. The address range assigned to subnet 202.44.7.64 is 202.44.7.65 to 202.44.7.96. Again, you'll see that the host addresses are equal to the subnet plus host portions of the classless address (64 + 1 through 64 + 31). The pattern is fundamental to all subnetted networks and is repeated on

Table 11.2 Classless and classful addresses.

Classless	Classful
202.44.7.32:3	202.44.7.35
202.44.7.32:10	202.44.7.42
202.44.7.32:21	202.44.7.53
202.44.7.32:29	202.44.7.61

each subnet; it includes subnet 0 (mask 000) and subnet 224 (mask 111) on networks that support all 0s and all 1s for subnet addresses.

All hosts on a given subnet have a bit pattern in the host portion of their IP addresses (the subnet addresses) that's unique to the hosts on that subnet. Routers within the network are configured with a subnet mask to recognize the bit patterns, allowing each subnet to be uniquely identified and routed to within the network. The process is the same whether you subnet a Class A address by masking the second and third octets, or you subnet a Class C address by masking the four high-order bits in the fourth octet. Once you understand the process, you'll learn common patterns and become familiar with conventions and rules that provide the quickest paths to managing subnets efficiently.

By convention, subnet masks are assigned with contiguous bits, starting with the high-order bit in an octet. The decimal value of the rightmost bit in the mask can be used to determine the start of the range of available subnet addresses in an octet. Each address in the range is a multiple of the starting address up to, but not including, the multiple that has the same decimal value as the subnet mask. This is illustrated in Figure 11.6.

Planning Subnets

Before creating subnets on your network, you need to develop a strategy based on the following suggestions:

➤ Accommodate subnet needs by rounding up the maximum number of hosts currently needed to the nearest power of two, after determining the maximum number of subnets needed. For instance, if you determine that you need nine subnets and your network supports subnet addresses 0 and 1, 2^3 (or eight) subnets do not provide enough subnet addressing space. You must round up to 2^4 (or 16) subnets to provide for your current needs.

➤ You should also ensure that you are providing subnet addressing space that will accommodate network growth. In this case, even providing for 16 subnets when you currently need 9 may prove inadequate if your

---

Example 1:   IP Address = 203.88.6.0
             Subnet Mask = 255.255.255.240
             Available Subnet Addresses = 2^4 - 2 = 14

             16
             ▽
             11111111.11111111.11111111.11110000

The decimal value of the rightmost bit in the mask is 16. The subnet addresses are obtained by starting with address 16 and adding 16 to each successive address in the sequence. The final address is the highest multiple of 16 that is less than the value of the subnet mask.

The available subnet addresses obtained by using this mask are:
16, 32, 48, 64, 80, 96, 112, 128, 144, 160, 176, 192, 208, 224

Example 2:   IP Address = 183.60.0.0
             Subnet Mask = 255.255.192.0
             Available Subnet Addresses = 2^2 - 2 = 2

             64
             ▽
             11111111.11111111.11000000.00000000

The decimal value of the rightmost bit in the mask is 64. The subnet addresses are obtained by starting with address 64 and adding 64 to each successive address in the sequence. The final address is the highest multiple of 64 that is less than the value of the subnet mask.

The available subnet addresses obtained by using this mask are:
64 and 128

Figure 11.6   Using the rightmost bit in the subnet mask to determine the subnet addresses.

network is growing rapidly. It may be better to plan for 2^5 (or 32) maximum subnets to ensure adequate addressing space in the future.

➤ Ensure that your strategy includes enough host bits to accommodate all hosts on your largest subnet. Again, round up the maximum number of hosts currently needed to the nearest power of two to determine how many host bits will be required. For instance, if your largest subnet must support 35 hosts, 5 host bits will provide for only 2^5 (or 32) host addresses. You'll need 2^6 (or 64) maximum addresses to accommodate the subnet with 35 hosts. You should consider planning to accommodate growth by providing address space for more hosts per subnet as well as planning for additional subnets.

Assigning Subnet Addresses

You should make subnet and host address assignments in a way that allows you to create additional subnets or support additional hosts without having to reassign existing addresses. You can do this by assigning subnet addresses starting with the leftmost of the subnet address bits and assigning host addresses starting with the rightmost of the host address bits and progressing in numeric order.

In Figure 11.7, subnet addresses have been assigned starting from the left of the subnet address field. Although a maximum of 16 subnets are available, only 5 have been assigned. This means that only the first three bits are used to make all subnet address assignments. If the number of available hosts needs to be increased, the existing subnet and host addresses remain valid when the subnet mask is changed to 224. The mask is altered by changing the fourth bit in the subnet address field from 0 to 1, as shown in Figure 11.8.

If you start with a subnet mask of 224, you may eventually find that more subnets are needed and the number of hosts per subnet will probably not exceed 16. If the greatest number of hosts supported on any subnet is currently 10 and host addresses were assigned by starting with the rightmost bit in the host field, progressing in numeric order, only the four rightmost bits were used to make the host address assignments. This means that the unused host bit (fifth from the right) is available to increase the maximum number of subnets possible without necessitating any changes beyond changing the subnet mask to 240 by changing the fourth high-order bit from 0 to 1. If host addresses were assigned by starting from the left of the host address field, the host addresses using the fifth bit would need to be reassigned in order to make the bit available for assigning subnet addresses.

Following are the steps to take when creating subnets:

1. Determine the number of subnets needed and the number of hosts that must be supported on each subnet, taking into account current and

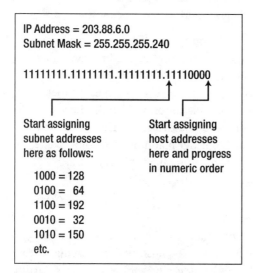

Figure 11.7 Assigning subnet and host addresses.

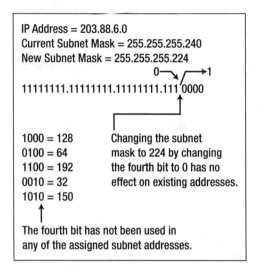

IP Address = 203.88.6.0
Current Subnet Mask = 255.255.255.240
New Subnet Mask = 255.255.255.224

11111111.11111111.11111111.111 0000

1000 = 128   Changing the subnet
0100 = 64   mask to 224 by changing
1100 = 192   the fourth bit to 0 has no
0010 = 32   effect on existing addresses.
1010 = 150

The fourth bit has not been used in
any of the assigned subnet addresses.

Figure 11.8   Changing the mask in a subnet address.

future needs. Calculate the maximum number that must be available to support your needs, using these general formulas:

➤ Number of Subnets = $2^n - 2$, where n is the number of masked bits

➤ Number of Hosts = $2^m - 2$, where m is the number of unmasked bits

2. Determine the subnet mask and subnet address assignments based on the maximum number of subnets needed. Once the mask is determined, the available subnet addresses will be multiples of the decimal value of the rightmost bit in the mask, up to, but not including, the decimal value of the mask. Assign subnet addresses starting with the leftmost bits in the subnet address field.

3. Assign IP addresses to subnet hosts, taking the following into account:

➤ All hosts on the network must have the same network address.

➤ All hosts on a subnet must have the same subnet address.

➤ All hosts on a subnet must have a unique host address.

➤ Host address fields cannot be all zeroes or all ones.

➤ Host addresses on each subnet must be assigned starting with the rightmost bit in the host address field and progressing in numeric order.

In the following section, you learn how to create a supernet by defining a single network with multiple Class C addresses.

Supernets

Supernets combine multiple Class C addresses into a block of addresses that can be assigned to hosts on a single network segment. Even though multiple Class C addresses are used to define the supernet, it's identified as a single network by routers.

Supernets were invented to address the following issues concerning the current IP addressing structure:

➤ Virtually all Class B network addresses have been assigned, whereas a relatively large number of Class C network addresses are still available.

➤ A single address supports a maximum of only 254 hosts.

➤ Continued growth of the routing tables in Internet routers will render them virtually unmanageable due to their enormous size.

➤ The existing IP address space must accommodate continued growth.

The process of creating a supernet mask to combine multiple Class C addresses is the reverse of the process involved in creating a subnet mask to subdivide a network. Instead of borrowing bits from the host portion of the IP address, bits are borrowed from the default network address and used to increase the number of host address bits.

Remember that the default subnet mask for a Class C network is 255.255.255.0 or 11111111.11111111.11111111.00000000. The first 24 bits are used to identify the network portion of the address, and the final 8 bits are used to identify the host portion of the IP address. Using the formula

```
2ᵐ - 2 = number of hosts
```

gives a potential $2^8 - 2$ (or 254) hosts within a Class C IP network.

By using a subnet mask that defines 23 bits for the network portion of the address (255.255.254.0), the number of unmasked bits defining the host portion of the address becomes 9. Substituting 9 for m in the formula provides a potential $2^9 - 2$ (or 510) hosts on a single network.

Combining Class C networks to create supernets is also referred to as *address aggregation*.

IP Address Requirements For Creating Supernets

For you to create supernets from Class C IP addresses, the network addresses must be consecutive and the third octet in the first address must be evenly divisible by two. This ensures that a single bit (the rightmost bit in the third octet) defines the difference between the two addresses. Using these criteria, for example, you can create a supernet with the Class C network addresses 211.34.16.0 and 211.34.17.0, but not with network addresses 211.34.19.0 and 211.34.20.0. The comparison of binary addresses shown in Figure 11.9 makes the difference between the two pairs more obvious.

Figure 11.9 shows that the addresses in the valid pair are contiguous at the binary level, meaning that the blocks of host addresses that they contain are also contiguous. The pair that cannot be used to create a supernet is not contiguous at the binary level (a fact that's not readily apparent when viewing the dotted decimal format) and the blocks of host addresses they contain are not contiguous.

To create a supernet from network addresses 211.34.16.0 and 211.34.17.0, assign a mask using 23 bits. The 24th bit becomes part of the host address space, allowing 510 hosts on the combined network instead of 254.

The router on the new supernet advertises only the first Class C address (211.34.16.0) and the subnet mask /23. Receiving routers read the IP address and mask and recognize that the mask is made up of 23 bits, indicating that one bit of the Class C address has been used to make a supernet. This information is used by the routers to identify 211.34.16.0 and 211.34.17.0 as two contiguous Class C networks that have been combined. The first network in the pair is identified as supernet 0, and the second is identified as supernet 1.

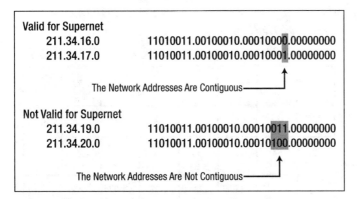

Figure 11.9   Comparison of valid and nonvalid pairs of network addresses for creating a supernet.

Combining More Than Two Class C Addresses

You can combine more than two Class C addresses by borrowing more bits from the network portion of the address to extend the host portion of the address. Figure 11.10 shows the effect of borrowing additional bits to support more hosts on a single network. You can use the information shown in Figure 11.10 to determine how many networks to combine or how many bits to borrow to support a given number of hosts.

 Become very familiar with the information in Figure 11.10. For example, you should know how many bits should be borrowed to support 4,098 hosts on a single network. (The answer is 5.)

Supernets And Classless InterDomain Routing (CIDR)

CIDR was invented to provide a process for enabling routers to identify nondefault or classless IP addresses. Because it allows routers to use subnet masks other than the defaults for Class A, B, and C networks, the routers can identify these addresses. Earlier routing schemes used the default mask to identify the network portion of an IP address. With CIDR, network addresses are identified by the number of bits in the network portion of the address. The IP address 211.34.16.0/23, for example, is read by routers as having a subnet mask of 11111111.11111111.11111110.00000000. The /23 in the address tells the router that the first 23 bits from the left make up the subnet mask.

Being able to combine networks and advertise all the address ranges combined together as one block greatly decreases the volume of information that a router is required to store and route on the Internet.

Note: *Do not create supernets without ensuring beforehand that your network routers support CIDR.*

Number of Bits Borrowed	7	6	5	4	3	2	1	0
Subnet Mask	128	192	224	240	248	252	254	255
Number of Contiguous Addresses to Combine	128	64	32	16	8	4	2	0
Number of Hosts Supported		> 8,192 < 16,384	> 4,096 < 8,192	> 2,048 < 4,096	> 1,024 < 2,048	< 1,024 > 512	> 256 < 512	< 256

Figure 11.10   Combining more than two Class C networks.

Practice Questions

Question 1

> Which of the following represents a subnet mask of 255.255.248.0?
>
> ○ a. 00000000.00000000.00001111.11111111
>
> ○ b. 11111111.11111111.11111000.00000000
>
> ○ c. 11.11111.11111.11.11111.11111.11.1111.0.0
>
> ○ d. 11111111.11111111.11110000.00000000

The correct answer is b. The decimal value of 11111111.11111111.11111000. 00000000 is 255.255.248.0. The other answers are incorrect, because answers a and c contain invalid formats for a subnet mask and answer d represents the subnet mask 255.255.240.0.

Question 2

> Which of the following are valid reasons for creating subnets? [Choose the three best answers]
>
> ❑ a. Reducing host CPU usage
>
> ❑ b. Reducing network congestion
>
> ❑ c. Adding more than the default number of hosts to a single network segment
>
> ❑ d. Extending the existing network

The correct answers are a, b, and d. Valid reasons for subnetting include the need to reduce host CPU usage, reduce network congestion, and extend the existing network. The need to add more than the default number of hosts to a single network segment is a valid reason to create a supernet, not a subnet. Therefore, answer c is incorrect.

Question 3

What's the default subnet mask for the following IP address?

11001101.01001011.10101111.00000101

○ a. 11111111.00000000.00000000.00000000

○ b. 11111111.11111111.00000000.00000000

○ c. 11111111.11111111.11111111.00000000

○ d. None of the above

The correct answer is c. The first three bits of the address shown indicate that it's a Class C address (initial bits are 110). Answer c is correct because it's the default mask for Class C network addresses. Answers a and b are incorrect because they are default masks for Class A and Class B network addresses, respectively. Answer d is incorrect because answer c is correct.

Question 4

Which of the following is not a valid subnet address when using the following subnet mask on a Class C network?

Subnet mask = 255.255.255.224

○ a. 206.77.1.48

○ b. 210.22.77.64

○ c. 196.123.221.96

○ d. 208.66.4.192

The correct answer is a. Valid subnet addresses using the mask 255.255.255.224 are multiples of 32, in the fourth octet, starting with subnet 32. They are 32, 64, 96, 128, 160, and 192. Only answer a does not have one of these values as the fourth octet. Answers b, c, and d are valid subnet addresses using the given mask and are therefore incorrect.

Question 5

> What are IP addresses called that do not use the default subnet mask?
>
> ○ a. Classful addresses
>
> ○ b. Unclassified addresses
>
> ○ c. Classless addresses
>
> ○ d. New Order addresses

The correct answer is c. IP addresses that do not use the default subnet mask are called classless addresses. IP addresses that use the default subnet mask are called classful addresses. Therefore, answer a is incorrect. Unclassified addresses and New Order addresses are not standard networking terminology. Therefore, answers b and d are incorrect.

Question 6

> Which of the following occur when the number of bits that define the subnet portion of an IP address is increased? [Choose the two best answers]
>
> ❑ a. The number of available hosts per subnet is increased.
>
> ❑ b. The number of available hosts on the network is decreased.
>
> ❑ c. The number of available subnets is increased.
>
> ❑ d. The number of available subnets is decreased.

The correct answers are b and c. Increasing the number of bits defining the subnet address allows more subnets to be defined but reduces the number of bits available to define host addresses. Answers a and d provide the opposite effect and are therefore incorrect.

Question 7

Which technique allows you to add more hosts to a single network segment than are allowed by the default mask?

○ a. Address aggregation

○ b. CIDR

○ c. Host bonding

○ d. Classless addresses

The correct answer is a. Supernetting is also commonly called *address aggregation* and is a technique that allows you to add more hosts to a single network segment than are allowed by the default mask. This is a trick question because both CIDR and classless addresses are requirements for supernetting; they are not, however, techniques. Therefore, answers b and d are incorrect. Host bonding is not a synonym for supernetting. Therefore, answer c is incorrect.

Need To Know More?

 Lewis, Chris. *Cisco TCP/IP Routing Professional Reference, 2nd Edition.* McGraw-Hill. New York, 1998. ISBN 0-07-041130-1. This book contains valuable information on routing TCP/IP.

 Parker, Timothy. *Teach Yourself TCP/IP in 14 Days, 2nd Edition.* Sams Publishing. Indianapolis, IN, 1998. ISBN 0-672-30885-1. This book is a great source of information on TCP/IP.

 www.garlic.com/~lynn/rfcietf.html is a good site for doing a search on subnets and supernets or for searching for specific RFCs by number (RFCs 1122, 950, 1338, 1518, and 1519 contain information about Internet standards, subnets, and supernets).

TCP/IP

Terms you'll need to understand:

✓ Transport Control Protocol/Internet Protocol (TCP/IP)

✓ File Transfer Protocol (FTP)

✓ Hypertext Transfer Protocol (HTTP)

✓ Simple Mail Transfer Protocol (SMTP)

Techniques you'll need to master:

✓ Understanding the layers of the Department of Defense (DoD) networking model and their functions

✓ Mapping the TCP/IP protocol suite to the DoD networking model and the Open Systems Interconnection (OSI) model

Communication protocols define rules for interaction between hosts on a network. When protocols are mapped to the OSI model, it's clearer how the interaction is to take place. In this chapter, we introduce you to the TCP/IP protocol suite as it relates to the Department of Defense (DoD) networking model and the OSI model.

The TCP/IP Protocol Suite

The Transport Control Protocol/Internet Protocol (TCP/IP) communications protocol suite can be mapped to the OSI model we discuss throughout this book. The protocol suite is based on the four-layer networking model developed by the DoD about ten years before the OSI model.

The TCP/IP protocol suite is used by hosts and networks to communicate globally on the Internet. The suite is an open standard managed by the Internet Architecture Board (IAB). The IAB does not make direct changes to the Internet standards but is the driving force behind the formation of workgroups that solve or address particular Internet problems, such as the soon-to-be IP address "shortage."

TCP/IP's versatility in connecting disparate networks makes it a perfect fit for the Internet, which connects global networks regardless of their Physical layer properties. The TCP/IP protocol suite operates above the Physical and Data Link layers of the OSI model while relying on other standards to handle the physical properties. That's why the XYZ Corporation, a token ring shop, can connect to the Internet along with Joe Smith, a home dial-up user.

Most people think of TCP/IP as a single entity. However, it's a protocol suite comprised of various communications protocols operating at various layers of the OSI model. The basic protocols that make up the TCP/IP protocol suite are the Transmission Control Protocol (TCP) and the Internet Protocol (IP). TCP initiates communications between two hosts on an internetwork and separates the data to be sent into pieces (called packets). TCP numbers the pieces so they can be arranged in order when they arrive at the destination. IP takes care of data transfer between two hosts by handling packet addressing to ensure that routers can pass the packets through the internetwork.

TCP/IP is also well suited to the Internet environment because of the many protocols it supports, such as the File Transfer Protocol (FTP), the Simple Mail Transport Protocol (SMTP), the Hypertext Transfer Protocol (HTTP), and so on. These protocols allow TCP/IP to easily render the basic functions of two communicating hosts.

Within TCP/IP, you'll find that FTP is commonly used on the Internet to transfer files back and forth. However, simply having TCP/IP installed on a computer and being connected to the Internet doesn't guarantee that you can use FTP to transfer files. You have to first connect to another FTP host on the Internet using the processes defined in the Process/Application layer of the DoD model (discussed in the following section). Once both your computer and the host are communicating using the same FTP, files can be transferred back and forth.

SMTP is another TCP/IP protocol widely in use on the Internet; it's used for email services. Two mail hosts can communicate and exchange email using this standard protocol.

> *Note: SMTP does not provide an end user interface, but rather the backend server process that moves messages between mail hosts of different companies.*

HTTP is widely used on the World Wide Web (WWW) for communication between hosts. Browsers send requests formatted using the HTTP protocol to Web servers that then process the requests using the same protocol. The information sent back to the browser will be rendered in the form of an HTML document.

The DoD Model

The DoD model contains four layers that map well to the OSI model. Starting at the lowest layer, the Network Access layer, we define the functions of each layer in the DoD model in the following sections.

Network Access Layer

The Network Access layer is the lowest layer of the DoD model. It includes the functions associated with the Physical and Data Link layers of the OSI model. This includes rules about how hosts on a network physically connect with one another. Information found at this layer pertains to Ethernet, token ring, Fiber Distributed Data Interface (FDDI), and other types of networks that define the physical interconnection.

Internet Layer

Moving up a layer, the Internet layer of the DoD model maps to the OSI Network layer. It specifies processes defined by TCP/IP protocols that operate at the Network layer of the OSI model. (The Network layer defines routing processes that occur between different hosts or networks.) The Internet layer is responsible for routing data between different networks. TCP/IP protocols at this layer include IP, Internet Control Message Protocol (ICMP), Bootstrap Protocol (BOOTP), and Address Resolution Protocol (ARP), among others.

Host-To-Host Layer

The Host-to-Host layer of the DoD model maps to the OSI Transport layer and specifies processes that are defined by TCP/IP protocols. As you'll recall from previous chapters, this layer provides reliable (error-free) end-to-end communications and delivery of data between hosts.

Process/Application Layer

The uppermost layer, the Process/Application layer, includes the functionality of the OSI model's Session, Presentation, and Application layers. This layer provides the user interface and means of transferring files between hosts. TCP/IP protocols at this layer include Telnet, FTP, and HTTP. Web browsers are a good example of this layer, because they use HTTP to communicate with Web servers either on an intranet or the Internet.

 Telnet, FTP, and HTTP are all TCP/IP protocols that map to the OSI Session, Presentation, and Application layer of the OSI Model, and to the Process/Application Layer of the DoD model.

Mapping The TCP/IP Protocol Suite And The DoD Model To The OSI Model

Figure 12.1 shows the TCP/IP protocol suite as it maps to both the OSI model and the DoD model. This figure illustrates the suite's versatility. As you can see by the number of protocols that fit into the various layers of the OSI model, the TCP/IP protocol suite contains functionality for almost any task you need.

					OSI Layers	DoD Layers
TELNET	NFS	SMTP	HTTP	FTP	Application	Process/Application
					Presentation	
					Session	
DNS		UDP		TCP	Transport	Host-to-Host
ICMP	BOOTP RARP		ARP RIP	IP	Network	Internet
Networks Ethernet, Token Ring, FDDI & Others					Data Link	Network Access
					Physical	

Figure 12.1 TCP/IP and how it fits into the OSI and DoD models.

Practice Questions

Question 1

> Which of the following DoD layers maps to the Physical and Data
> Link layers of the OSI model?
>
> ○ a. Network Access
>
> ○ b. Internet
>
> ○ c. Host-to-Host
>
> ○ d. Process/Application

The correct answer is a. The physical properties of communication are defined
in the Network Access layer of the DoD model. Answer b is incorrect because
the Internet layer maps to the Network layer of the OSI model. Answer c is
incorrect because the Host-to-Host layer maps to the Transport layer of the
OSI model. Answer d is incorrect because the Process/Application layer maps
to the upper three layers of the OSI model.

Question 2

> Which of the following TCP/IP protocols can be found within the
> Internet layer of the DoD model and, therefore, operate at the Net-
> work layer of the OSI model? [Choose the three best answers]
>
> ❏ a. FTP
>
> ❏ b. HTTP
>
> ❏ c. ICMP
>
> ❏ d. BOOTP
>
> ❏ e. ARP

The correct answers are c, d, and e. ICMP, BOOTP, and ARP all fit within the
Internet layer of the DoD model and can be mapped to the Network layer of
the OSI model. Answers a and b are incorrect because both of those protocols
operate at the Process/Application layer of the DoD model.

Question 3

Which of the following DoD layers is responsible for establishing
reliable end-to-end communications between systems?

○ a. Network Access

○ b. Internet

○ c. Host-to-Host

○ d. Process/Application

The correct answer is c. The Host-to-Host layer maps to the Transport layer
of the OSI model and is responsible for reliable communications between systems on an internetwork. Answers a, b, and d are incorrect because they define
other functions.

Question 4

Which of the following TCP/IP protocols provide services widely
used on the Internet? [Choose the three best answers]

❏ a. FTP

❏ b. HMTP

❏ c. SMTP

❏ d. HTTP

The correct answers are a, c, and d. FTP, SMTP, and HTTP are all used on the
Internet to facilitate services between hosts. FTP is used for file transfer, SMTP
is used for mail services, and HTTP is used for communication between hosts
on the Web. Answer b is incorrect because there is no such named protocol in
the TCP/IP suite.

Question 5

> Which of the following groups can request and spur action to create additions to the TCP/IP protocol suite standard?
>
> ○ a. IAB
> ○ b. RIPE
> ○ c. ARIN
> ○ d. WWW

The correct answer is a. The Internet Architecture Board (IAB) is a technical advisory board that operates to spur the formation of workgroups to solve Internet problems and to create new standards or add to existing ones. Answers b and c are incorrect because RIPE and ARIN are responsible for assigning and administering IP addresses in some parts of the world. Answer d is incorrect because the WWW is an internetwork of computers, not a group. This is a trick question because the groups RIPE and ARIN handle IP address administration but do not actually provide technical oversight to groups that create additions or changes to the protocol suite.

Question 6

> Which protocol within the TCP/IP protocol suite handles breaking data into pieces and numbering the pieces so they arrive at the destination in the correct order?
>
> ○ a. TCP
> ○ b. HTTP
> ○ c. SMTP
> ○ d. FTP

The correct answer is a. TCP is responsible for establishing communications between two hosts and for breaking up the data into pieces. Answer b is incorrect because HTTP is used on the Web for communications between hosts but is not part of the TCP/IP protocol suite. Answer c is incorrect because SMTP is for mail information, and answer d is incorrect because FTP operates at the upper layers of the OSI model to handle file transfers.

Question 7

> HTTP, Telnet, and FTP operate at which layers of the OSI model?
>
> ○ a. Physical, Data Link, Network
>
> ○ b. Session, Presentation, Application
>
> ○ c. Network, Transport, Session
>
> ○ d. Network Access, Internet, Host-to-Host

The correct answer is b. HTTP, Telnet, and FTP all operate at the upper three layers of the OSI model. Therefore, answers a and c are incorrect. Network Access, Internet, and Host-to-Host are DoD layers, not OSI model layers. Therefore, answer d is incorrect.

Need To Know More?

 Krol, Ed. *The Whole Internet, 2nd Edition.* O'Reilly & Associates, Inc. Sebastopol, CA, 1994. ISBN 1-56592-063-5. This book
contains a lot of information regarding the TCP/IP protocol
suite presented in a very easy-to-understand manner.

 Lewis, Chris. *Cisco TCP/IP Routing Professional Reference, 2nd
Edition.* McGraw-Hill. New York, 1998. ISBN 0-07-041130-1.
Chapter 2 of this book provides a very good overview of the
OSI model and the DoD networking model.

 Parker, Timothy. *Teach Yourself TCP/IP in 14 Days, 2nd Edition.*
Sams Publishing. Indianapolis, IN, 1998. ISBN 0-672-30885-1.
Chapter 1 includes additional information on the topics of stan-
dards and protocols that is pertinent to this chapter

 www.iab.org has information about the Internet Architecture
Board as it relates to Internet standards.

IP Routing Protocols

Terms you'll need to understand:

√ Autonomous system

√ Interior gateway protocols (IGPs)

√ Exterior Gateway Protocol (EGP)

√ Routing Information Protocol (RIP)

√ Designated router (DR)

√ Backup designated router (BDR)

√ Link state update (LSU) packet

√ Link state advertisement (LSA) packet

√ Autonomous system border router (ASBR)

√ Stub area

√ Transit area

Techniques you'll need to master:

√ Understanding the routing process as it applies to the TCP/IP protocol suite

√ Understanding the route discovery process and metrics used by RIP

√ Understanding the enhancements to RIP offered by RIP II

√ Understanding the route discovery process and metrics used by Open Shortest Path First (OSPF)

√ Understanding the various OSPF logical groupings

√ Identifying the benefits OSPF has over RIP on IP networks

Like all Network layer-aware protocol suites, TCP/IP must have a routing protocol to determine the best path for packets to take across an internetwork. TCP/IP has two primary protocols that perform this task: RIP and OSPF. In this chapter, you'll learn the details of RIP and OSPF and the advantages OSPF has over RIP.

IP Routing Overview

As you've learned in previous chapters, the Internet Protocol (IP) is the member of the TCP/IP suite that's responsible for addressing and forwarding packets using connectionless communications services. Along these lines, IP is also responsible for Layer 3 packet switching. However, IP is not a comprehensive Network layer protocol because it relies on other protocols in the suite for address resolution, dynamic route discovery, communication prioritization, and process messaging.

Of course, because of the structure of the TCP/IP suite and IP's role within the suite, IP is uniquely suited for large, complex internetworks. An IP internetwork can easily be divided into individual, logical groups called *autonomous systems*. An autonomous system is a group of networks within an internetwork that's administered as a whole by a single authority. An example is a company with campuses in four cities around the country. Each campus can be designed to operate as an autonomous system while maintaining connectivity to the whole corporate network.

Routing protocols that operate within an autonomous system are referred to as *interior gateway protocols (IGPs)*, which are protocols that operate completely within the autonomous system and are responsible only for routing local information. In this context, the words *router* and *gateway* are virtually interchangeable; therefore, routing protocols are sometimes called *gateway protocols*.

> *Note: This is where the term default gateway originates. However, a router should not be confused with a translational gateway, such as those that change IP to IPX. This is another case in networking where the same term applies to two separate functions.*

To communicate between autonomous systems, IP uses exterior gateway protocols, such as the Border Gateway Protocol (BGP) and the very aptly named Exterior Gateway Protocol (EGP). An EGP provides a method of communication between routers at the edges of their respective autonomous systems. The original EGP was designed when networks were relatively small and, like distance vector routing protocols, EGP does not scale well into large, complex enterprise internetworks. BGP is designed as an enhancement to EGP and operates

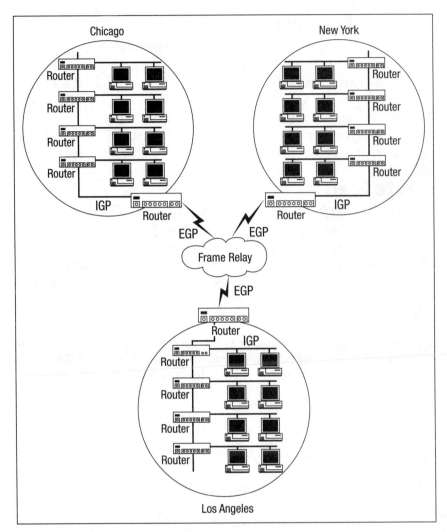

Figure 13.1   IGPs and EGPs work together to provide connectivity between autonomous systems.

as an interdomain routing protocol. Interdomain routing protocols give administrators a more extensive layer of control in large internetworks. Figure 13.1 shows a sample internetwork and the relationship between IGPs and EGPs.

RIP

The Routing Information Protocol (RIP) is an IGP in the TCP/IP protocol suite, and it acts as TCP/IP's distance vector routing protocol. As you learned in Chapter 7, a distance vector routing protocol, such as RIP, uses a straightforward routing algorithm to discover routes and maintain its routing information tables.

Route Discovery

On a network such as the one shown in Figure 13.2, RIP uses a simple route discovery process. When the routers are powered on, they distribute information to all routers on the network regarding the networks to which they're attached. On distance vector networks, as the routers learn about other routers and networks, they distribute their entire routing tables. Eventually, barring a network failure, each router is broadcasting similar routing tables, with only the hop count changed.

Route Metrics

Like most distance vector routing protocols, RIP uses the number of routers between the source and destination as the cost for a particular route. The number of routers involved in a particular path is called the *hop count*. The hop count, or cost, can be from 1 to 16, with 16 representing an unreachable network. Recall from Chapter 7 that to distance vector routing algorithms, 16 is infinity. Tables 13.1, 13.2, and 13.3 are examples of the routing information tables for Router 1, Router 3, and Router 4, respectively, from Figure 13.2.

Table 13.1 The routing information table for Router 1.		
Network	**Cost**	**Next Hop**
AAA	1	N/A
BBB	1	N/A
CCC	1	N/A
DDD	2	RT2
EEE	2	RT2
FFF	3	RT2

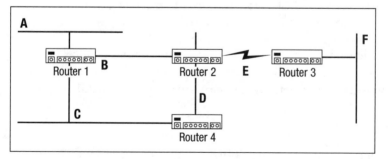

Figure 13.2 A sample network using RIP.

Table 13.2   The routing information table for Router 3.

Network	Cost	Next Hop
AAA	3	RT2
BBB	2	RT2
CCC	2	RT2
DDD	2	RT2
EEE	1	N/A
FFF	1	N/A

Table 13.3   The routing information table for Router 4.

Network	Cost	Next Hop
AAA	2	RT1
BBB	2	RT2
CCC	1	N/A
DDD	1	N/A
EEE	2	RT2
FFF	3	RT2

In their routing information tables, the routers keep track of the destination network, the cost to get to the network, and the next router in line to the destination. For example, on Router 3, Network A (whose address is AAA) is three hops away through Router 2.

To communicate amongst themselves, routers broadcast their routing tables. On any particular LAN, there may be RIP-enabled devices that can read the routing tables sent by the routers to let the devices decide which router to use to send packets destined for particular networks. For example, on the network mentioned in the earlier example, a server residing on Network C will receive broadcast messages from both Router 1 and Router 4, and will make its own determination on which router to send its packets to. If traffic is destined for Network A, it will clearly choose Router 1 because the cost is one, whereas Router 4's cost to Network A is two. However, if traffic is destined for Network E, the server could choose either Router 1 or Router 4, because their costs are the same. Most of the time it doesn't matter which router is used in this situation, but there may be situations in which one particular router is preferred. In this case, one router can be configured with a higher cost to ensure that the other router is used for a particular path.

RIP Disadvantages

As you learned in Chapter 7, the two biggest drawbacks to distance vector routing protocols, such as RIP, are the time it takes for routers to synchronize their routing tables (called *convergence*) and, consequently, their exposure to the count-to-infinity problem.

Networks using RIP as their routing protocol realize slower convergence than networks using other routing protocols, because distance vector algorithms require each router to recalculate its entire routing table before passing up-dated information on to the other routers on the network.

Another consequence of a slow convergence is the count-to-infinity problem. On a network similar to the one shown in Figure 13.3 (and discussed in Chapter 7), Router 4 knows that Network A is four hops away, Router 3 knows that it's three hops away, Router 2, two hops, and Router 1, one hop.

If, at some point, Router 1 fails or a failure occurs on Network B, Router 2 must update its routing table. Router 2 does not understand that Network A is no longer available, but accepts the information provided by Router 3, which indicates that Network A is now four hops away (three, plus one for itself). After Router 2 recalculates its routing information, it sends its entire routing table to Router 3, which now thinks that Network A is five hops away. Router 3 then sends its entire routing table to Router 4 and Router 2. When Router 2

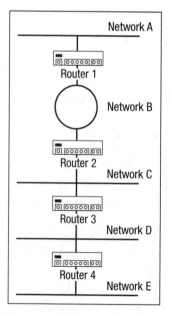

Figure 13.3 A network susceptible to the count-to-infinity problem.

receives the updated information, it recalculates its routing information table again, and the whole process starts all over, to infinity. Of course, the cost cannot actually reach infinity, because there's a maximum limit to the number of hops a particular route can have, usually 16.

> A route with a cost of 16 is considered unreachable and will not be used by networking devices or included in a router's routing information table.

Solutions

Two options are available that help reduce the effects or combat the count-to-infinity problem: split horizon and poison reverse. Here's a description of each:

➤ **Split horizon** To combat the count-to-infinity problem, networking protocol designers developed split horizon. Quite simply, on routers using split horizon, destinations are not advertised to ports from which they are received. For example, on the network shown in Figure 13.4, Router 3 broadcasts different information down each of its three ports. On Port 1, Router 3 sends a broadcast informing Router 2 that it's attached to or knows how to reach Networks D, E, F, and G. On Port 2, the broadcast consists of routes to Networks A, B, C, E, and F. And on Port 3, the routing table sent only includes routes for Networks A, B, C, D, and G. In this way, the routers on the network can recompute their routing tables without the interference of erroneous information from other routers.

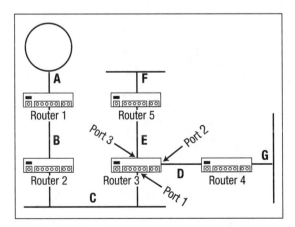

Figure 13.4   A network can employ split horizon to avoid the count-to-infinity problem.

Using split horizon decreases the size of the broadcasts being sent between the routers, but it increases the convergence time required in the event of a network failure.

➤ **Poison reverse** Poison reverse is the second method developed to reduce the effect of the count-to-infinity problem. On a network with poison reverse enabled, all routes learned from a particular network are rebroadcast back to that network with a cost of 16, meaning they're unreachable from that router. For example, on the network shown in Figure 13.5, Router 2 broadcasts that Network C is one hop away. When Router 1 receives this information, it sends a broadcast back across Network B saying that, on that port, Network C is 16 hops away. This way, if Router 2 fails, the hosts on Network B will not attempt to access Network C through Router 1, but will instead remove Network C from their routing tables. By default, poison reverse is enabled when split horizon is disabled.

Using poison reverse on a network reduces convergence time, but increases the amount of RIP traffic on the network because complete routing tables are transmitted.

RIP II—Additional Support

The first iteration of RIP, called simply RIP or RIP I, provided few specifications. Every 30 seconds, a router broadcasts all its routing tables to the other

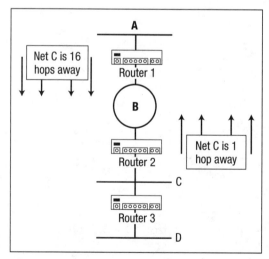

Figure 13.5 A network using poison reverse.

routers on the network, including the cost of each route. The routing table is accepted by the next router in line, and the receiving router calculates its routing table and forwards the entire table. To enhance the features provided by RIP, version 2 (known as RIP II) was introduced.

RIP II provides four primary features not seen in RIP I. First, RIP II includes authentication features that allow you to utilize a password for authentication and specify a key to authenticate routing information received from another router. This prevents someone from attaching to your network and sending bogus route information to your router to disrupt traffic. RIP II also supports variable-length subnet masks, which allow you to increase the number of hosts or subnets on a particular internetwork. With RIP I, subnet masks were only able to be configured along octet boundaries, thus limiting the configurations to Classes A, B, and C. You should note, however, that Open Shortest Path First (OSPF), which is discussed later in the chapter, is more efficient when variable-length subnet masks are required. In addition, RIP II supports a more extensive Next Hop Address field. With RIP I, the router from which the update was received was considered the next hop by default. However, with RIP II, this field can be configured to ensure that packets are not forwarded through extra routers in the system to reach their destination. Finally, RIP II routers support multicast packets that are used only to speak to other RIP II routers. Multicast packets are used to reduce the load on network hosts not using RIP II. When determining your network configuration, you should consider whether some or all of your networking devices support RIP II and plan accordingly.

Note: The multicast address for RIP II packets is 224.0.0.9.

IP Link-State Routing Overview

If you'll recall from Chapter 7, link-state routing involves each router on the internetwork sending a brief message with a list of its directly connected networks and their statuses. As the routers on the network receive these packets from the other routers, they build a detailed, firsthand map of the network and make determinations on which routes packets should take. This type of configuration minimizes the amount of data sent by each router and keeps the size of each router's information tables small.

OSPF

OSPF is the most frequently used link-state routing protocol on IP networks. Like other link-state protocols, the OSPF Hello Protocol is responsible for creating and maintaining router adjacency relationships, called *neighbor relationships*, between routers on the same network segment. For example, on the network shown in Figure 13.6, Router 2's Hello Protocol is responsible for recognizing that Router 1 and Router 3 are its neighbors.

Route Discovery

To facilitate the process of neighbor recognition, each router periodically multicasts a hello packet. Routers receiving hello packets automatically recognize there are other OSPF routers on the network. As mentioned, as a router receives information packets from other routers on the network, it builds a database representing a map of the internetwork. When a router on the internetwork detects that the status of one of its interfaces has changed, such as from disabled to enabled or if congestion is detected, the router sends new information to the other routers on the internetwork through a process called *flooding*. When a router receives this type of packet, it updates its routing table with the most recent information. Perhaps the biggest difference between RIP and OSPF is that at this point, each OSPF router constructs a shortest path tree through the network for each destination network.

OSPF Neighbor Router Identification

The first step in the route discovery process is identifying the routers on the network and their neighbors. As mentioned, a router uses hello packets to initiate a conversation between itself and another router. The hello packet is used to obtain neighbor information and maintain two-way communication between neighbors. The information that's gathered from the hello packet is added to the router's database.

When a hello packet is sent, it announces itself to the other router and thereby determines the router's neighbors. The packet itself includes the router's IP address and subnet mask and the interval at which each router sends hello

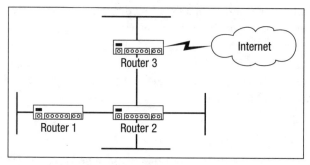

Figure 13.6 A sample OSPF network.

packets. The hello interval specifies the frequency at which hello packets are sent. If a router doesn't receive a hello packet from its neighbor within the hello interval, it declares that its neighbor is down. Because hello packets are such an integral part of monitoring the network's state, all OSPF routers must use the same hello interval. If not, they may not recognize each other as neighbors or may think that a neighbor is down when it's not.

The hello packet is also used to identify the designated router (DR) and backup designated router (BDR) on the network. The OSPF router with the highest priority on the network is named the designated router. In addition, routers use hello packets to elect a backup designated router. This election is won by the router with the second-highest priority. As routers exchange hello information, the DR and BDR are identified throughout the network.

If a router with a higher priority is powered on after the DR has been determined, the DR and BDR assignments do not change. The router with the higher priority will only become the DR or BDR in the event that the existing DR or BDR becomes inactive. If the DR becomes inactive, the current BDR becomes the DR, and the new system with the highest priority will become the BDR. If the current BDR goes offline, the new router will become the BDR.

A router's priority can be configured in OSPF to ensure that a particular router is always the DR or BDR. To configure a router so it can never be the DR or BDR, the router's priority should be set to 0.

Link-State Advertisement Database Synchronization

The second step in the route discovery process takes place after all routers have identified their neighbors and the DR and BDR have been determined. Once these two things have taken place, all routers on the network must create and synchronize their link-state advertisement databases with the DR and BDR. This process changes the relationship between the routers on the network. Before they begin the synchronization process, routers communicate in what is known as the *two-way state*. After synchronization, routers communicate in the full-neighbor state in which all routers are considered to be adjacent with each other. Here are the steps involved in synchronization:

1. The router starts in the two-way state. It sends a summary of its link-state database to the DR. The packets used for this communication are called *database description packets (DDPs)* and contain only summary information.

2. When the DR receives the DDPs, it sends its own summary DDPs to the routers on the network.

3. When the routers receive the DDPs from the DR, they compare the information received with the information already in their routing tables from the neighbor discovery process.

4. If one of the summary entries contains new or more up-to-date information than what's already in its database, the router sends a link-state request (LSR) packet to the router with the updated information.

5. When the router receives the LSR packet, it responds with the requested information via a link-state update (LSU) packet.

6. Upon receiving the LSU packet, the requesting router updates its routing table and acknowledges receipt by issuing a link-state acknowledgement (LSA) packet.

The state of the routers on the network plays a very important part in the OSPF process operation and communication between the routers. The DR and BDR should be in full-neighbor state with each other. All non-DR routers should be in full-neighbor state only with the DR or BDR, not with another non-DR router.

Route Selection

Like route selection on RIP networks, OSPF determines the best route for a packet to take based on the cost of that route. However, costs on OSPF networks are calculated differently than on RIP networks. An OSPF router's link-state advertisement databases represent the network from the router's perspective. When creating the routing table, OSPF assigns a cost to each interface. Then, the OSPF routing algorithm determines the interfaces a packet must travel through to reach a destination network and adds the costs of the interfaces to the total cost of the path. If there are multiple paths to the destination available, the path with the lowest cost is listed as the best path and is added to the routing table.

Unlike RIP, which recalculates its routing table each time it receives a broadcast from another router (every 30 seconds), OSPF only rebuilds the routing table when a change in the link-state advertisement database occurs. In addition, OSPF uses a hold-down interval to allow a cluster of changes to be added to the link-state advertisement database before recalculating the routing table. This minimizes the number of calculations that must be performed by the router in the event of major network changes.

Routing Database Maintenance

Once all routers in the network have synchronized their databases, they concentrate (though not too hard) on maintaining their routing tables. After the router calculates its routing table, it periodically issues LSU packets when changes occur in the network. By default, this takes place every 30 minutes. No, that's not a typo—it's 30 *minutes*, as opposed to the 30 *seconds* between each RIP update.

If there are no changes to the network, the routers issue LSUs less frequently. Periodically, each router will send LSU packets for each entry it's responsible for using a process called *flooding*. When flooding, the router sends a packet to the DR, which then floods the packet to the local network. If a router receives the flooded packet from the DR on one interface and has a neighbor router down another interface, the router forwards the packet to the other network. The DR on the other network then initiates another flood. This process continues until the packet is received by all routers on the internetwork.

When a router receives the LSU packet, it compares the information included in the packet to its link-state advertisement database. It resets the aging timer for the entries in the LSU packets. A change in the link-state database will only occur at this stage if the aging timer reaches four times the router dead interval, which can be configured on each router. At the same time the router receives the LSU packet, it sends an acknowledgment packet to the router that sent the LSU to ensure the packet was delivered.

OSPF routers will only go through a complete resynchronization process during full state changes. These types of changes should only occur when routers lose synchronization with the DR or BDR. At that time, the complete exchange of DDPs must again occur and adjacencies must be reestablished. For this reason, it's imperative that all routers on the OSPF network be in agreement on the link state, or *topology*, of the autonomous system.

OSPF Logical Groupings

For OSPF to route information effectively within an internetwork, it must be properly configured. Within the OSPF structure are four logical network groupings that are used to more effectively route data between networks: areas, autonomous systems, autonomous system border routers, and backbones. These groupings are discussed in the following sections.

Areas

For many networks, their size is such that distributing routing data throughout the network and maintaining an accurate network map is not difficult. However, as networks grow to include hundreds of routers, it becomes more and more difficult for each router to maintain an accurate link-state advertisement database and routing table due to storage limitations and the time it takes to reconfigure all routers in the event of a link-state change. In this type of environment, large enterprise internetworks are often divided into smaller contiguous segments called *areas*. An area is similar to an autonomous system and generally corresponds to an administrative domain such as a department or building.

OSPF routers treat areas as autonomous systems and do not require routers within an area to maintain link-state information for routers in other areas. This serves to limit the number of LSAs that are sent throughout the network and the size of the network map maintained by each router. This also decreases the amount of time required to recompute the routes when the state of the network changes.

Autonomous Systems

As mentioned, an autonomous system (AS) is a group of networks and their routers that exchange routing information using a common protocol. All routers in an autonomous system, such as the one shown in Figure 13.7, are managed as a single administrative unit.

Autonomous System Border Routers

Autonomous systems are connected to other autonomous systems, such as the Internet or a campus in another city, by specifically configured routers called *autonomous system border routers (ASBRs)*. An internetwork's ASBR communicates with other ASBRs and distributes routing information about external destinations to the AS. For example, in Figure 13.7, the router that connects the AS to the Internet is the ASBR. This router accesses routing information from the internal network using OSPF and from the Internet using EGP.

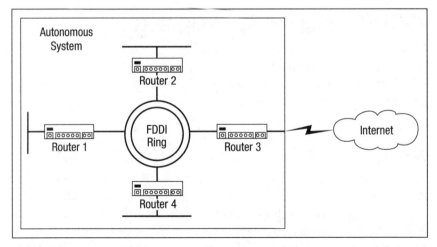

Figure 13.7   An autonomous system connected to the Internet.

Note: You may also see ASBRs called autonomous system boundary routers.

Backbone

In an OSPF environment, the *backbone* is the location area in the network where all areas connect. For example, in the network shown in Figure 13.8, the

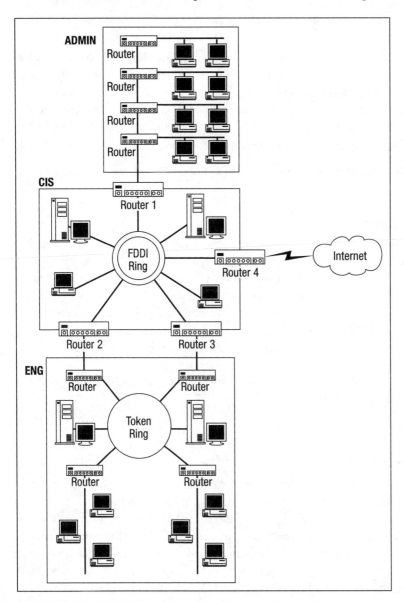

Figure 13.8   An OSPF network.

network in the CIS building is the backbone for the entire OSPF autonomous system. To be a backbone, the area must be connected to all other areas of the internetwork and must have an area address of 0.0.0.0.

> *Note: Although OSPF area numbers look like IP addresses, they're not. Some early implementations of OSPF used standard integers to represent areas (100938), but this got confusing. Because OSPF is only used with IP, it was determined that a similar numbering scheme would be best.*

The routers that connect one area to another in an OSPF network are called *area border routers (ABRs)*. The routers within a particular area receive information regarding the rest of the network from the ABR. The ABRs also exchange information about the areas with the backbone. It should be noted that ABRs require more memory and CPU power than routers within an area and, therefore, should not be low-end routers.

There are two types of areas that can be connected to the backbone: stub areas and transit areas.

Stub Area

Quite simply, a *stub area* is a section of the internetwork that has only one connection to the backbone, meaning it has only one ABR. In this type of configuration, all routes to destinations outside the local area are handled by the ABR, and the ABR advertises itself as the default route for these destinations. This network topology limits the size of the topological database within the area and reduces the amount of bandwidth required for area maintenance. In Figure 13.8, the Administration (ADMIN) building is in a stub area.

 An autonomous system border router cannot be located within a stub area.

Transit Area

As you can imagine, if an area with one connection to the backbone is a stub area, an area with more than one connection to the backbone is a transit area. These types of areas have slightly greater overhead requirements because they must determine the best route for particular paths, but the priority assignments on the routers can be configured to ensure that one router acts as the primary gateway, with the other router acting as the backup. An example of this type of area is the Engineering (ENG) building in Figure 13.8.

Advantages Of OSPF Over RIP

OSPF offers many advantages over RIP in most networking environments. The first, and perhaps most important in today's networking world, is its support for large, enterprise internetworks. OSPF is able to support networks of any size and is not limited to transmission through 15 routers the way RIP transmissions are. Remember that a router with a cost of 16 in RIP is considered unreachable, whereas an OSPF metric can be as high as 65,535. Could you imagine trying to connect all the devices on the Internet to be within 15 hops of each other? For this reason, OSPF is used in many larger internetworks, including the Internet.

Like RIP II, OSPF supports variable-length subnet masking. However, as mentioned earlier, OSPF is more efficient than RIP II in this realm. All LSAs include the subnet mask information about the network in question. The network administrator is able to assign different subnet masks for each network segment to more efficiently manage subnets and hosts on a single network address.

When properly designed and implemented, an OSPF network reconfigures itself much more quickly than a RIP network of the same size. The OSPF protocol is able to quickly detect changes to the internetwork and easily calculate new routes. The convergence time required is very short and involves minimal overhead, particularly when compared to RIP. Due to its design, OSPF does not suffer from the count-to-infinity problem at all. Along these same lines, the design of OSPF ensures that minimal bandwidth is used to maintain the network topology maps kept by each router, particularly when there are no changes to the network state. Whereas RIP routers broadcast entire routing tables every 30 seconds, OSPF routers broadcast only if there's a change and send hello packets only every 30 minutes.

 OSPF networks do not suffer from the count-to-infinity problem.

Practice Questions

Question 1

> Which of the following types of protocols is used to communicate
> within an autonomous system?
>
> ○ a. AS
>
> ○ b. IGP
>
> ○ c. ASRP
>
> ○ d. EGP

Answer b is correct. An interior gateway protocol (IGP), such as RIP, is used to communicate among routers in an autonomous system (AS). There really is no AS routing protocol, although many IGPs could, technically, be considered autonomous system protocols. Therefore, answer a is incorrect. Likewise, there is no autonomous system routing protocol (ASRP). Therefore, answer c is incorrect. An exterior gateway protocol, such as EGP or BGP, is used to communicate between autonomous systems. Therefore, answer d is incorrect.

Question 2

> During normal OSPF network operation, the DR and BDR should
> be in the _____ state.
>
> ○ a. two way
>
> ○ b. store-and-forward
>
> ○ c. full neighbor
>
> ○ d. full duplex

Answer c is correct. Once all information has been transferred between OSPF routers, the DR and BDR should be in full-neighbor state with each other. When synchronizing their databases, OSPF routers start in the two-way state. Therefore, answer a is incorrect. Store-and-forward is a type of switch, not a state for an OSPF router. Therefore, answer b is incorrect. Full duplex is an operating mode for a switch, not a routing state. Therefore, answer d is incorrect.

Question 3

> In which type of OSPF area does the ABR broadcast itself as the default gateway?
>
> ○ a. Backbone
>
> ○ b. Transient
>
> ○ c. Transit
>
> ○ d. Stub

Answer d is correct. A stub network is connected to the backbone by only one router. Therefore, it's the only route between the area and external destinations, so it can broadcast itself as the default gateway. The backbone connects all areas on a network. Therefore, answer a is incorrect. There is no transient area, but a transit area provides more than one connection to the backbone. In this configuration, no single router is necessarily the default route. Therefore, answers b and c are incorrect.

Question 4

> What's the default time between periodic updates for OSPF routers?
>
> ○ a. 30 seconds if there are no network updates
>
> ○ b. 30 minutes if there are no network updates
>
> ○ c. 30 minutes if there are network updates
>
> ○ d. 30 seconds if there are network updates

Answer c is correct. Routers running OSPF send LSUs every 30 minutes if there are changes to the network. It's very important to keep this information straight. RIP sends updates every 30 seconds, regardless of network state, whereas OSPF sends updates only if there's a change in network status. Therefore, answers a, b, and d are incorrect.

Question 5

> Which of the following enhancements are part of both RIP II and OSPF?
>
> O a. Extended Next Hop fields
>
> O b. Variable-length subnet masks
>
> O c. Password authentication
>
> O d. Multicast packets

Answer b is correct. All the enhancements listed have been included with RIP II, but only variable-length subnet masks are featured in OSPF. The other options were not required due to OSPF's design. Therefore, answers a, c, and d are incorrect.

Question 6

> Which of the following statements accurately describes a solution to an OSPF network's count-to-infinity problem?
>
> O a. OSPF increases infinity to 65,534 from 16 to eliminate this problem.
>
> O b. OSPF uses split horizon to eliminate the count-to-infinity problem.
>
> O c. OSPF uses poison reverse to eliminate the count-to-infinity problem.
>
> O d. OSPF networks do not suffer from the count-to-infinity problem.

Answer d is correct. OSPF networks are not affected by the count-to-infinity problem. Although the maximum cost of an OSPF route is 65,535, this is not a solution for count-to-infinity. Therefore, answer a is incorrect. RIP networks can use either split horizon or poison reverse to reduce the effects of count-to-infinity, but they are not available on OSPF networks. Therefore, answers b and c are incorrect.

Question 7

Which of the following types of routers is used to connect areas
to the backbone?

○ a. ABR

○ b. RIP

○ c. ASBR

○ d. AS

Answers a is correct. An area border router (ABR) is used to connect OSPF
areas to the backbone network. RIP, of course, is a routing protocol and does
not support areas. Therefore, answer b is incorrect. An autonomous system
(AS) is connected to another system by an autonomous system border router
(ASBR). Therefore, answers c and d are incorrect.

Need To Know More?

 Clarke, David James IV. *CNE Study Guide for Core Technologies.* Novell Press. San Jose, CA, 1996. ISBN 0-7645-4501-9. The Internet TCP/IP section of Chapter 10 deals with the protocols of the TCP/IP suite, including RIP and OSPF.

 There are numerous RFCs that define RIP, RIP II, and OSPF. For more information regarding these protocols, refer to any of the many RFC databases on the Internet, such as **www.rfc-editor.org** and **info.internet.isi.edu/1/in-notes/rfc**. Specifically, look at RFC 1387 (RIP Version 2 Protocol Analysis), RFC 1245 (OSPF Protocol Analysis), and RFC 1246 (Experience with the OSPF Protocol).

14

Other TCP/IP Protocols

Terms you'll need to understand:

√ Router discovery

√ Address Resolution Protocol (ARP) table

√ Relay agents

√ Management Information Base (MIB)

√ Simple Network Management Protocol (SNMP) traps

√ SNMP community name

√ Protocol analysis

√ Next generation Internet Protocol (IPv6)

Techniques you'll need to master:

√ Identifying the main components of the TCP/IP protocol suite

√ Describing the relationship of the TCP/IP protocol suite components to the OSI and DoD models

√ Explaining the function of the main TCP/IP protocols operating at the Internet, Host-to-Host, and Application/Presentation layers of the DoD model

√ Determining the proper TCP/IP protocol to implement to provide a needed functionality or to correct an error condition on your network

√ Explaining how protocol analyzers can be used to manage a TCP/IP network

√ Describing the features of the next generation Internet Protocol (IPv6)

The TCP/IP protocols specify networking functions that operate at the Network layer and above of the Open Systems Interconnection (OSI) model and at the Internet layer and above of the Department of Defense (DoD) model. The TCP/IP protocol suite, often referred to as the *Internet Protocol suite*, is currently the most popular set of communication protocols used to connect heterogeneous systems in mixed network environments. This is due in large part to the fact that the Data Link and Physical layer protocols are not specified within the protocol suite. This means that virtually any physical network platform is supported.

Another reason for the success of the TCP/IP protocol suite is the popularity of its Internet services, which include File Transfer Protocol (FTP), Simple Mail Transport Protocol (SMTP), and Hypertext Transfer Protocol (HTTP). In fact, any host that accesses the Internet or is accessible from the Internet must use TCP/IP.

In this chapter, you'll learn about the main TCP/IP protocols that specify functions operating at the Internet, Host-to-Host, and Process/Application layers of the DoD model. In addition, we'll cover the specifics of protocol analysis and provide you with a brief overview of the next generation Internet Protocol—IPv6.

Understanding The Internet Layer Protocols

The processes operating at the Internet layer of the DoD model are responsible for moving information across internetworks. Because the information sent between hosts is in the form of packets, which must often be forwarded through many routers, the Internet layer protocols provide the routing and packet-switching functions necessary to ensure that the packets are delivered to their final destinations. In addition, these protocols have the ability to fragment and reassemble packets when necessary—a feature made possible by the inclusion of sequencing information in the packet headers.

The Internet Protocol (IP)

IP is the DoD Internet layer protocol that provides connectionless, nonguaranteed delivery of Transport layer packets, often referred to as *transport protocol data units (TPDUs)*, across the internetwork. IP standardizes the routing, fragmentation, and reassembly of packets on a network.

Remember from Chapter 2 that a layer process communicates with its peers across the network through information included in protocol-specific headers attached to the data units it handles. Remember also that a layer process provides services to processes operating in layers above it, and requests the services of processes operating in the layers below it. In the case of IP, the service provided to the Transport layer processes is the connectionless, nonguaranteed delivery of TPDUs to the appropriate Transport layer processes at the destination address.

When IP receives a TPDU from the Transport layer, it fragments the TPDU into smaller parts, where required, and adds sequencing information to the IP header so the packet can be reassembled along the way or at its destination. It then attaches the IP header, which also includes protocol-specific information, such as the type of service, the length of the packet, the source address, the destination address, and so on, that will be read by its IP peer (see Figure 14.1).

Note that the fields IP Header Length (IHL), Don't Fragment (DF), and More Fragments (MF) in Figure 14.1 are used to communicate fragmentation and reassembly information. The TPDU or TPDU fragment is then delivered to a lower-layer protocol for transmission across the network as a frame. When the TPDU reaches its destination, the IP peer reads the header, reassembles the TPDU, if necessary, and delivers it to the appropriate Transport layer process.

You may wonder how a connectionless, nonguaranteed delivery protocol such as IP can provide transport services for a connection-oriented Transport layer protocol such as TCP. What appears at first glance to be an unlikely relationship actually turns out to be a situation that provides the best of both worlds.

When viewed from the perspective of TCP, the data units that it handles are always delivered to and received from IP transparently. (From the TCP point of view, the TPDUs could be thought of as being placed in a pneumatic tube that transports them directly to and from the destination peer process without the involvement of any "middlemen.") TCP has no knowledge of or concern for what IP may be doing with the TPDUs.

If TCP detects a transmission error, it's detected through communication with its TCP peer (remember that the protocol-specific header can only be read by a peer protocol). Any error recovery is handled through the same communication channel. IP never gets blamed for the transmission errors. In fact, if TCP detects an error that requires retransmission of a group of packets, the retransmission request is made to a TCP peer; IP doesn't see it as a retransmission at all—it's just another bunch of packets to deliver.

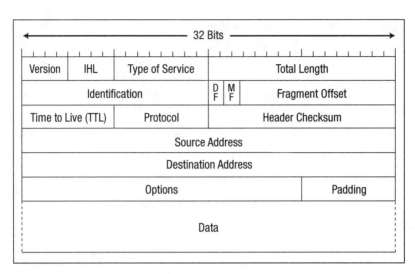

Figure 14.1   The IP frame format.

Let's return to the original question of how a connectionless, nonguaranteed delivery protocol such as IP can provide transport service for a connection-oriented Transport layer protocol such as TCP. As it turns out, IP is able to move tremendous amounts of data with relatively few critical errors. Because TCP is able to manage its own error recovery, the occasional errors associated with IP's connectionless, nonguaranteed delivery represent a small price to pay for the tremendous performance benefits gained by employing it for data transport.

 The key things you need to remember about IP are that it's a connectionless, nonguaranteed protocol that reassembles and fragments data packets.

The Internet Control Message Protocol (ICMP)

ICMP is a protocol supported in all implementations of TCP/IP. ICMP and IP work together to provide error and control information to upper-layer protocols such as TCP. Such control information is contained in ICMP messages, which are sent out by IP hosts in the following situations:

➤ A host has been asked to forward a packet and it knows of a better alternate route.

➤ A packet can't be placed in the buffer for some reason.

➤ A packet's destination is determined to be unreachable.

➤ The IP host needs to report congested or failed links to the internetwork.

➤ A problem exists with some parameter in the IP header.

➤ When the time to live (TTL) of a packet expires.

➤ When the IP host is trying to determine whether another host on the network is available.

➤ When the IP host is trying to determine which network it's on.

Some of the more common ICMP messages and their meanings are shown in the following list:

➤ **Destination Unreachable** Indicates that transmission problems have prevented a packet from being forwarded to its destination.

➤ **Echo Request and Echo Reply** A request/reply message pair that's used to determine whether a host can communicate with another host.

➤ **Redirect** Sent by an intermediate router to the source to inform it of a better alternate route to the destination.

➤ **Source Quench** Indicates that the destination or an intermediate node cannot keep up with the data rate and the source needs to slow its transmission down.

➤ **Time Exceeded** Indicates that a packet has been "thrown away" because its TTL has expired.

ICMP also supports router advertisements and solicitations, making it possible for hosts to discover neighboring routers. When a host comes online, it can transmit an ICMP multicast packet (224.0.0.2) asking neighboring routers to identify themselves. Neighboring routers that support Open Shortest Path First (OSPF) router discovery respond to the packet by returning their addresses. The host may then request packet forwarding through a discovered router (although the router may respond with an ICMP redirect message if it knows of a better route).

Be sure you know all the special IP addresses—such as the multicast address used by ICMP for router discovery (224.0.0.2). It's also good to know that ICMP router discovery can be configured to work with the generic broadcast address 255.255.255.255.

The Various Address Resolution Protocols (ARPs)

Because the MAC header of a frame only contains a hardware destination address, a problem arises when a packet is being sent to another network. A method that enables the network address to be mapped to the hardware address is necessary in order for the packet to get to the destination network properly.

Address Resolution Protocol (ARP)

The most popular method used to provide address resolution is ARP. ARP is used in the TCP/IP protocol suite to map a 32-bit software-based IP address to a 48-bit hardware-based Data Link address, also known as a MAC-layer address.

All hosts on the network maintain a table, called the *ARP table* or the *ARP cache*, that associates IP addresses with hardware addresses. The ARP protocol places entries into this table on an as-needed basis.

When a destination IP address does not have an associated hardware address entry in a host's ARP table, an ARP broadcast is sent to all hosts on the network. This broadcast requests the network address for the hardware interface associated with the given IP address. If the target host is on the network and it supports ARP, it responds to the broadcast by entering the source station's hardware address in its own ARP table and creating a response packet with its own hardware address in the source address field. It then sends the response packet directly to the source station. The ARP process at the source station receives this response packet and then copies the address in the source address field (along with the associated IP address) into its own ARP table.

ARP responses do not have to come from the destination address—intermediate routers can supply their own hardware addresses to allow them to move a packet to the next network segment on the route between sender and receiver. Users remain unaware of this process.

In the unlikely event that ARP is not supported on a destination device, you can add an entry for the destination to your ARP table manually. Once an entry is in the ARP table, that destination address becomes reachable even if it doesn't support ARP directly.

An IP router doesn't need to help the ARP process get MAC addresses; however, ARP does affect IP routers, as follows:

➤ IP routers and other products that support ARP have ARP enabled by default. This means that, by default, IP routers recognize and respond to ARP requests.

➤ IP routers are occasionally required to respond (via a response known as Proxy ARP) to ARP requests on behalf of a host located on another subnetwork.

The Reverse Address Resolution Protocol (RARP) And The Bootstrap Protocol (BOOTP)

The Reverse Address Resolution Protocol (RARP) is an extension of ARP that's used to discover the IP address associated with a particular hardware address. RARP is most important on networks that support diskless workstations because network address information can't be stored locally. The Bootstrap Protocol (BOOTP) is also used to discover the IP address associated with a particular hardware address. It's a newer protocol that's much more widely used today than RARP.

With BOOTP (and RARP), each network host's physical and logical addresses are stored on a BOOTP server. When a host, such as a diskless workstation, comes online and needs to learn its own IP address, it broadcasts an address request packet to the BOOTP server. The server responds with the network address information for the host itself.

As with ARP, the process does not require the assistance of IP routers as long as the host and BOOTP server both reside on the same network segment. When the BOOTP server and the host that's requesting address information reside on different networks, the assistance of an IP router is required. In that situation, IP routers between the host and the BOOTP server need to be configured to forward BOOTP requests to the BOOTP server. The router configuration includes providing the router with the addresses of the BOOTP servers on the internetwork to which the routers will be asked to forward requests.

The Dynamic Host Configuration Protocol (DHCP)

Manual configuration and administration of IP addresses on a TCP/IP-based network can be time-consuming processes that demand more administrative overhead than can reasonably be justified. Processes designed to provide automatic configuration of IP addresses alleviate this administrative requirement, and make network administrators' lives easier.

The Dynamic Host Configuration Protocol (DHCP) accomplishes this by providing IP address configuration parameters to Internet hosts. The protocol is based on a client/server model in which the server provides initialization parameters through DHCP to any client that requests such parameters from the server.

DHCP is actually implemented with two protocols: One protocol provides the host with its host-specific configuration parameters, and the other assigns the host its IP address. IP address assignments can be made in one of the following three ways (in decreasing order of likelihood, or frequency, of such use):

➤ **Dynamic allocation** An IP address is assigned to a host for a well-defined lease period (or until the host gives up this address).

➤ **Automatic allocation** A permanent IP address is assigned to a host.

➤ **Manual allocation** The network administrator assigns IP addresses, and DHCP delivers them to their respective hosts each time these hosts come online.

Understanding The DHCP Process

DHCP uses a process to configure hosts and assign IP addresses. First, a host requests configuration information with a broadcast packet that's picked up by a listening DHCP server. Next, the DHCP server reads the request packet to determine from which network segment the request originates. Finally, the DHCP server responds with all requested IP configuration information specific to that host and the network segment from which the request originates (unless it has no configuration information for that network segment; in that case, the DHCP server ignores such a request).

DHCP Relay Agent

Because DHCP requests are made with broadcasts, and routers do not forward broadcast packets, special assistance is required so DHCP servers can receive DHCP requests from other network segments. The assistance is provided by *DHCP relay agent* software that runs on a router. The relay agent forwards DHCP requests to the DHCP servers and then forwards the resulting DHCP replies back to the DHCP clients who originated those requests.

Understanding Host-To-Host Layer Protocols

Host-to-Host protocols specify the processes that provide reliable, full-duplex, connection-oriented service for communications between peer processes residing on different networks.

The Transmission Control Protocol (TCP)

The primary TCP/IP Transport layer protocol is TCP. TCP supports the following transport mechanisms or characteristics:

➤ **Acknowledged** This means that individual protocol data units (PDUs), or groups of PDUs, may be explicitly acknowledged as having been received successfully or unsuccessfully—in the latter case, a retransmission request will usually be issued.

➤ **Connection oriented** This means that both parties to the connection can negotiate and establish an ongoing exchange of information with an explicit beginning, middle, and end phase.

➤ **Flow controlled** This means that both parties to the connection can exchange information to increase or decrease the rate of data flow between them.

➤ **Full duplex** This means that data can move in both directions between both parties to the connection at the same time on a single carrier.

In short, data can move from one TCP peer to another TCP peer in a remote network station for messages of any size passed down from an upper-layer protocol (ULP). TCP optimizes the use of transmission bandwidth by supporting multiple, concurrent ULP conversations.

Flow control management is important because it prevents a faster system from overrunning a slower one while providing a mechanism to ensure that both systems are able to negotiate at an optimal pace. Numerous reliability features are specified in fields of the TCP protocol header (see Figure 14.2). The fields in the header that are used to support TCP reliability features include URG (urgent), ACK (acknowledgement), PSH (push), RST (reset), SYN (synchronize), and FIN (finish).

The User Datagram Protocol (UDP)

UDP, like TCP, provides transport services. Unlike TCP, UDP is not connection oriented, it doesn't acknowledge data receipt, and it doesn't provide related error handling abilities. UDP simply accepts datagrams from a ULP and transports them to their destinations.

UDP is a transport protocol of choice for many ULPs because its efficiency isn't compromised by the overhead involved in establishing and breaking connections, controlling data flow, or performing other functions that TCP must handle. Because it's not encumbered with such overhead, UDP is usually much faster than TCP.

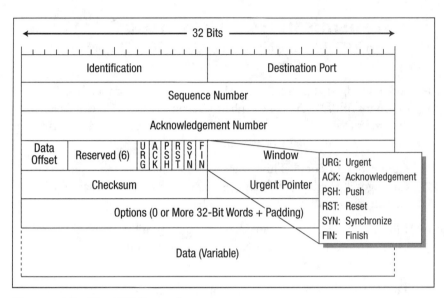

Figure 14.2 The TCP frame format.

The UDP header, shown in Figure 14.3, contains four fields:

➤ Source port

➤ Destination port

➤ Length

➤ Checksum (optional)

Note the relative simplicity of the UDP frame format when compared to a TCP frame. The total number of bytes in the entire UDP datagram is specified by the length field. The other fields are functionally the same as the matching fields in the TCP header.

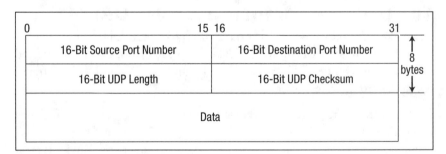

Figure 14.3 The UDP frame format.

Understanding The Process/ Application Layer Protocols

Every TCP/IP implementation provides numerous applications that are compatible across all versions of TCP/IP. In fact, one of the best-appreciated capabilities of the TCP/IP protocol suite is its support for a well-documented, interoperable set of standard applications across a wide variety of operating systems and platform types.

The File Transfer Protocol (FTP)

FTP is one of the most popular of the Process/Application layer protocols. It uses virtual circuits to establish a reliable path between hosts to enable file-related services. FTP depends on TCP's connection-oriented services for transport. Although FTP provides a variety of session control functions, its primary function is to enable users to move copies of files from one TCP/IP host to another.

The other session control functions included in FTP are as follows:

➤ Command execution

➤ Directory scans

➤ File manipulation

➤ Login

Part of the reason for FTP's enduring popularity is that its functions do not depend a host operating system or any particular hardware platform. Any TCP/IP host, regardless of its underlying operating system or platform, can use all FTP functions.

 FTP file transfers require a user account and password authentication, unless an administrator has configured the server to allow anonymous access. Anonymous access usually means supplying the word "anonymous" as the account, and the user's email address as the password (but no password is actually required).

The Trivial File Transfer Protocol (TFTP)

TFTP is another TCP/IP file transfer protocol. It allows users to transfer files between two TCP/IP hosts without requiring an account or password. Unlike FTP, TFTP cannot be used to scan files or directories, but it can be used to download files that are not restricted (most TFTP implementations allow restrictions to be placed on the types of files a host can access). TFTP also differs from FTP in that it does not require the services of a reliable transport protocol—it can use the services of any unreliable packet delivery system, such as UDP.

The Hypertext Transfer Protocol (HTTP)

HTTP provides access to information on the World Wide Web and on intranets through a request/response mechanism. HTTP is also used to enable communication capabilities between agents that use different TCP/IP protocols (such as SMTP, FTP, and Gopher) by acting as a common generic protocol.

An HTTP client accesses information by sending a request to a server. Incorporated into each such request is basic search and retrieval functionality, along with information about the purpose of the request. The following information fields are included in the request:

➤ **Identifier** This field contains the Uniform Resource Identifier (URI) that indicates the resource to which the request is to be applied.

➤ **Message Type** This field indicates a single request method—**GET**.

➤ **Method** This field indicates how the information is to be retrieved.

➤ **Protocol Version** This field contains the HTTP version. If the field is empty, the version is assumed to be HTTP/0.9.

➤ **Uniform Resource Locator (URL)** This field contains the name, location, and so on, used to identify a network resource. URLs are also referred to as Web addresses and Universal Document Identifiers.

The Simple Mail Transfer Protocol (SMTP)

SMTP specifies how messages move from one host to another across an internetwork. SMTP serves as a standard for exchanging mail between servers. SMTP is implemented as an email-routing application that relies primarily on the services of TCP to move email messages between network hosts.

> *Note: SMTP does not provide a local mail user interface or local delivery; it only specifies a process for passing messages from host to host. A local mail application is required to provide an interface to allow users to compose messages, set up mailboxes, and deliver messages to local users. Two of the protocols used for local delivery of mail from an SMTP host to a local user are the Post Office Protocol (POP, version 3, a.k.a. POP3) and the Internet Messaging Access Protocol (IMAP).*

Remember from previous discussions that gateways are hardware, software, or combinations of hardware and software that translate between dissimilar network platforms, protocols, or formats. An SMTP gateway performs the translation necessary to enable the exchange of email between SMTP and other email messaging systems.

The Simple Network Management Protocol (SNMP)

SNMP allows you to use a single workstation on your network, called an *SNMP manager*, to monitor an entire network. From the SNMP manager, you can query any other network devices that are running where an SNMP agent is available. Agents can reside on routers, TCP/IP hosts, printers, and in other SNMP managers.

Each SNMP agent includes a collection of Management Information Base (MIB) objects that contain the information that the manager can request from that host. The types of objects supported depend on the vendor's implementation of SNMP, but they typically include the following:

➤ ARP tables

➤ Event counters

➤ Hardware addresses

➤ Network addresses

➤ Routing tables

➤ Statistics

SNMP managers can examine and/or modify the objects contained within an agent's MIB. For example, from an SNMP manager, you could examine a host's ARP table and delete or change an incorrect entry.

> *Note:* *Because there are multiple version of SNMP in use today, and because not all vendors support all possible MIB objects, certain devices may not support queries or operations that other devices will support through an SNMP manager. Be wary of such inevitable inconsistencies.*

Commands

SNMP defines five types of commands that can occur in management communications between the SNMP managers and SNMP agents. These SNMP-defined command types are as follows:

➤ **GetNextRequest** Allows the manager to obtain information located in a table or array. The manager issues this command repeatedly until the desired information or full contents of the array have been retrieved.

➤ **GetRequest** Issued by the manager to request information from an agent.

➤ **GetResponse** Used by an agent to respond to a request made by the manager.

➤ **SetRequest** Used by the manager to modify the value of an MIB parameter on the agent.

➤ **Trap** Used by the agent to report the occurrence of special events to the manager.

SNMP Traps

An SNMP manager can configure SNMP agents to notify the manager or a group of managers when specified events occur. Such notification takes the form of a trap message sent by the agent to an SNMP manager. SNMP agents can be set to send trap messages for any condition that lies within their detection capabilities. For example, a LANalyzer agent on a network segment can be configured to send a trap message to an SNMP management console when bandwidth utilization on the segment remains above 40 percent for more than five minutes.

The following list describes the typical events that can cause an SNMP agent to send a trap message to the manager:

➤ **Authentication failure** An authentication failure trap occurs on a server when an unknown community name accompanies an SNMP request.

➤ **Cold or warm boot** An agent must reinitialize its configuration tables when it restarts because its configuration could have been altered by the cold start.

➤ **Enterprise specific** Trap messages occur when IP applications recognize specified events. The vendor's implementation of the protocol determines which events can trigger a trap, and the types of trap messages that may be sent.

➤ **Loss of an EGP neighbor** This type of trap message is sent when an SNMP agent can no longer communicate with an Exterior Gateway Protocol (EGP) peer.

➤ **When a link comes up or goes down** A server sends these trap messages to notify the manager whenever an IP fails or comes back to life.

SNMP Community Names

Any time an SNMP manager sends a request to an agent, it includes a community name with that request. The community name is a case-sensitive text string of up to 32 characters. This name functions in some respects like a password. If the community name accompanying a request is not recognized, or is not authorized to accompany that particular request, it triggers an authentication failure trap.

SNMP community names belong to certain categories, as follows:

➤ **Control community** Supplying the control community name gives the SNMP manager the right to read and write to a limited set of objects within the MIB. Any manager that provides the control community name for a server, for instance, can modify its routing table, enable or disable an interface, or enable or disable routing on the server. The manager cannot, however, modify counters that indicate the number of packets that have been processed.

By default, the control community name is disabled. This prevents unauthorized managers from making modifications to the MIB.

➤ **Monitor community** Supplying the monitor community name gives the SNMP manager the right to read information from the MIB of an agent. The default monitor community name is set to "public."

➤ **Trap community** The trap community name is included with all trap messages originating from an agent. For an SNMP manager to receive trap messages, it must be configured to accept traps from the trap community. The trap community name is set to "public" by default.

Receiving SNMP Trap Messages

Trap messages must have specified targets. For example, if your server has been configured to transmit trap messages, you must specify where those messages should be sent.

The default target for the traps is your local system (127.0.0.1).

By supplying their addresses as targets, you can set up multiple management consoles to receive trap messages. On a large network, assigning multiple management consoles makes it easier to define management boundaries and isolate SNMP traffic.

Protocol Analyzers

Protocol analyzers are designed to provide you with valuable protocol-specific information about network performance, behavior, and traffic that you can use to troubleshoot and manage a network. A protocol analyzer can be a software-only program, such as Microsoft's Network Monitor or the AG Group's EtherPeek, or it can be a standalone device that incorporates a combination of hardware and software components, such as Network General's Sniffer or Novell Customer Connection's (NCC's) LANalyzer.

The following list contains examples of the types of features available from protocol analysis tools used at different levels of the OSI model and how the information they gather can be used:

➤ **Network layer** Protocol analyzers operating at this level are designed to determine the distance between clients and servers. The information collected here might reveal the need for cable reconfiguration to improve router efficiencies.

➤ **Transport layer and above** Protocol analyzers operating at this level can examine applications by capturing the traffic between a client and a server during an application download. Developers require such functionality when testing and debugging applications that generate network traffic; network professionals find such functionality useful when attempting to characterize or analyze traffic and usage patterns on their networks.

IP Next Generation—IPv6

The rapid growth of the Internet ensures that the current version of IP (IPv4) will soon prove incapable of addressing the needs of TCP/IP-based networks. In fact, it's inevitable that the Internet will eventually run out of usable addresses. A new version of IP, called IPv6 and IPng (IP Next Generation), is designed to address these current growth trends, and to extend IPv4's security features and functions as well.

The features of IPv6 include the following:

➤ **Anycast address** This new type of address represents defined sets of nodes that are the target of packet delivery.

➤ **Enhanced security capabilities** Packet extensions that support authentication, data integrity, and encryption have been defined as options. Current work on IP Secure (IPsec) already demonstrates benefits for these technologies.

➤ **Expanded routing and addressing capabilities** IP addresses have been increased in size from 32 bits to 128 bits to provide an almost unlimited number of available addresses. In addition, autoconfiguration of the addresses has been simplified.

➤ **Expanded support for options** The rules defining header options are more flexible to make it easier to incorporate new options as needed, and the length limits are not strictly designed in order to allow new options to be more easily accommodated. Also, the way that the options are encoded has been changed to allow more efficient forwarding.

➤ **Header format simplification** Unused header fields have been either eliminated or, for those fields that are used by some implementations and not by others, have been made optional.

➤ **Quality-of-service capabilities** Information indicating the type of data traffic can be included with the packets.

Practice Questions

Question 1

Which DHCP method of IP address assignment involves auto-matically assigning an address to a host for an administratively defined lease period (or until the address is relinquished by the host)?

○ a. Automatic allocation

○ b. Dynamic allocation

○ c. Manual allocation

○ d. All of the above

The correct answer is b. With dynamic allocation, an IP address is assigned to a host for an administratively defined lease period (or until the address is relinquished by the host). With automatic allocation, a permanent IP address is assigned to a host. Therefore, answer a is incorrect. With manual allocation, the network administrator assigns the IP address, and DHCP delivers it to the host each time the host comes online. Therefore, answer c is incorrect. This is a trick question because the wording of the question makes answer a an attractive choice.

Question 2

What is the default target for traps?

○ a. Management Information Base (MIB)

○ b. Directory Information Base (DIB)

○ c. 127.0.0.1

○ d. The nearest SNMP manager

The correct answer is c. The default trap target is your local system (IP address 127.0.0.1). Therefore, answers a, b, and d are incorrect.

Question 3

> Which Internet layer protocol provides connectionless, non-
> guaranteed delivery of Transport layer packets, often referred
> to as transport protocol data units (TPDUs), across the
> internetwork?
>
> ○ a. IP
>
> ○ b. UDP
>
> ○ c. FTP
>
> ○ d. TFTP

The correct answer is a. IP provides connectionless, nonguaranteed delivery of
Transport layer packets across the internetwork. UDP, FTP, and TFTP are
not Internet layer protocols. Therefore, answers b, c, and d are incorrect.

Question 4

> Which protocol informs upper-layer protocols when a packet's
> destination is determined to be unreachable?
>
> ○ a. SMTP
>
> ○ b. RIP
>
> ○ c. ICMP
>
> ○ d. Trap

The correct answer is c. ICMP informs ULPs when a packet's destination has
been determined to be unreachable. SMTP specifies how messages are passed
from one host to another across the internetwork. Therefore, answer a is incorrect. RIP is the Routing Information Protocol. Therefore, answer b is incorrect.
Trap is a command used by the agent to report the occurrence of special events
to the manager. Therefore, answer d is incorrect.

Question 5

> What is the default trap community name?
>
> ○ a. Public
>
> ○ b. Admin
>
> ○ c. Supervisor
>
> ○ d. Manager

The correct answer to this question is a. If a trap community name is not specified, the name *public* is used as the default. Therefore, answers b, c, and d are incorrect.

Question 6

> Which of the following fields are included in a UDP header? [Choose the four best answers]
>
> ❑ a. Source port
>
> ❑ b. Checksum
>
> ❑ c. Acknowledge
>
> ❑ d. Length
>
> ❑ e. Urgent
>
> ❑ f. Destination port

The correct answers are a, b, d, and f. UDP is not connection-oriented and does not acknowledge data receipt. The header fields contain only the information necessary to accept and transport datagrams from a ULP with checksum error checking provided as an option. Acknowledge (ACK) and Urgent (URG) are TCP header fields that help provide connection-oriented transport with selectable class of service. Therefore, answers c and e are incorrect.

Question 7

Which feature of IPv6 virtually ensures that IP address space will not be exhausted in the foreseeable future?

- ○ a. Expanded support for supernetting options
- ○ b. Expanded address space that allows a total of 128 address classes
- ○ c. The new 64-bit addressing scheme
- ○ d. 128-bit IP addresses

The correct answer to this question is d. In IPv6, the IP addresses have been increased in size from 32 bits to 128 bits to provide an almost unlimited number of available addresses. Answers a, b, and c are not features of IPv6 and are therefore incorrect.

Need To Know More?

 Lewis, Chris. *Cisco TCP/IP Routing Professional Reference, 2nd Edition.* McGraw-Hill. New York, NY, 1998. ISBN 0-07-041130-1. Chapter 4 of this book includes a section that provides a very good overview of IPv6.

 Parker, Timothy. *Teach Yourself TCP/IP in 14 Days, 2nd Edition.* Sams Publishing. Indianapolis, IN, 1998. ISBN 0-672-30885-1. Read Chapter 3 for additional information on IP, Chapter 4 for information on Transport layer protocols, and Chapter 13 for an excellent overview of SNMP.

 info.internet.isi.edu/in-notes/rfc/files/rfc1945.txt is where you can find RFC 1945, "Hypertext Transfer Protocol—HTTP/1.0." This is a good introduction to HTTP.

 info.internet.isi.edu/in-notes/rfc/files/rfc821.txt is where you can find RFC 821, "Simple Mail Transfer Protocol." This a good place to start if you want more information on SMTP.

 info.internet.isi.edu/in-notes/rfc/files/rfc1924.txt is where you can find RFC 1924, "A Compact Representation of IPv6 Addresses." This RFC has detailed information on IPv6.

The IPX Protocol Suite

Terms you'll need to understand:

√ Internetwork Packet Exchange (IPX)

√ Sequenced Packet Exchange (SPX)

√ Protocol suite

√ IPX header

√ SPX header

√ Network address

√ Node address

Techniques you'll need to master:

√ Understanding the role of the IPX/SPX protocol suite

√ Identifying the components of an IPX address

√ Understanding the function of IPX header information

√ Understanding the function of SPX header information

Both the Internetwork Packet Exchange (IPX) and Sequenced Packet Exchange (SPX) protocols have been with NetWare since its inception. These two Novell protocols provide the means by which two network devices can communicate with one another in a NetWare environment. IPX and SPX are parts of the IPX/SPX protocol suite that operate in conjunction with other protocols, such as the Routing Information Protocol (RIP) and the Service Advertising Protocol (SAP). In this chapter, we discuss the IPX/SPX protocol suite and provide an explanation of how it functions on a network.

IPX/SPX Protocol Suite Overview

Two devices on a network must agree upon a protocol or set of rules before they can communicate. IPX/SPX is a protocol suite that allows this communication to occur. It was developed in the early 1980s by Novell and was based on the Xerox Network Systems (XNS) protocol suite of the 1960s. IPX, a connectionless protocol, addresses and routes packets, whereas SPX, a connection-oriented protocol, reliably transports the packets. RIP and the NetWare Link Services Protocol (NLSP) collect routing information to help IPX deliver the packets.

When a network device needs to transmit a packet on a network, it passes the data to IPX, which adds addressing and routing header information at the beginning of the packet and then passes the packet to the network board driver. Next, the packet is sent across the network, where it's routed by other IPX routers along its path to its source destination. Other network devices must support the IPX protocol in order to read and route the packet. Because IPX is a connectionless protocol, there's no "return receipt" guarantee that the packet is delivered. This delivery means that IPX addresses and routes the packet but never receives a return notification that it was delivered. In addition, the packets may arrive at the destination in any order.

SPX is another protocol in the IPX/SPX protocol stack, and it's designed to guarantee the delivery of the packet. SPX forms a connection like a pipe to both the transmitting device and the receiving device whereby the data is sent. Therefore, devices sending packets do receive notification that their packets arrived without (or with) errors and in the proper sequence. This extra guarantee (called *connection-oriented delivery*) costs more in network overhead, because two-way communication occurs between the sending and receiving devices; therefore, there are more packets traversing the network.

RIP and NLSP are both routing protocols in the IPX/SPX stack that provide routing information to IPX as to which routes are available for packet delivery. RIP provides distance vector route discovery, and NLSP provides link-state route discovery.

SAP is another protocol in the IPX/SPX stack. It allows for service advertising on a network, which enables devices to know which services are available where.

You'll learn more about RIP and SAP in Chapter 16 and about NLSP in Chapter 17. In this chapter, we focus on IPX and SPX.

Relating The IPX/SPX Protocol Suite To The OSI Model

A *protocol suite* is simply a collection of protocols that all perform specific networking functions. Protocol suites work in the Open Systems Interconnection (OSI) model's structure to enable communication on a network. Figure 15.1 shows a diagram of the IPX/SPX protocol suite as it compares to the OSI model.

As you can see in Figure 15.1, the IPX/SPX protocol suite is made up of the following protocols:

➤ **NetWare Core Protocol (NCP)** This protocol operates at the upper layers (the Session, Presentation, and Application layers).

➤ **Service Advertising Protocol (SAP)** This protocol operates at the upper layers (the Session, Presentation, and Application layers).

➤ **Sequenced Packet Exchange (SPX)** This protocol operates at the Transport layer.

➤ **Internetwork Packet Exchange (IPX)** This protocol operates at the Network layer.

➤ **Router Information Protocol (RIP)** This protocol operates at the Network layer.

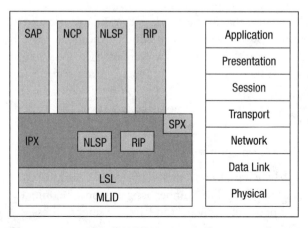

Figure 15.1   The IPX/SPX protocol suite vs. the OSI model.

➤ **NetWare Link State Protocol (NLSP)** This is a routing protocol that operates at the Network layer.

In Chapter 2, we discussed the function of each of the layers of the OSI model in detail. The IPX/SPX protocols function in the same manner as their corresponding layers of the OSI model.

IPX Addresses

The U.S. post office cannot deliver a package for you unless you address the package properly. For instance, you cannot address a postal package destined for a city in the U.S. using the French postal addressing scheme. Also, the address on your package must be unique; otherwise, the post office won't know to which recipient to deliver the package. Similarly, IPX addresses must be properly formatted and unique for routers to deliver packets correctly.

Whenever a packet is sent on a network, it contains information such as the source address and the destination address. Various protocols build packets differently and insert address information in different bit positions of packets. Whereas IPX places source address information, another protocol may place its destination address. To decipher packets on a network, two network devices must use the same protocol to communicate. A workstation using TCP/IP doesn't understand a packet destined for an IPX workstation. However, NetWare 5's Compatibility Mode changes this. Novell now provides tools, such as the Migration Gateway (also called a Migration Agent), that allow organizations to use IP as a transport protocol. The Migration Gateway allows customers to change from IPX/IP to TCP/IP and still maintain functionality.

IPX addressing is simple on small networks that will never connect to other networks—it's not hard to number addresses with just two servers. On the other hand, networks that will hook up to larger networks have to provide a unique address for each node on the internetwork. However, just because the numbers are unique within your network scheme doesn't mean they will be unique when you connect to another network or even another organization. Therefore, to be certain that your numbers are unique, you can register your IPX addresses with Novell's Network Registry (call 408-577-7506 or send email to **registry@novell.com**). Again, this is not necessary if your network is a small, standalone LAN.

IPX addresses contain the following information:

➤ **Network address** A 4-byte hexadecimal number (such as C40E30AC) that identifies a logical network. The number assigned must be unique. No two nonconnected network segments can have the same address, whereas all connected network segments *must* have the same address. For example, if you have two file servers and each server has two network boards in it (LANCARD A and LANCARD B in each server) and you use LANCARD B in each server to physically connect the two of them, then each LANCARD A must have a unique address, and both LANCARD B boards need to have the same address:

➤ Server 1 LANCARD A = Network Address 1

➤ Server 1 LANCARD B = Network Address 2

➤ Server 2 LANCARD A = Network Address 3

➤ Server 2 LANCARD B = Network Address 2

The problem most administrators have is that they'll give LANCARD A the same network address on both servers, and then they have a routing problem that they may never get an error message about.

➤ **Internal network address** A 4-byte hexadecimal number (such as 02CAB10E) used by the server for internal routing.

➤ **Node address** A unique 6-byte hexadecimal number (such as 000000243EF2) programmed into a network board by its manufacturer. Also known as *MAC* and *physical address*.

➤ **Socket number** A 2-byte number that defines processes and services, such as NLSP (9001), NCP (0451), SAP (0452), and RIP (0453).

On an IPX network, the network address and the node address have to be unique. Node (MAC) addresses are set by the network board manufacturer and are, therefore, usually unique. With some exceptions, such as ARCNet, Omninet, LANPac, and so on, the node address is still unique (between 1 and 254), but it's set manually on the network board via switches. The network address, on the other hand, is set by the administrator, so care and forethought must be given when assigning this number.

IPX Addressing Rules

IPX has two types of addresses: internal and external. An external number is also called the *network number* or *network address* and must be the same for all the workstations or nodes within a network segment. The segment is the only thing to which you assign the address—all devices physically attached to that segment inherit its network address.

An internal number represents a NetWare file server and must be unique.

Both internal and external numbers contain up to 4 bytes (represented in hexadecimal notation) and can be assigned with a combination of numbers (0 to 9) and letters (A to F). The only addresses you're not able to use are 00000000, FFFFFFFE, and FFFFFFFF.

IPX Packets

You need to know that an IPX address is different than an IPX packet. Within an IPX packet, you have the packet header and the data being transmitted, including the IPX address information. Figure 15.2 shows the bit positions of an IPX packet header and should make this point much clearer to you.

Notice in Figure 15.2 that there are source and destination IPX addresses and that the information must be in certain bit positions of the IPX packet. If just one bit is off or shifted for any reason, the entire packet could be sent to the wrong recipient or dropped altogether. The total length of the packet header is 30 bytes.

The following list identifies the functions of the IPX packet header contents, as shown in Figure 15.2:

➤ **Checksum** Two bytes of information, which are usually set to the value FFFF; unless checksums are enabled, because a CRC check is done on the entire packet.

➤ **Length** Two bytes of information that contain the IPX packet header plus the data. There is no Ethernet frame field information because of the method used to compute packets by that frame type. In those packets where there's an odd number of data bytes, the LAN driver appends 1 byte to the packet to make it even.

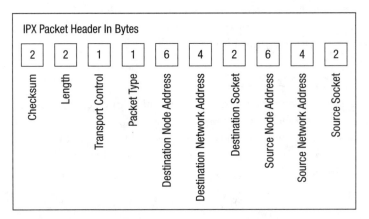

Figure 15.2 The structure of an IPX packet.

➤ **Transport Control** A 1-byte field that designates the hop count (number of routers) a packet traverses. Each router increases the hop count by one, with the originating node setting the count to zero. A packet may go through 15 routers, but when the packet hits the 16th router, it's tossed into the bit bucket, never to be seen again.

➤ **Packet Type** A 1-byte field that contains information about the type of service a packet will use—for example, IPX=0 or 4, SPX=5, and NCP=17. Note that if a node uses SPX for transport, this field will contain the number 5.

➤ **Destination Node Address** The 6-byte field of the destination node that's to receive the packet. IPX does not guarantee delivery and therefore supports broadcast packets intended for all nodes. In this case, the destination node address is set to all F's.

➤ **Destination Network Address** A 4-byte field that represents the network address where the destination node is located.

➤ **Destination Socket** A 2-byte field that contains the socket number of the process—for example, NCP=451, SAP=452, and RIP=453.

➤ **Source Node Address** The 6-byte address of the node sending the data.

➤ **Source Network Address** A 4-byte network address to which the source or sending node belongs.

➤ **Source Socket** A 2-byte field containing the socket number of the transmitting process.

SPX Packets

An SPX packet contains the 30 bytes of the IPX header information plus 12 bytes of its own information, as shown in Figure 15.3, for a total of 42 bytes.

SPX only needs to be used by processes, such as printing, that need guaranteed delivery of the packet. It does create some overhead, but it's more reliable for data transmission. Before transmission occurs, both sending and receiving nodes must perform some handshaking activities and establish a connection.

The following list identifies the functions of the SPX packet header contents, as shown in Figure 15.3:

➤ **Connection Control** One byte of information handling the two-way communication. Remember that SPX provides for guaranteed delivery, which in turn means that data will be flowing back and forth between the source and destination nodes. There must be some handshaking and acknowledgements of data.

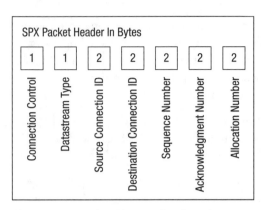

Figure 15.3 The SPX packet header.

➤ **Datastream Type** A 1-byte field designating handshaking information within the packet. This field will contain information, such as a request to close the connection between nodes.

➤ **Source Connection ID** A 2-byte field containing information that keeps track of the virtual connections between the sending SPX node and the destination node. Keep in mind that several virtual connections can be opened at the same time.

➤ **Destination Connection ID** A 2-byte field set after both source and destination nodes perform handshaking activities. This number represents the connection ID on the destination node.

➤ **Sequence Number** Two bytes of information representing the cumulative number of packets sent by the source node. SPX is in charge of making sure the packets arrive in the correct order; therefore, it must keep track of packets as they are transmitted. When a packet is transmitted, an acknowledgement is sent. Once the acknowledgement is received, the sequence number is incremented.

➤ **Acknowledgement Number** A 2-byte field indicating sequencing of the packets to determine errors in data transmission. This number contains the next sequence number that's expected. Therefore, as stations transmit and receive data, there's a sequence number associated. When packet #1 is transmitted and received, 2 is placed in this field to say that the receiver is expecting packet #2. The sending node examines this field to compare the value to that of the expected value. If the sender is ready to send packet #3 but sees that the receiver is expecting packet #2, the sender assumes there's been a transmission error and resends packet #2.

➤ **Allocation Number** A 2-byte field designating the number of receive buffers available in a node. Because zero indicates the first buffer available, always add one to the total count.

Now that you understand IPX and SPX and how their packets are formed, it's time to tie it all together and see how the media access information is added to the entire packet as it traverses the network.

The IPX header information is squeezed in between the media access frame and the data, as shown in Figure 15.4.

The packet is sent through the internetwork, and if it crosses a router along its path, the media access information is replaced with the new destination information. The hop count is increased by one for each router it crosses. Looking at the simple network shown in Figure 15.5, you can see how a packet travels across a network.

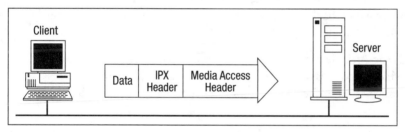

Figure 15.4   How the IPX header fits into the entire packet.

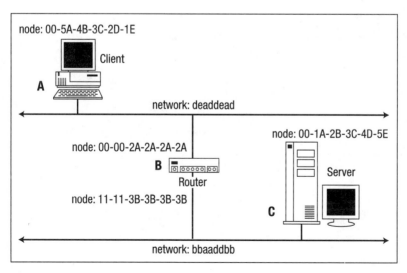

Figure 15.5   A simple network diagram to show a packet's path.

Nodes A, B, and C reside on an Ethernet network. Node A is the client, Node B is the router, and Node C is the server. Notice that Node B has two node addresses because it has two network boards to serve as the IPX router.

Node C tells everyone about its available services by broadcasting routing information and service advertisements to other nodes on the segment using either RIP/SAP or NLSP. Node B, in turn, sends this information to the networks to which it's connected so as to notify other nodes of the addresses of Node C's file and print services. A packet travelling across the network shown in Figure 15.5 would follow these steps:

1. For Node A to access Node C, Node A must place Node C's internal network number in its IPX header field. Node A must find out how to reach Node C, so it broadcasts a routing request, which is picked up by Node B—the router.

2. Node B knows how to route the packet on to Node C, so Node B sends information back to Node A that tells Node A to send the packet to Node C's node address (MAC address).

3. Node A sends the information on to Node B. Node B strips off the Media Access layer information and places Node C's media access information in the packet and routes the packet to Node C.

Practice Questions

Question 1

> Which of the following statements best describes the purpose of IPX?
>
> ○ a. To guarantee delivery of packets through a network
>
> ○ b. To route packets through a network
>
> ○ c. To compress packets for faster transmission through the network
>
> ○ d. To send its route tables to its neighboring router

The correct answer is b. IPX's main purpose is to transmit packets through a network. Answer a is incorrect because IPX does not guarantee the delivery of the packets. This is handled by SPX. Answer c is incorrect because IPX does not compress the packet but rather adds a header to the packet. Answer d is incorrect because IPX uses its RIP routing protocol to send route table information to neighboring routers.

Question 2

> Which of the following are IPX address components? [Choose the three best answers]
>
> ❑ a. Network address
>
> ❑ b. Internal network address
>
> ❑ c. MIC address
>
> ❑ d. Socket number

The correct answers are a, b, and d. IPX address components consist of a network address, an internal address, a node address (or MAC address), and a socket number for network services. Answer c is incorrect because there's no such thing as a MIC address—it's a MAC address.

Question 3

> Which of the following statements most accurately defines IPX addressing rules?
>
> ○ a. Node numbers must be unique, but network numbers can be the same.
>
> ○ b. Network numbers must be unique, but node numbers can be the same.
>
> ○ c. Network numbers must be unique, and node numbers must be unique.
>
> ○ d. Network numbers can be the same, and node numbers can be the same.

The correct answer is c. On an IPX network, network numbers must be unique, and the node numbers must be unique. Otherwise, IPX would not know where or to whom a packet is to be delivered. Therefore, answers a, b, and d are incorrect.

Question 4

> Which field in an SPX packet header represents the next expected sequence number of the packet to be transmitted?
>
> ○ a. Connection Control
>
> ○ b. Sequence Number
>
> ○ c. Acknowledge Number
>
> ○ d. Allocation Number

The correct answer is c. This is a trick question because your first impulse would be to select Sequence Number, because it seems like the most logical answer to the question. However, that field does not contain the next "expected" sequence number, the Acknowledge Number field does. Therefore, answers a, b, and d are incorrect.

Question 5

> Which of the following statements is correct?
>
> ○ a. The IPX header contains 42 bytes and the SPX header contains 30 bytes. Total bytes equals 72.
>
> ○ b. The IPX header contains 60 bytes and the SPX header contains 42 bytes. Total bytes equals 102.
>
> ○ c. The IPX header contains 30 bytes and the SPX header contains 12 bytes. Total bytes equals 42.
>
> ○ d. The IPX header contains 30 bytes and the SPX header contains 42 bytes. Total bytes equals 72.

The correct answer is c. The IPX header contains 30 bytes of data, and the SPX header contains 12 bytes. Answers a and b are incorrect because their numbers aren't accurate. Answer d looks close because it contains the number 42, but if you remember, that's actually the total byte count of the two headers summed (IPX+SPX).

Question 6

> IPX is a connectionless protocol responsible for making sure that the packets arrive in the proper order.
>
> ○ a. True
>
> ○ b. False

The correct answer is b, false. Part of the statement is correct, but not all of it. IPX is a connectionless protocol, but it does not care what sequence the packets arrive in.

Question 7

Which of the following IPX header fields contains the number 5 if the node is using SPX for transport?

- ○ a. Transport Control
- ○ b. Packet Type
- ○ c. Source Socket
- ○ d. Source Network Address

The correct answer is b. The number 5 is assigned to SPX for transport. If the Packet Type field contains the number 5, then SPX is being used as the transport protocol. Therefore, answers a, c, and d are incorrect. If you weren't sure, you may have guessed answer a, which seems logical because of its name. However, this answer is actually incorrect.

Need To Know More?

 Chappell, Laura A., Dan E. Hakes. *Novell's Guide to NetWare LAN Analysis*. Novell Press. San Jose, CA, 1994. ISBN 0-7821-1362-1. Chapter 14 discusses the IPX/SPX protocol in great detail.

 Clarke, David James IV. *Novell's CNE Study Guide for Core Technologies*. Novell Press. San Jose, CA, 1996. ISBN 0-7645-4501-9. Chapter 10 discusses this subject in good detail.

 Sheldon, Tom. *Encyclopedia of Networking Electronic Edition*. Osborne/McGraw-Hill. Berkeley, CA, 1998. ISBN 0-07-882333-1. This book provides a good overview of the IPX/SPX protocol stack under the listing "Novell NetWare Protocols."

 www.novell.com is Novell's Web site. Go to this site's search engine and type in the keywords "NLSP" and "RIP" to locate white papers and further details on the information discussed in this chapter.

16

IPX Routing With RIP And SAP

. . . .

Terms you'll need to understand:

√ Routing Information Protocol (RIP)

√ Service Advertising Protocol (SAP)

√ Distance vector routing

√ Routing information table

√ Split horizon algorithm

√ Services table

√ Routing cost

√ SAP filtering

Techniques you'll need to master:

√ Explaining the two types of RIP packets

√ Explaining how RIP builds the routing information table

√ Knowing the default RIP broadcast time interval

√ Defining routing cost and how it's determined

√ Describing the types of devices sending RIP and SAP packets

√ Explaining how SAP devices build a services table

√ Describing SAP filtering and why it may be used

Networks provide shared resources, whether we're talking about a few systems in one office or hundreds of systems in dozens of offices. Finding remote resources requires intelligent routing to guide packets efficiently from one part of the network to another.

Routing efficiency is a different concept today than it was a decade ago. IPX was built at a time when networks were local and linked together by NetWare servers over physical cabling. Bandwidth wasn't the problem then. Now, networks routinely link over third-party routers tied to telecommunications links a hundred times slower than local connections. Bandwidth must be used efficiently, and this has driven new NetWare routing techniques.

In this chapter, you'll learn about IPX routing using the Routing Information Protocol (RIP) and the Service Advertising Protocol (SAP). You'll also learn the details of how each of these protocols transmits packets and builds tables.

RIP/SAP Routing

Routing Information Protocol (RIP) is an IPX *distance vector routing* protocol that provides routing information to other routers; the Service Advertising Protocol (SAP) was developed by Novell to provide information about which services are available on a network.

> *Note:* The name distance vector comes from the distance vector algorithm used to learn and maintain the routing information table by counting the number of hops between one network and another.

Together, these protocols help IPX build and maintain routing information and service tables. RIP dynamically learns and maintains a routing information table, and SAP dynamically learns and maintains a table of available services. These tables provide workstations with information about available services, and allow the workstations to connect to the available services. In this chapter, you'll learn how to set up preferable routes when there are options between two points.

The Routing Information Protocol

RIP is a distance vector routing protocol that, like IPX, is based on the Xerox Network Systems (XNS) protocol. RIP is used to exchange routing information with routers on the same network segment. RIP determines the best route by counting the number of intermediate routing points, or *hops*, between the workstation and the desired destination.

When more than one route is available between two devices, a *routing cost* can be assigned to each route to push packets toward the more favorable route. The number of hops between two points and the tick count (time) determine the routing cost. Different costs can be assigned to different routes to influence traffic patterns.

RIP-enabled devices send network information for five reasons:

➤ During router initialization, RIP routers broadcast packets to announce their availability.

➤ When a router receives a request from another routing device, it transmits its entire routing table to the requesting station.

➤ Every 60 seconds, RIP routers broadcast their entire routing tables to ensure that all other routers have the most complete routing information.

➤ When a route changes, each router broadcasts its entire routing table.

➤ When a router is downed, it broadcasts that fact by declaring that all of its routers are now 16 hops away.

RIP/SAP opponents claim that IPX is a bandwidth hog because of these broadcasts (which are not used often in today's WAN world).

Request And Response RIP Packets

There are two main types of RIP packets—Request and Response—and both use identical packet formats. The following are fields found in RIP packets:

➤ **Hops Away** This field lists the number of routers crossed to reach another network.

➤ **Network Address** This field contains either the network destination address or a broadcast address.

➤ **Packet Type** This field designates whether the packets are Request (indicated by a value of 1 byte) or Response (indicated by a value of 2 bytes).

➤ **Time-in Ticks** This field contains the number of ticks (about 1/18 of a second) needed to make it to the remote network. This is often not used with RIP, but IPX keeps track of this in the Response packet to assign a time value to the number of hops.

Note: Information on up to 50 networks can be contained in a single RIP Response packet.

Router Information Transmissions

Routing tables in each RIP device hold information about all the discovered routers on the network. Routers use this table to determine the correct router to use for forwarding received packets, if those packets are not local. NetWare routers require the network board for each segment to report the time delay on that segment by the number of ticks.

Building The Routing Information Table

RIP routers learn about the network through secondhand information relayed by other routers. The alternative is for each router to explore the complete network, which can create enormous amounts of traffic.

When a router asks, "Where am I?" accurate responses come back saying, "You are here, relative to me." A routing information table is built by a router using the following method:

1. The router broadcasts its known routes.

2. The router then broadcasts a Route Request packet to routers close to it, asking for copies of their routing information tables.

3. Each router responds to the Route Request packet by forwarding the information it has about the rest of the internetwork.

4. The original router that requested the information updates its routing information table.

5. The newly updated router then advertises the updated routing information table but follows the *split horizon algorithm* by not broadcasting the updates back to the same routers that provided the updates.

Note: The split horizon algorithm pulls out the links supplying information to a router before the router passes that information on. This is a slight technical improvement over the earlier poison reverse method, listed in the NetWare configuration files, that added a flag in the packets being sent back to the information-providing routers so they would know that the routing table was a copy of the information they sent.

The Service Advertising Protocol

SAP provides information about which services are available on a network. This information is kept in a *services table*. SAP table information is stored in the NetWare bindery in NetWare 2.x and 3.x, and in the NDS database for

NetWare 4.x. When the client requests information about available services, the server responds based on the SAP information in its database. Every service—for example NetWare file servers, print servers, access servers, gateway servers, and PCs running Internet Access Server 4.1 routing software—sends information about its services to other network nodes using SAP.

Clients looking for a service, such as a printer, contact the nearest router SAP agent when the service is needed, if that resource isn't already listed in the services table. The services table fulfills many client requests, because clients remember the latest SAP broadcast information, so they contact the SAP agent still in their services table buffer when they need that service.

One distinct advantage of IPX over TCP/IP is the dynamic listing of network resources, because each new network resource announces itself with a SAP broadcast to the network. TCP/IP resources aren't dynamically allocated, because the network resources are defined in text files on each system. The downside of this dynamic announcement is the broadcast traffic it causes. Routers send only local SAP broadcasts, whereas SAP agents (servers) broadcast their information across the entire internetwork.

To examine RIP/SAP information on a NetWare server, type "TRACK ON" at the server console.

SAP Packets

Like RIP packets, SAP packets are wrapped in IPX and use MAC protocols for transport around the network. SAP packets also have Request and Response packet types, including Get Nearest Server Request and Get Nearest Server Response (these fall under the heading of Service Queries and Service Responses packet types). The packet type's flag is set in the Operations packet field. The four possible settings for the Operations field in a SAP packet are:

➤ Request

➤ Response

➤ Get Nearest Server Request

➤ Get Nearest Server Response

There are three types of SAP packets used by NetWare: Information Broadcasts, Service Queries, and Service Responses. We cover each of these in the following sections.

Up to eight servers worth of information can be included in a single SAP message.

SAP Information Broadcasts

Every server type that uses SAP packets broadcasts server information at startup to inform the network about its availability. Every 60 seconds (the default time value), each SAP-based server broadcasts this information using a Service Identification packet. This includes the expected NetWare services: file server, print queue, print server, advertising print server, job server, archive server, remote bridge server, and unknown.

The formula for calculating total network bandwidth used by SAP Information Broadcast packets is:

```
32 bytes of header + 64 bytes per SAP device
```

Imagine 10 SAP devices (servers and routers) on the network. Each SAP Information Broadcast packet would have 640 bytes of service information (10 devices × 64 bytes each) plus the 32 bytes of header, for a total of 672 bytes per packet.

SAP Service Queries

Clients looking for services send a SAP Service Query Packet. For example, when the client first logs on to the network, it sends a request for the identity of the nearest server. This uses the Request packet type and is broadcast by the client looking for a service. It has to be a broadcast packet, because the new client has no idea where the services are available so the new client can't address the station providing the service directly.

SAP Service Responses

Service Queries are answered by Service Responses from appropriate SAP-enabled servers. General Service Responses are sent in answer to broadcasts, such as from the new client example in the preceding paragraph. Nearest Service Responses are only sent to answer queries directed at a particular station.

Building The Services Table

SAP builds a table of known services information in the same manner as RIP handles routing information. Service information is requested, remembered, and updated constantly. SAP-enabled routers follow these steps:

1. A router (server) advertises its services, if it has any.

2. A router (client) broadcasts packets containing a Service Request (query). The expected reply is the list of known services (for the type of query) on the network.

3. Each router and server on the same segment as the initial broadcaster (based on hop counts so only neighboring systems get involved) replies with the service information it has about the network.

4. The original requesting router updates the services table with the new information.

5. The router advertises the new services information it acquired.

 The SAP aging timer clears the server information table after four minutes, to ensure only recent information is included. This handles the problem of a router going down without warning.

SAP Filtering

Local networks have no trouble supporting the relatively small amount of SAP broadcast traffic because they have so much available bandwidth. It's fair to say that IPX, RIP, and SAP work best for small- and medium-sized local networks. However, when your network starts growing and WAN links are added, the situation changes.

SAP traffic is a potential headache because the SAP broadcast default time is 60 seconds, the entire services table is sent in every packet, and WAN link bandwidth is limited. SAP filtering of inbound and outbound traffic helps the bandwidth problem.

 Novell allows SAP filtering of both inbound and outbound traffic to help deal with the bandwidth problem.

Network hardware and software is considerably more reliable today than it was when Novell engineers set the default SAP broadcast rate at 60 seconds. Increased reliability makes it relatively safe to stretch the SAP broadcast rate from 60 seconds to many minutes. Start with 5 minutes (300 seconds) and see if that works well with your network. Set all IPX filters in the FILTCFG program. Choose Define IPX Filters|Outgoing SAP Filters|Filters to change the default settings.

Practice Questions

Question 1

> When do IPX routers use RIP transmit packets? [Choose the three best answers]
>
> ❏ a. When a router boots and initializes
>
> ❏ b. When another router requests a copy of the route table
>
> ❏ c. When a new user logs in to the network
>
> ❏ d. When a server mounts a new volume
>
> ❏ e. When an existing route becomes unavailable or a new route appears

The correct answers are a, b, and e. Routers always broadcast when they join a network, and they always respond to requests for routing information. When routers learn of new or deleted routes, they transmit that information. Users and volumes have no bearing on network routes and do not trigger any type of RIP activity. Therefore, answer c is incorrect. A new server volume activates SAP packet transmission, but not RIP packets. Therefore, answer d is incorrect.

Question 2

> Which two types of RIP packets are used?
>
> ○ a. Broadcast and Respond
>
> ○ b. Request and Repeat
>
> ○ c. Request and Respond
>
> ○ d. Reboot and Query
>
> ○ e. Query and Comment

The correct answer is c. Both RIP packet types are identical except for the Packet Type field. Whereas some of the other answers may sound correct, Novell nomenclature demands Request and Response.

Question 3

> Which of the following are steps used in building the routing information table? [Choose the two best answers]
>
> ☐ a. A router broadcasts its name and address.
>
> ☐ b. A router requests copies of routing information tables.
>
> ☐ c. A router queries NDS for a list of other routers.
>
> ☐ d. A router reads a text list of other routers in its configuration files.
>
> ☐ e. A router updates its routing information table based on information from other routers.

The correct answers are b and e. Routers broadcast their routing information table when queried or every 60 seconds. More than the names and addresses are sent (the entire routing table is included in every broadcast). Therefore, answer a is incorrect. NDS does not contain routing information tables. Therefore, answer c is incorrect. Because IPX is dynamic, no configuration files are necessary to tell routers about the network. Therefore, answer d is incorrect.

Question 4

> Which of the following devices use SAP to inform other network nodes of their services? [Choose the three best answers]
>
> ☐ a. Disk volumes
>
> ☐ b. File servers
>
> ☐ c. Gateway servers
>
> ☐ d. Managed wiring concentrators
>
> ☐ e. Internet Access Server 4.1 systems

The correct answers are b, c, and e. Disk volumes are subsets of file servers, and don't send SAP packets themselves (but they are a service listed as belonging to their host server). Therefore, answer a is incorrect—and the reason why this is a trick question. Managed wiring concentrators use protocols other than SAP. Therefore, answer d is incorrect.

Question 5

> Which of the following are SAP packets? [Choose the three best answers]
>
> ❑ a. Information Broadcasts
>
> ❑ b. Service Echoes
>
> ❑ c. Service Queries
>
> ❑ d. Service Rebroadcasts
>
> ❑ e. Service Responses

The correct answers are a, c, and e. SAP devices do not echo packets of any type. Plus, there's no such thing as a SAP Service Echo. Therefore, answer b is incorrect. SAP devices only respond to queries and send information broadcasts at set intervals and do not rebroadcast information. Therefore, answer d is incorrect.

Question 6

> Which of the following are steps in building a SAP services table? [Choose the three best answers]
>
> ❑ a. A router broadcasts a Service Request.
>
> ❑ b. A server queries each active disk volume for information.
>
> ❑ c. Routers and servers respond to service queries from other SAP devices.
>
> ❑ d. Servers query the NDS SAP Repository for updates.
>
> ❑ e. SAP devices fill in their services table with information from SAP Service Responses.

The correct answers are a, c, and e. Disk volumes do not have SAP information. Therefore, answer b is incorrect. NDS does not track SAP details. Therefore, answer d is incorrect.

Need To Know More?

 Dickie, Mark. *Routing in Today's Internetworks*. Van Nostsrand Reinhold. New York, 1994. ISBN 0-442-01811-8. Chapter 10 covers RIP for IPX.

 In the NetWare 5 online documentation, search for "Configuring RIP and SAP," "Configuring RIP," and "IPX Routing and Service Protocols" for detailed information on both protocols.

IPX Routing With NLSP

In this chapter, you'll learn about the NetWare Link Service Protocol (NLSP) and how it improves IPX routing. We'll also describe the various routing methods and components of NLSP. Finally, we'll explain the differences between NLSP and the Routing Information Protocol (RIP), and we'll discuss the Open Shortest Path First (OSPF) protocol.

NLSP Routing Overview

Expanding networks requires enhanced routing services, so Novell developed NLSP. Novell based NLSP on the Intermediate System to Intermediate System (IS-IS) protocol, defined by the International Standards Organization (ISO). NLSP is designed to replace Routing Information Protocol/Service Advertising Protocol (RIP/SAP) communications between IPX routers. NLSP improves IPX routing similarly to the way Open Shortest Path First (OSPF) protocol reduces network traffic and speeds routing with TCP/IP (see Chapter 13).

NLSP is a link-state routing protocol and an improvement over RIP's distance vector protocol. Here are some of the improvements:

➤ NLSP routers track the status of other routers and links between networks, and update packets are sent only when the network topology changes, thus reducing broadcasts on the network.

➤ NLSP adapts more quickly to network changes than RIP, making it more effective for large, complex networks. Less overhead and more scalability equals a protocol that runs faster and jumps higher, especially in large and growing internetworks.

➤ NLSP supports SAP and RIP within the same network, and a single NetWare MultiProtocol Router can support both protocols at once. These features make the conversion process much easier.

➤ Support for Simple Network Management Protocol (SNMP) is included, along with the appropriate Management Information Bases (MIBs) to support network management applications. The SNMP support makes it easier for management consoles to provide services to network routers.

➤ NLSP now includes hierarchical routing domains. This may sound complicated, but it just means that a network can be chopped into logical routing areas. (The first version of NLSP did not include hierarchical routing domains.) Each router knows all about its own area, or *domain*, but only summarizes information about remote areas.

➤ Costs determine routing choices with NLSP, rather than hops and ticks from one router to another. Link speed determines the cost, but managers may modify the cost for certain links to encourage or discourage traffic through that link.

➤ Broadcasts aren't eliminated with NLSP, but they are cut down significantly. The default time between routing table updates is 7,200 seconds, or 2 hours. This delay of two hours for routing information is a drastic improvement over RIP's rate of half a minute between certain types of broadcasts.

Figure 17.1 shows the various databases NLSP uses to track the state of the network routers and links between networks. This system is more complicated than RIP, because the networks it must manage have grown considerably in size and complexity.

NLSP Operation

NLSP uses a set of terms to define link-state routing components and operations. In many cases, these are not the same terms used in IS-IS definitions. If you're familiar with IS-IS routing, pay close attention to the next few sections because the following NLSP-equivalent terms are defined and used:

➤ **Adjacency** This term describes the router's immediate neighbors.

➤ **Designated router (DR)** This is a special router on the network, with special responsibilities, that's elected to represent other network routers. Each network using NLSP has a DR.

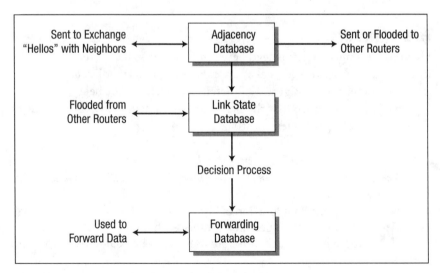

Figure 17.1 NLSP databases and their links.

➤ **Link** This is an acknowledged physical link between two adjacent routers that's established when the routers (neighbors) recognize and acknowledge each other.

Note: This section is concerned with NLSP running on a local set of internetworks. WAN links add extra NLSP details that are not covered in this portion of the book.

Like RIP routers, NLSP routers must initiate a discovery process to learn about the routers and services on their network. There are several steps in this continual learning and updating process.

 Are you familiar with the game "Six Degrees of Separation," where people at parties figure out how they connect to famous people around the world? Each person knows a person who knows a person, and so on. Apply that principle to link-state routing.

Discovering Routes, Services, And Adjacent Neighbors

The tools used for discovering routes and adjacent neighbors are named, appropriately enough, *hello packets*. Hello packets are sent from each NLSP router upon initialization and then periodically thereafter to ensure the router's adjacency database is accurate.

Hello Packets

Hello packets must be exchanged between two routers before they can establish adjacency. Each router makes an entry into its own adjacency database about the other router. Figure 17.2 details the exchange of hello packets. In Figure 17.2, you'll notice that the hello packets contain the MAC address of each router as a type of "identification."

Note: You'll also see priority settings in Figure 17.2. Priority settings are covered later in this chapter in the "Designated Router Election" section.

 One important function of hello packets is to ensure bi-directional communication between routers. Both routers must send and receive hello packets before their adjacency database is updated.

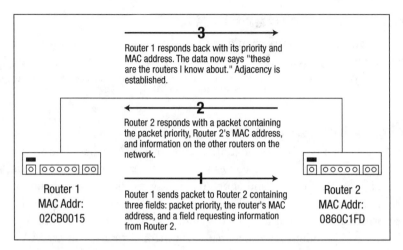

Router 1 responds back with its priority and MAC address. The data now says "these are the routers I know about." Adjacency is established.

Router 2 responds with a packet containing the packet priority, Router 2's MAC address, and information on the other routers on the network.

Router 1
MAC Addr:
02CB0015

Router 1 sends packet to Router 2 containing three fields: packet priority, the router's MAC address, and a field requesting information from Router 2.

Router 2
MAC Addr:
0860C1FD

Figure 17.2   Hello packets are exchanged and adjacency is established.

Link State Packets (The Adjacency Database)

A Link State Packet (LSP) is also the adjacency database; therefore, the adjacency database is an LSP. An adjacency database is created to keep track of link information and various attributes between two neighboring systems (for example, Router D and Router M), which are the results of the exchange of hello packets. Table 17.1 explains what would appear in a sample adjacency database for Router D.

Links in NLSP are either up, down, or initializing. The first hello packet starts the process by recognizing a new (or down) link as up.

Table 17.1 What appears in an adjacency database.		
Field	**Sample Result**	**Explanation**
Holding Time	30 seconds	The length of the wait period for another hello packet from the adjacent router listed in the database. The default setting is 30 seconds. If a hello packet doesn't appear in that time, the router assumes the adjacent router is unavailable.
MAC Address	XX-XX-XX	The adjacent router's MAC address.
Priority	64	The value used to determine the DR. The highest value becomes the DR.
System ID	M	The internal IPX address of the source router.

Designated Router Election

The DR for an NLSP network should be the most powerful and reliable router available. However, you should specify more than one router—having a single router makes your network vulnerable because that router can become a single point of failure.

Administrative Designation

NLSP "elects" routers based on a configurable priority number. The router with the highest priority value becomes the DR. When a router is elected as the DR, it bumps its priority number up 20 points, which lowers the chance of another router taking over the DR job by accident. If two routers have the same priority number, the unit with the higher MAC address becomes the DR. Because MAC addresses are incremented by manufacturers, a higher MAC address usually indicates a newer system.

 To ensure a new router on the network becomes the DR, set its priority number 21 points above the existing DR's number.

DR Responsibilities

Once elected, the DR serves in three major capacities:

➤ It creates a pseudonode.

➤ It manages database synchronization.

➤ It receives and translates IPX RIP/SAP information from other routers.

These responsibilities make it clear why the most reliable router available should be the DR. Continuity in all these functions helps the network run more smoothly.

Pseudonode Creation

Work continues once each router compiles its own adjacency database and a DR has been chosen. The routers must create their link-state databases, which are the routers' views of the internetwork topology.

For packets to be forwarded correctly, each router in the internetwork must have an identical link-state database. The key to synchronizing link-state databases is relying on the DR to create a pseudonode.

Pseudonode: Description And Purpose

A *pseudonode* is an imaginary, or fictitious, node on the network to which all routers believe they are connected. In fact, each router believes it's connected only to the pseudonode and that the pseudonode, in turn, is connected to every router on the network.

This pseudonode trickery reduces the size of each router's LSP (adjacency database). Link-state information is kept for one connection only—the pseudonode—rather than for every node across the network. Smaller LSPs transmit faster and are resolved more quickly.

Let's examine a network with six routers, as shown in Figure 17.3. If there's no pseudonode, each router must track five other routers and keep their information in its adjacency database. With a pseudonode, however, each router tracks only the pseudonode, or just one other router.

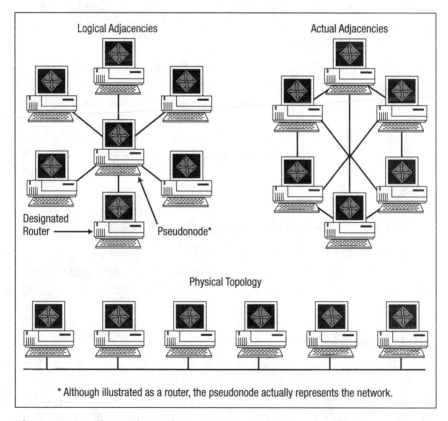

Figure 17.3   Physical topology, actual adjacencies, and the logical adjacency with the pseudonode.

A pseudonode isn't critical for a six-router network, but the adjacency databases for larger networks grow so quickly that having a pseudonode is critical. With 20 routers, each router would have a much larger database to control and no central copy available for backup. If you have a pseudonode, your LSP will be smaller, and it will therefore transmit faster.

Role Of The DR

Because the pseudonode is not real, the DR acts in place of the pseudonode. The DR maintains an LSP, including the links from the pseudonode to each router on the network. The DR continues this activity until it's removed from the network or replaced. Of course, the new DR takes over these functions.

Replacing The DR

Remember that every NLSP network must have a DR. When a DR drops off the network, a new DR must be elected immediately—for example, when the current DR is taken down for routine maintenance. The current DR helps elect and support the new DR.

Three steps are involved in electing the new DR. First, the old DR sends an LSP advertising the fact that it no longer works on behalf of the pseudonode, and it purges the existing pseudonode's LSPs. Once the new DR is elected, it purges the old DR's LSPs from the link-state database and creates new LSPs for the pseudonode. Because the DR has changed, all the adjacency databases need to be replaced. Finally, the old DR and the other routers generate a new LSP and then flood the network to indicate the link containing the new pseudonode.

Building The Link-State Database: Mapping The Internetwork

Routers exchange LSPs that include their connection to the pseudonode. All other routers on the internetwork must receive this information for packet forwarding to work.

LSP Information

Each LSP includes more than just the link to the pseudonode; it also includes the services available on the router, the router name, and the network number. Details about other network services, such as NetWare Management System consoles and printers, are handled by the pseudonode. The pseudonode creates LSPs and exchanges them with the other routers to spread the services information.

LSP Exchange

Routers add their connection to the pseudonode and then prepare to send their LSPs. Each router sends out its LSPs with details included, thus flooding the internetwork. (*Flooding* is covered in the "Flooding Process" section later in this chapter.) Routers receiving these LSPs add the LSP entries to their link-state databases. Once the routers are finished swapping LSPs, they will have identical link-state databases. Using the entries in the link-state database, every router can build a map of the entire internetwork. The next step is intelligent routing of packets.

> *Note: Flooding is used in all link-state databases to transmit area information.*

Selecting Routes

All routes through a network are not equal. Selecting the proper route in a complex internetwork requires a forwarding database.

The Forwarding Database

Much like the RIP routing information table, the forwarding database consists of routes identified as the ways to reach all the networks in the internetwork. The forwarding database has several improvements over the routing information table.

One improvement is the fact that the forwarding database is separate from the link-state database. NLSP routers don't need to go through the forwarding database calculations to flood new link-state database information. Forwarding databases are the result of a calculation done on the link-state database. Part of the calculation includes a cost metric (covered in the following section).

Cost And Equal-Cost Routes

In the forwarding database, a *cost metric*, rather than hops or ticks, is used to define route selection. The cost metric is a value assigned to each interface, and the best route is defined as the one with the lowest cost. The default costs for NLSP for various LAN types are shown in Table 17.2.

Up to eight equal-cost routes to a given network may be kept in the forwarding database. You want to keep several routes defined on a network because this makes it much easier to split the load among different paths. You can call this *path splitting* for NLSP, but it's the same as *load balancing*.

Routes are added and dropped from the database, depending on cost values and availability. If there are four equal-cost routes between Network A and

Table 17.2 The default costs for NLSP for various types of LANs.		
Type of LAN	**Speed**	**Default Cost**
Fiber Distributed Data Interface (FDDI)	100Mbps	14
Token ring	16Mbps	19
Ethernet	10Mbps	20
Token ring	4Mbps	25
E1	2.048Mbps	26
T1	1.544Mbps	27
ISDN (U.S. and European)	56-128Kbps	45

Network B, all four would be listed in the forwarding database. All four routes would be kept to offer multiple path options for heavy traffic loads.

If a new route between Networks A and B appears that costs less than the four equal-cost routes, that new route would be listed in the forwarding database as the best path option. The four equal-cost routes would no longer be the paths of choice. If the new lower-cost route disappears, the forwarding database is regenerated and the four equal-cost routes would once again be the paths of choice.

Rebuilding The Forwarding Database

In the previous sections, the concept of regenerating, or *rebuilding*, the forwarding database came up. You do this whenever a change occurs in the link-state database. However, changes to the link-state database come in bunches, because one change triggers a flood of LSPs. This constant rebuilding of the forwarding database during this LSP flood can overload the router, or at least impede traffic, which is why NLSP uses a hold-down interval to smooth out forwarding database regeneration.

SPF Hold-Down Interval

Officially called the *Shortest Path First (SPF) hold-down interval*, this configurable value sets a delay, in seconds, before a forwarding database rebuild is started after the link-state database receives a network change. The default is five seconds, and we suggest you don't change that value. Increasing a hold-down interval leads to network routing problems, and decreasing it leads to intensive forwarding database activity.

The Creation Process

Once the hold-down interval is past, a new forwarding database is generated. After the link-state database is created, the NLSP router starts the calculation algorithm. The algorithm calculates the cost for each possible route to a destination network by adding the cost of each link that a packet will need to cross to reach the destination network. Remember that each link has a cost, and the total of all links in one path will be compared to the costs of other paths. The list of usable network routes will be prioritized, with the lowest-cost path listed as the first-choice route in the forwarding database. Forwarding database entries include the routes, indicated by network numbers. Also included are the next router in the path and its associated cost.

The maximum path cost in NLSP is 1,023. An interface cost (a speed rating, essentially, because higher speeds translate to lower costs) can range from 1 to 63.

Route And Service Information Maintenance

Every routing service requires constant maintenance and updating to ensure that information remains accurate. NLSP is no exception, although the improvements found in NLSP make it more reliable than earlier routing protocols. Routing information maintenance includes keeping all routers synchronized and informing all routers of any network changes.

Router Synchronization And Communication

Another job for the DR is to keep all the other routers synchronized with the current link-state database. Large networks can change regularly; therefore, the DR initiates a regular process of verifying that every router has the most current link-state database. Here's a sample conversation between a DR and another router:

1. DR: Here's what's in my link-state database.

2. R1: Looks like I'm missing an entry for Network 22. Please send it.

3. DR: Here's the information on Network 22.

4. R1: Thanks. I have some newer information on Network 43. Here it is.

Packet Exchange (CSNP, PSNP, And LSP)

As with all networking technologies, NLSP has many acronyms. NLSP uses three types of databases—forwarding, link state, and adjacency—and four types of packets—hello packet, LSP, complete sequence number packet (CSNP), and partial sequence number packet (PSNP). In the conversation in the previous section, the packet types sent by the DR are as follows:

> ➤ **CSNP** This packet includes a summary of the DR's link-state database, not a copy of the entire link-state database.

> ➤ **PSNP** This packet is a request to the DR for more complete information.

> ➤ **LSP** This is the complete adjacency database, which provides all the information the DR has about the internetwork links.

 NLSP packet types are hello, LSP, CSNP, and PSNP.

Using the properly named packets, the conversation between the DR and R1 in the previous section goes, officially, like this:

1. DR: Here's what's in my link-state database. (The DR sends a CSNP.)

2. R1: Looks like I'm missing an entry for Network 22. Please send it. (R1 sends a PSNP in response.)

3. DR: Here's the information on Network 22. (The DR sends the LSP for Network 22.)

4. R1: Thanks. I have some newer information on Network 43. Here it is. (R1 sends the LSP for Network 43.)

The DR sends the CSNP every 30 seconds, by default. If the information in the CSNP matches the router's link-state database (which is the case most of the time), the router does nothing.

 Do not change the CSNP default setting of 30 seconds. Playing with defaults for routing packets can have disastrous consequences for large networks.

Router Notification After A Network Change

All network changes aren't the result of a router going down. For example, unloading RCONSOLE from a server changes the list of services on that router, and that change is flooded out to the network.

Flooding Process

A router that just unloaded the RCONSOLE program will notify the other routers by flooding an LSP containing the new information. The other routers will know that this is an update to the link-state database, because the sequence number has changed from the previous LSP.

If an LSP arrives at a router with the same sequence number as an earlier LSP, the router rejects it. Using the sequence number gives NLSP routers a quick way to determine whether the LSP includes a change.

 When new information is presented, routers will flood the information to make sure all other routers receive the changes. Typically, one router floods sooner than the others, so the other routers stop their flooding when they see the LSPs with the updated information available.

If a router receives the LSP with a higher sequence number (indicating a change has been made in the link-state database), that router forwards the packet through all available interfaces (except, of course, the interface that received the new LSP in the first place).

Convergence

Convergence is a fancy term for the process of every router being synchronized with a current link-state database. NLSP converges faster than RIP (one of its big advantages over RIP) because NLSP routers forward new information before they update their own databases.

There's no reason to track the hops to ensure a packet doesn't fall into the count-to-infinity problem. NLSP routers have a complete map of the network, so they know of any alternative paths.

The Aging Timer And LSP Validation

One of the easy ways to tell when an LSP is valid is through the use of an aging timer, similar to the way the RIP routing information table uses an aging timer. Every two hours (which is the default), an LSP flood confirms the status of the LSP for all NLSP routers. Network changes trigger the LSP flood as well, but the two-hour timer provides a backup method of ensuring that the latest and most accurate information is used.

Unreachable Routes And LSP Purging

Large dynamic networks, especially those with WAN links, generate plenty of route changes as groups of routers beyond a downed link become unreachable and then become reachable again. If NLSP routers re-created their entire link-state databases every time a link was out of reach for a few minutes, the processing overhead would become an annoyance and possibly a burden to the router host.

NLSP intelligently does not purge any LSPs that have been declared "unreachable." Rather, the routers merely flag those LSPs as "unavailable." This updates the link-state databases with the important information, but it doesn't cause any recalculations or LSP flooding.

LSPs are purged if an unavailable link is still listed as missing in action when the aging interval expires. Because the normal interval is two hours, links that go up and down during testing or because of network problems don't generate extra work for all the other routers. Links that drop and recover in a few minutes will almost always miss the aging interval boundary.

Handling RIP Traffic

NLSP does handle RIP traffic, but it treats this traffic differently than NLSP traffic. In fact, NLSP routers consider RIP traffic paths as external routes. Only the DR can translate and transmit RIP/SAP information through an NLSP internetwork. If there's a choice between an NLSP route and a RIP route, NLSP will always assign a lower cost to the NLSP route.

Comparing And Contrasting RIP And NLSP

Is NLSP just a new and improved RIP? Are there valid reasons to migrate to NLSP? Let's compare and contrast NLSP and RIP to see where the advantages are.

Major Differences

As you might expect from two approaches to performing the same function, many of the differences between RIP and NLSP involve enhancements to similar features. Here are some specifics:

➤ Both RIP and NLSP use a hop and tick count to determine optimum routes. With RIP, it's an actual hop number and time tick count, whereas with NLSP, it's a cost value assigned to a link.

➤ NLSP routers have first-hand knowledge of the entire internetwork, although it's derived by reading LSPs from other routers rather than each router searching the network itself. Support for multiple routes to the same remote network eliminates the count-to-infinity problem in RIP routers.

➤ RIP sends the entire routing information table with each update. This chews up bandwidth and router processing time. NLSP only sends the changes.

NLSP's Advantages Over RIP

One of NLSP's advantages over RIP is its ability to support larger IPX internetworks. This is a result of the number of hops supported by NLSP (126 hops is the maximum; 127 hops indicates an unreachable network). RIP has a maximum hop count of 15 (remember that, here, 16 indicates an unreachable route). More hops equal a larger internetwork.

 NLSP's maximum hop count is 126; RIP's maximum hop count is 15.

NLSP sends only link-state database changes after a network event rather than the entire database. This helps lower bandwidth demands while speeding up network convergence (all the routers being synched together). This is particularly true of WAN links, where the constant SAP traffic demands much more bandwidth and uptime than NLSP.

Path splitting, or load balancing, makes efficient use of bandwidth while speeding performance for users. Up to eight equal-cost routes may be defined within NLSP.

NLSP offers more network management information to applications, such as ManageWise and SNMP management consoles, than RIP. Problems such as inactive routers or links, duplicate network numbers, and even failed network boards are found using NLSP.

It all boils down to a simple matter of NLSP putting less routing and service traffic out on the internetwork than RIP, while still providing more information and speed. A worthwhile update, but one that can be phased out, because NLSP works with RIP/SAP routers.

Comparing OSPF And NLSP

What NLSP is to RIP with IPX, OSPF (Open Shortest Path First) is to RIP with TCP/IP. OSPF was developed to replace RIP in large, complex internetworks by saving bandwidth and speeding information transfer. The tradeoff is CPU time, because OSPF is much more CPU-intensive than RIP.

OSPF, which was built for IP networks, focuses on worldwide internetwork issues. There are more packet types in OSPF, and the protocol is more complex. The reputation for complexity precedes OSPF everywhere. In fact, in Christian Huitema's book *Routing in the Internet*, the title of Chapter 5 is "Why Is OSPF So Complex?"

Like NLSP, OSPF is a link-state protocol. OSPF tracks the operational state of all routers in the network, tracking details about the network map provided by each router. Knowing all the links between all the routers makes it relatively easy, after some computation, to plan the shortest path through a network.

Packet Types

OSPF has a variety of packets that don't match up exactly to NLSP packets, but they cover all the same jobs, and more. A similar relationship exists with the assorted databases for keeping track of routing information. Table 17.3 shows the NLSP and corresponding OSPF packet types.

You'll find nothing out of the ordinary in Table 17.3, except that the OSPF has a packet that NLSP doesn't—the link-state acknowledgement (LSA) packet.

Database Types

Just as OSPF has an extra packet type, there's an extra database type as well. Some of the nomenclature is a bit further afield than that seen in the packet type comparison, but it makes sense. Table 17.4 shows the NLSP and corresponding OSPF database types.

Router Types

OSPF uses the concept of "areas" and the network backbone to segment the network into digestible chunks. This adds to the complexity of designing OSPF networks, but it also adds an extra handle for large network management.

Table 17.3   NLSP and OSPF packet types.

NLSP Packet	OSPF Packet	Information
CSNP	DDP	Database description packet (only on demand).
Hello	Hello	The OSPF packet includes a subnet mask.
LSP	LSU	Link-state update (link-state announcements).
PSNP	LSR	Link-state request.
	LSA	Link-state acknowledgement (a reply from the router that receives an LSU or DDP).

Table 17.4   Matching NLSP and OSPF databases.

NLSP	OSPF	Information
Adjacencies DB	Neighbors list	Adjacent routers
Forwarding DB	Routing table	Network map
Link-state DB	Link-state advertisement DB	Tracks announcements about link states
	Interfaces list (includes cost and router type)	

One detail tracked by OSPF is a packet's route to and from the backbone network. This makes sense, because large networks always have a backbone, and tracking where to get on and off influences routing decisions.

Internal routers connect only to networks in the same area. Area border routers (ABRs) link more than one area, such as linking one defined area to a backbone. ABRs must learn and remember details about both areas they serve. A backbone router has interfaces to the backbone and provides information about the backbone area to other areas down the line. Autonomous system border routers (ASBRs) link to external networks. One router may perform multiple jobs in an OSPF network.

Note: You may also see ASBRs called autonomous system boundary routers.

Is OSPF (and NLSP) worth the extra overhead over RIP? OSPF needs five different messages and three procedures to accomplish what RIP does with two messages. RIP routers need only a routing table, whereas OSPF needs to maintain a link-state database as well as a routing table.

Does this extra work make a difference? Consider this scenario: In June 1994 (before the Web took off), there were 20,000 external routes off the NSFNET backbone borders. RIP had to repeat them every 30 seconds (24 octets per route times 20,000 routes is a lot of overhead every 30 seconds). With OSPF, the route packets were smaller, and they were sent every 30 minutes, thus cutting the packet storm by a ratio of 60:1 (two packets an hour in place of 120).

Note: See Chapter 13 for more information on OSPF.

Practice Questions

Question 1

> Which of the following are components of NLSP? [Choose the
> three best answers]
>
> ❑ a. Adjacency database
>
> ❑ b. Link-state database
>
> ❑ c. Alternate route table
>
> ❑ d. Flood-packet database
>
> ❑ e. Forwarding database

The correct answers are a, b, and e. The adjacency database, link-state database, and forwarding database are the three databases used by NLSP. An alternate route table sounds like a good option for tracking higher-cost routes, but those routes are discarded out of memory and are not kept in a table. Therefore, answer c is incorrect. Flood packets are not tracked—they announce network changes. Therefore, answer d is incorrect.

Question 2

> Which of the following terms are unique to NLSP? [Choose the
> two best answers]
>
> ❑ a. Routing table
>
> ❑ b. Number of hops
>
> ❑ c. Adjacency
>
> ❑ d. Network number
>
> ❑ e. Designated router

The correct answers are c and e. Adjacency is a link-state routing concept, and the designated router (DR) has specific functions within NLSP, such as creating the pseudonode. Routing tables are common in both RIP and NLSP, as is the number of hops (RIP relies on hops strongly, but NLSP effectively ignores them). Therefore, answers a and b are incorrect. Both protocols use network numbers to identify routers. Therefore, answer d is incorrect.

Question 3

> Which of the following is the value initially used to elect a desig-
> nated router?
>
> ○ a. MAC address
> ○ b. Most recent router addition to the network
> ○ c. Size of the adjacency database
> ○ d. Priority value in the hello packet
> ○ e. Number of backbone connections

The correct answer is d. Priority levels can be set, and the physical or MAC address (answer a) is used as a tiebreaker when two routers have the same priority level—the highest MAC address wins. Therefore, answer a is incorrect—and the reason this is a trick question. New routers joining the network will not displace an active designated router just by joining the network, even if their priority numbers are higher. Therefore, answer b is incorrect. The size of the adjacency database is the same for all routers, and the number of backbone connections has no bearing on the designated router election or function. Therefore, answers c and e are incorrect.

Question 4

> Which of the following is *not* a feature of the forwarding database?
>
> ○ a. The link-state database is separate from the forwarding database.
> ○ b. Up to eight equal-cost routes can be tracked in the forwarding database.
> ○ c. Routes are based on cost calculations figured on each router interface.
> ○ d. Hops and ticks are added to the cost calculation to break any ties.

The correct answer is d. NLSP routers do not use hops and ticks when calculating routes through the network. The link-state database is separate from the forwarding database, so an NLSP router doesn't need to calculate the route algorithm before flooding a network change. Therefore, answer a is incorrect. Eight routes can be tracked, and all can be used for load balancing. Therefore, answer b is incorrect. The cost calculations are weighted so faster interfaces have lower costs and are therefore chosen most often by routers. Therefore, answer c is incorrect.

Question 5

> Which of the following is the goal of the hold-down interval?
>
> ○ a. It slows the wave of traffic during flooding.
>
> ○ b. It allows time for a group of changes to be integrated into the link-state database before rerunning the calculation algorithm.
>
> ○ c. It keeps the size of the link-state database from growing.
>
> ○ d. It cuts down the number of spurious hello packets.

The correct answer is b. Holding recalculations to every five seconds allows groups of changes to be assimilated. Although you might think answer a is a good answer, the goal is to keep the router's overhead down by stopping it from calculating every change that appears in a big group of changes. Therefore, answer a is incorrect—and the reason this is a trick question. The size of the link-state database is a direct result of the number of routers in the network, and hello packets have nothing to do with the hold-down interval. Therefore, answers c and d are incorrect.

Question 6

> Which of the following are not methods used to synchronize routers on a network? [Choose the two best answers]
>
> ❏ a. Replying with newer Link State Packets (LSPs) if the received information is old
>
> ❏ b. Sending a partial sequence number packet (PSNP) requesting more information
>
> ❏ c. Sending the router information table to all other routers
>
> ❏ d. Requesting the MAC address of all routers
>
> ❏ e. Sending a complete sequence number packet (CSNP)

The correct answers are c and d. The router information table is not sent separately by NLSP; part of NLSP's advantage over RIP is that it sends only the information that changes. The MAC address is part of the LSP already, and there's no reason to request that separately. CNSPs, PSNPs, and LSPs are the three packet types used by NLSP to organize and synchronize all routers. Therefore, answers a, b, and e are incorrect.

Question 7

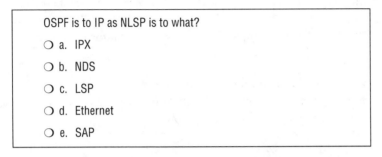

OSPF is to IP as NLSP is to what?

○ a. IPX

○ b. NDS

○ c. LSP

○ d. Ethernet

○ e. SAP

The correct answer is a. OSPF (Open Shortest Path First) provides IP with a link-state protocol, just as NLSP provides IPX with a link-state protocol to replace RIP. Novell Directory Services (NDS) has nothing to do with routing protocols, LSP is the Link State Packet, Ethernet is a physical medium rather than a protocol, and SAP relies on RIP. Therefore, answers b, c, d, and e are incorrect.

Need To Know More?

 Dickie, Mark. *Routing in Today's Internetworks*. Van Nostrand Reinhold. New York, 1994. ISBN 0-442-01811-8. Chapter 10 covers RIP for IPX, and Chapter 11 discusses NLSP in depth.

 Huitema, Christian. *Routing in the Internet*. Prentice Hall. Englewood Cliffs, NJ, 1995. ISBN 0-13-132192-7. Chapter 5, "Why Is OSPF So Complex?" provides detailed information on OSPF.

 www.ietf.org/html.charters/wg-dir.html covers all the various working groups of the Internet Engineering Task Force, including those covering routing and the Internet.

Other NetWare Network Services And Protocols

18

Terms you'll need to understand:

√ NetWare Core Protocol (NCP)

√ Multiple Link Interface Driver (MLID)

√ Link Support Layer (LSL)

√ Application services

Techniques you'll need to master:

√ Identifying upper-layer connection-oriented protocols supported by NetWare

√ Explaining how NCP function calls are used by NetWare clients

√ Describing the Open Data-Link Interface (ODI) architecture

√ Explaining the function of the MLID

√ Explaining the function of the LSL

√ Understanding how protocol analyzers can be used to manage an IPX/SPX network

NetWare supports a large number of connection-oriented upper-layer protocols that use IPX/SPX transport services. In this chapter, you'll learn about the NetWare services that provide this support. You'll also get a general overview of protocol analysis tools you can use to manage your IPX/SPX-based network.

Understanding The NetWare Core Protocols (NCPs)

The NetWare Core Protocols (NCPs) are the NetWare operating system kernel components that make NetWare server application functions available to users. Examples of server application functions include file and print services as well as messaging services. The NCP components consist of function calls that support these and other network services through client/server connections using standard request and reply packets.

NetWare client software running on a workstation uses the NCP function calls to request network services. The particular service being requested is identified with a service-specific function code that's included in the NCP request packet. The service provider that responds to the request uses an NCP reply packet that also includes the service function code. The communication established between the client and the service provider by exchanging the request and reply packets represents an NCP connection that's identified by the NCP socket address and the service function code.

The NCP function calls provide network service access that's transparent to the client; in fact, all network services appear to be locally provided when viewed from the client's perspective. For example, a directory listing of files on a NetWare server volume appears to be a local drive scan, and a print job sent to a NetWare print queue appears to be sent to a local printer port.

Implementations of NCP include the following Novell products:

➤ NetWare client requesters (NetWare DOS Requester, Client 32, and others)

➤ The NetWare core operating system

The available NCP services include, but aren't limited to, the following:

➤ Accounting services

➤ AppleTalk file services

➤ Auditing services

➤ Connection services

➤ Directory services

- Extended file attribute services

- File services

- File server environment

- Message services

- Novell Directory Services (NDS)

- Packet Burst protocol

- Print and print queue services

- Security services

- Synchronization services

- Transaction-tracking services

Open Data-Link Interface (ODI) Specification

Cross-platform compatibility is an important issue in any mixed-network environment. Heterogeneous network environments have become increasingly common as more and more networks are merged to provide more broad-scale connectivity. The Open Data-Link Interface (ODI) specification defines a process for supporting multiple communication protocols on a single network. The process allows a single network board to support multiple protocols while using only one network board driver. An ODI-compliant driver can communicate with any ODI-compliant protocol stack, such as IPX or TCP/IP, meaning that a single network board can support multiple clients on the network.

The ODI architecture specifies three components: the Multiple Link Interface Driver (MLID), the Link Support Layer (LSL), and the protocol stacks discussed in the previous section. We'll take a look at the first two components in the following sections.

Multiple Link Interface Driver (MLID)

The MLID specifies the network board installed in a computer. It's implemented as a network board driver developed to the ODI MLID specifications. The ODI-compliant driver controls communication between the network board and the LSL. It operates at the MAC sublayer of the Open Systems Interconnection (OSI) Data Link layer.

The MLID has three components that provide support for the selected media, topology, and hardware platform:

➤ **Media Support Module (MSM)** This module implements the media-specific functions of the ODI-compliant LAN drivers. It provides general card initialization, builds the network board configuration table, maintains the send queue, and handles most of the I/O control functions.

➤ **Topology Support Module (TSM)** This module supports the selected topology by managing the Event Control Buffers (ECBs) and collecting associated statistics.

➤ **Hardware Support Module (HSM)** This module contains developer-specific code that handles the network board details, such as moving packets on and off the board, managing control functions, and initializing and resetting the board.

Link Support Layer (LSL)

The LSL defines processes operating at the Logical Link Control (LLC) sublayer of the OSI Data Link layer. The LSL is implemented as software that acts as a switchboard between the MLID below it and the ODI-compliant communication protocol stack above it. The LSL allows a single driver to support multiple protocols by accepting data packets from the MLID and then determining to which protocol stack to deliver the packet. The LSL also performs the switchboarding operation in the opposite direction to allow a single protocol to use multiple drivers.

Application Services Provided By NLMs

The NetWare operating system provides support for application modules that can be selectively added to or removed from the active operating system. These application modules, called *NetWare Loadable Modules (NLMs)*, are typically designed to provide additional network services. The NLMs are written to use the NetWare Core Protocol (NCP), TCP/IP, IPX/SPX, or any other appropriate lower-layer service.

NLMs that provide these additional application services are available from Novell as well as from third-party vendors and developers. The application services currently available include the following:

➤ Communication services

➤ Database services

➤ Email

➤ File sharing

➤ Other transport protocols

➤ Printer sharing

Protocol Analysis And The OSI Model

Protocol analysis is a network management technique that involves gathering, storing, and displaying protocol-specific statistical information that can help you better understand how your network is currently running. Protocol analysis can help you perform the following tasks:

➤ Monitor network performance

➤ Troubleshoot network problems

➤ Optimize network performance

➤ Plan for growth

Protocol analysis requires the use of devices designed to collect and/or display information about specific protocols. The devices, called *protocol analyzers*, can be combinations of hardware and software or they can consist of software only. The major differences between "high-end" protocol analyzers and "low-end" protocol analyzers can be found in such factors as the following:

➤ The number of protocols they can be used to analyze

➤ Their ability to generate test traffic

➤ Their speed

➤ The comprehensiveness of the information they provide

Because protocols specify the rules for the networking processes operating at any given functional level of the OSI model, a general overview of protocol analyzer capability is most meaningful within that framework. The following list provides examples of the features that should be incorporated into protocol analyzers designed to operate at a particular layer of the OSI model:

➤ **Physical layer** At this layer, a protocol analyzer tests for media faults, such as cable breaks or shorts. The industry standard tool that's incorporated into many analyzers to provide analysis at this level is called a Time Domain Reflectometer (TDR).

➤ **Data Link layer** Analyzers operating at this layer must be able to examine the traffic on the network segments. The depth of the information available depends on the vendor-implemented features, the physical and logical topologies involved, and the media access method employed on the network. Error reports at this level could include information on the following:

➤ Beaconing

➤ Collisions

➤ Invalid Cyclic Redundancy Checks (CRCs)

➤ Network board jabber errors

➤ Receiver congestion

➤ Short and/or long packets

➤ **Network layer** Analyzers at this layer are used to figure out the distance between clients and servers in order to evaluate the need for cable and/or router reconfigurations.

➤ **Transport layer and above** Analysis at this level includes the examination of Transport, Session, Presentation, and Application layer protocols. Typical protocols that might be examined in a NetWare environment would include the following:

➤ NCP

➤ NetWare Link Services Protocol (NLSP)

➤ Packet Burst

➤ Routing Information Protocol (RIP)

➤ SPX

The following is a list of protocol analyzers that provide some or all of the previously mentioned features:

➤ LANalyzer for Windows

➤ ManageWise (numerous components)

➤ Novell Customer Connections (NCC) LANalyzer

➤ Time Domain Reflectometers (TDRs)

Remember that most protocol analyzers require some initial configuration and also assume a certain degree of operator skill for meaningful use. The operator must know the type of information to request and how to request it. In addition, the operator needs to be able to incorporate that information into a specific solution to a specific problem.

Practice Questions

Question 1

> Which of the following is not a component of the MLID?
>
> O a. LSL
>
> O b. MSM
>
> O c. TSM
>
> O d. HSM

The correct answer is a. The MLID is a MAC sublayer process; therefore, the MLID components are also MAC sublayer processes. Because the Link Support Layer (LSL) is an LLC sublayer process, it cannot be an MLID component. The MSM, TSM, and HSM are all components of the MLID and are therefore incorrect answers.

Question 2

> A network protocol analyzer works at which layer(s) of the OSI model?
>
> O a. The Physical and Data Link layers
>
> O b. The Transport layer and above
>
> O c. All seven layers of the OSI model
>
> O d. At the layer or layers containing the protocols it's designed to analyze

The correct answer is d. A protocol analyzer is used to collect protocol-specific information. The analyzer works at the same layer of the OSI model that the protocol under analysis operates. Some analysis products include protocol support for processes operating at any layer of the OSI model (for example, ManageWise), whereas others are specific to a single layer (for example, a TDR at the Physical layer). Therefore, answers a, b, and c are incorrect. This is a trick question because, at first glance, answer c appears to be the correct choice, because protocols operating at any layer of the OSI model are subject to analysis by an appropriately designed protocol analyzer. The question, however, provides no information about the design of the analyzer; therefore, it's not possible to assign the analyzer's operation to any particular layer or layers of the OSI model.

Question 3

> Which of the following are services made available through the
> NetWare Core Protocols (NCPs)? [Choose the two best answers]
>
> ❏ a. Email
> ❏ b. Messaging services
> ❏ c. Database services
> ❏ d. Transaction tracking
> ❏ e. Printer sharing

The correct answers are b and d. NCP function calls allow NetWare clients to
access messaging and transaction-tracking services (among others). Email,
database services, and printer sharing are all application services provided as
add-on enhancements that are made available by running the appropriate
NLMs. Therefore, answers a, c, and e are incorrect.

Question 4

> The NetWare Core Protocol (NCP) is assigned the NetWare socket
> number of 0x0451. How does a NetWare client request a specific
> NCP-provided service if all request packets are delivered to the
> same socket?
>
> ○ a. The client request includes the NDS object name and the
>   context for the requested resource.
>
> ○ b. The client request packet includes a pointer to the SAP
>   address of the requested service.
>
> ○ c. Because NCP runs concurrently on the client and server,
>   a function call for any service causes NCP socket
>   synchronization between the client and server. This
>   makes all services momentarily available on a dedicated
>   basis for the duration of the request cycle. The effect is
>   analogous to turning on a light switch to make the
>   objects in a room visible.
>
> ○ d. All NCP message packets (including the client request
>   packet) contain a function code that identifies the
>   particular service being requested or replied to.

The correct answer is d. Although NCP is assigned the NetWare socket number of 0x0451, individual service function calls within NCP are specified by

referencing the assigned service function code. Answers a, b, and c are incorrect because they do not describe actual processes that occur during a client service request.

Question 5

> Which of the following could not be included as part of the description of a particular vendor's MLID?
>
> O a. It is software.
>
> O b. It complies with the Novell ODI architecture.
>
> O c. It's an ODI-compliant network board.
>
> O d. It supplies the code that allows a single interface on a network board to utilize multiple protocols.

The correct answer to this question is c. The MLID is a piece of software written for a particular network board (typically by the board's manufacturer) that complies with the Novell Open Data-Link Interface (ODI) architecture. It supplies the necessary code to allow a single interface on the network board to utilize multiple protocols. Because the MLID is not the network board itself, the statement in answer c cannot be used as part of the MLID description and is therefore the correct answer. The statements in answers a, b, and d can be used in the MLID description and are therefore incorrect.

Question 6

> Which NetWare protocol functions as the interface between an MLID and various upper-layer protocols?
>
> O a. LANalyzer for Windows
>
> O b. LSL
>
> O c. NCP
>
> O d. MSM

The correct answer to this question is b. The Link Support Layer (LSL) functions as the interface between an MLID and various upper-layer protocols. LANalyzer for Windows is a protocol analysis product. Therefore, answer a is incorrect. NetWare Core Protocols (NCPs) consist of client requests and server replies. Therefore, answer c is incorrect. A Media Support Module (MSM) is one of the MLID components. Therefore, answer d is incorrect.

Need To Know More?

 www.novell.com/documentation/mw26.html is the location of Novell's ManageWise product documentation. Here, you can get plenty of details concerning the capabilities of network protocol analysis and network management products.

 Start at **www.novell.com/documentation/lg/nw5/docui/index.html** and follow the links in the NetWare 5 documentation to LAN driver statistics and monitoring network traffic to learn more about MLID components.

 www.novell.com/documentation/lg/nw5/docui/index.html is the NetWare 5 online documentation. Select Contents from the NetWare 5 documentation main menu and then select Network Services to view detailed information about many of Novell's application services.

 www.novell.com/documentation/lg/nw5/docui/index.html#../product/topic_fi.html^false is where you can find information on NCP-provided services.

19

X.500 Directory Services And LDAP

Terms you'll need to understand:

✓ Directory Services (DS)

✓ Directory Service Agents (DSAs)

✓ Directory User Agents (DUAs)

✓ Request for comment (RFC)

✓ Distributed database

✓ Replication

✓ Synchronization

✓ Directory Information Tree (DIT)

✓ Directory Information Base (DIB)

✓ Object

✓ Attribute

✓ Distinguished name (DN)

✓ Relative distinguished name (RDN)

✓ Lightweight Directory Access Protocol (LDAP)

Techniques you'll need to master:

✓ Understanding Directory Services and its features

✓ Identifying the structure and components of an X.500 directory

✓ Learning LDAP and mapping it to the OSI model

Have you ever installed a local area network (LAN), defined all the usernames and security accesses, and then had to install the same usernames again when you installed another application (such as email)? This happens because most network operating systems and applications maintain their own databases of user information and services. X.500 Directory Services (DS) is meant to eliminate duplication of user information and services across a global network by providing a distributed database schema that standardizes naming conventions and structure. In this chapter, we discuss what you need to know about the underpinnings of X.500 Directory Services.

X.500 Directory Services Overview

X.500 Directory Services (DS) is a Consultative Committee on International Telegraphy and Telephony (CCITT), now called ITU (International Telecommunication Union), standards recommendation designed to provide a global directory service with an international authority as its root or top level. The concept is similar to the white pages of a local telephone service—it allows you to look up information or call a local operator who searches an online database. One difference is that location and the local telephone company restrict white pages, whereas the X.500 DS is a global lookup of people and services.

Although some entities on the Internet currently support global naming schemes, most of them use a centralized database rather than a distributed database. This causes bottlenecks on the processors during peak lookup times because of the high amount of traffic.

The computer industry has never embraced X.500 DS, and no one international authority has ever assumed the root authority. However, some organizations, such as Novell, have implemented a variant based on the X.500 recommendation in their network operating systems.

 Request for comment (RFC) 1309, "Technical Overview of Directory Services Using the X.500 Protocol," provides a brief history and overview of DS. It can be found at **info.internet.isi.edu/in-notes/ rfc/files/rfc1309.txt**.

RFCs are notes about all aspects of computing related to the Internet. Anyone can submit an RFC. However, before it can be published, the RFC must go through both the Internet Engineering Task Force (IETF) and the IETF's Steering Group (IESG) or through the RFC editor. RFCs take the format of RFC *<number>*. For example, RFC 1308 and RFC 1309 pertain to Directory Services.

You can read all about RFCs in general at **www.rfc-editor.org**, or you can search for specific RFC numbers at **www.rfc-editor.org/rfc.html**.

Features

X.500 has the following features that make it attractive to organizations:

➤ Replication

➤ Scalability

➤ Synchronization

We discuss each of these features in the following sections.

Replication Of The Database

When the X.500 database is replicated, an exact copy of the database is made; therefore, local copies of the database can exist anywhere on the network. This increases performance in complex searches and provides a high degree of fault tolerance. The distributed nature of the database means that if one database fails, users can retrieve information from another copy of the database residing elsewhere.

Scalability Using DSAs

The database can be divided into Directory System Agents (DSAs) and distributed to other processors. (Novell calls these *NDS partitions*.) The DSAs are stored as local databases, which allows them to be changed and queried faster and more efficiently. DSAs are distributed over several processors and locations; however, they appear as one directory. This provides scalability as an organization grows because the entire directory tree does not have to grow as one large database on one processor. Instead, as the organization grows, it can add more network resources to the tree and split the tree up over several processors and locations.

Synchronization Of The Database

The X.500 distributed database provides for synchronization; all other Directory Services servers are updated with the latest changes whenever changes are made to the directory. Changes made to the main directory server can be synchronized downward to all other servers, or changes can be made to any server in the distribution that will be propagated to all other servers in a predetermined sequence. It's also possible to prohibit changes to the directory, but that can pose problems. There's obviously some latency and delay introduced in synchronization, so it's possible that at any given point, the entire directory may not be fully synchronized.

 The three features of X.500 that make it desirable both on the Internet and in organizations are replication, scalability, and synchronization.

The X.500 Directory Tree

We all know that real-world trees have their roots in the ground and grow upward. The X.500 Directory Information Tree (DIT) is like a tree turned upside-down so its roots are in the air. The only difference is that in a DIT, only one root is at the top. Figure 19.1 depicts the basic hierarchical DIT structure.

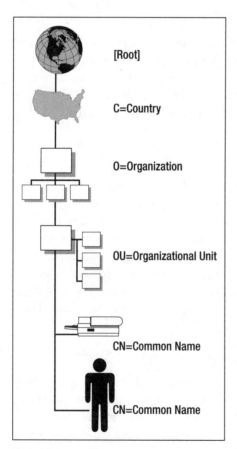

Figure 19.1 Hierarchical structure of the X.500 DIT.

Understanding The DIT

Working from the top of the DIT (the root) and proceeding downward, we'll define the designators or labels used in the tree:

➤ **Root** Represents the top of the tree. This is typically designed for an international authority.

➤ **C** Represents "Country" and is designed for a country code, such as US for United States.

➤ **O** Represents "Organization" and is designed to refer to an organization or company, such as Novell.

➤ **OU** Represents "Organizational Unit," which is designed to further divide the organization (for example, "SALES" and "MKT" for sales and marketing departments).

➤ **CN** Represents "Common Name." Common names describe leaf objects (discussed later in this chapter). If "person" is the leaf object, the common name might be "JSmith."

Each of the fixed designators has a place in the tree hierarchy. For example, you can't have the root in the middle of the tree.

DIB Entries

The X.500 DIT information also stores its information in an information base called the *Directory Information Base (DIB)*. This information base is similar to the way Simple Network Management Protocol (SNMP) stores data in a Management Information Base (MIB). Entries in the DIB include two types of objects and their attributes:

➤ **Intermediate objects** Intermediate objects are used only for organizational purposes of the tree, but they can contain other objects. These objects are similar to directories and subdirectories in a computer.

➤ **Leaf objects** Leaf objects represent the actual item on the network, and they can't contain any other objects. These objects are similar to the files on a computer. They are structured in the DIT by the intermediate objects.

➤ **Attributes** Each object and its associated information (known as its *attributes*) is an entry in the DIT. Each attribute contains one piece of information about the object. For example, you might have an object called "person" with the attributes "surname," "telephonenumber," and "address." The value of each attribute is the actual information. For example, in the object "person," the attribute "surname" might have the value "Jones," which is a string of characters. However, another attribute called "picture" might have an image as the value.

 | Intermediate objects are used to structure the tree, whereas leaf objects represent the actual items on the network.

Object Relationship Restrictions

How do you designate people with the same name in the DIT? Due to the DIT's structure, it's possible to have ten John Smiths defined as "JSmith," as long as they're in different parts of the tree. The path from the object to the root is different for each occurrence of JSmith. Let's use a familiar example. On a computer, it's possible to have five copies of the file RESUME.DOC, as long as they're not all in the same directory:

```
C:\MYFILES\RESUME.DOC
C:\MYFILES\JOBS\CURRENT\RESUME.DOC
C:\LATEST\RESUME.DOC
C:\LATEST\REV2\RESUME.DOC
C:\RESUME.DOC
```

In this example, it's possible for all the RESUME.DOC files to be identical because they reside in different subdirectories. They can also contain different information. It doesn't matter either way. What's important is that they all share the same file name. How you reference the file depends on where on the hard disk you're presently situated. For example, if you're viewing the subdirectory C:\MYFILES, you could reference the file simply as RESUME.DOC, and the operating system knows which version of RESUME.DOC you're requesting. However, if you're in another subdirectory where there's no file called RESUME.DOC (such as C:\TAXES, for example), you need to tell the operating system the full path to the RESUME.DOC file you're requesting so it knows which version to retrieve.

Schema

The schema of X.500 directories lays out what information is held in the directory and how that information is structured. Administrators of individual directories then determine the structure of each directory as it relates to their organization.

Naming Conventions

X.500 standards define the structure of the tree, but the naming of the objects is up to each administrator. If two or more objects share the same name, the context of the location within the tree is considered, depending on what other information is given. The following two sections discuss the use of a distinguished name (DN) versus a relative distinguished name (RDN) to determine the location of an object. In the following sections, we'll use this example:

```
CN=SmithJ
OU=SALES
O=LANWrights
```

Distinguished Name

In X.500 terms, objects are referenced with either a DN or an RDN. Using the previous example, a DN would be the full path to CN=SmithJ.OU=SALES.O= LANWrights, whereas an RDN would simply be SmithJ.

Relative Distinguished Name

An RDN is "relative" to where you are in the directory structure. Therefore, John Smith could exist many times in the directory as an RDN. Each RDN would simply contain the information "John Smith." However, there can be only one DN that points to a specific "John Smith." There can be ten DNs pointing to John Smiths, but each DN must be unique in its construct.

For example, you could have the following list of DNs for John Smith:

```
CN=SmithJ.OU=SALES.O=LANWrights
CN=SmithJ.OU=MKTG.O=LANWrights
CN=SmithJ.OU=AUTHORS.O=LANWrights
```

 There can be multiple instances of the same RDN within the DIT; however, there can be only one unique DN for each RDN.

Understanding Protocols And Agents

Now that you understand the tree structure, let's look at how clients interact with the database, and vice versa. Again, if you're familiar with the SNMP protocol, you're familiar with protocols and agents. The protocol governs how the communication takes place between two devices. Any time communication occurs on a network, there must be an agreed upon set of rules governing that interaction. This set of rules is known as the *protocol*. An agent is merely a piece of software that resides on a computer and carries information back and forth between devices.

DUA And DSA Communication Ports

X.500 uses agents placed on the clients (*Directory User Agents*, or *DUAs*) and on the database (*Directory System Agents*, or *DSAs*) that talk to each other using the Directory Access Protocol (DAP). The DUA software interface may resemble a browser or a command-line prompt, or it may have a forms-based look and feel.

X.500 uses three main protocols to communicate from the DUA to the DSA: Directory Access Protocol (DAP), Lightweight Directory Access Protocol (LDAP), and Connectionless Lightweight Directory Access Protocol (CLDAP). This means that X.500 clients and databases must communicate with each other using one or more of these protocols.

When clients need to access information in the database, their DUA prepares a request to the DSA on the server, which then accesses the DIB for information and passes that information back to the DUA. DUAs can talk only to DSAs, but DSAs can talk to other DSAs as well as DUAs.

> *Note:* *Most users don't use the DAP because it's resource intensive on the desktop. Most users only perform simple reads and writes to the X.500 DS, so they don't need DAP's extensive features.*

Security Levels

X.500 provides public/private key authentication technology to prevent unauthorized users from accessing data in the tree or in portions of the tree. The public key certificate, unlike the private key certificate, includes a specified time period during which the key is valid. The standard includes a method of revoking the public key certificate if it's required before the time period of the certificate is completed. In addition to these authentication methods, X.500 also provides for digital signature authentication.

The Lightweight Directory Access Protocol

As mentioned earlier, clients need to make requests to the database. When low maintenance and simple requests for read/write access are in order, LDAP is used instead of the resource-intensive DAP. DAP is implemented using the entire OSI protocol stack; LDAP requires only another connection-oriented protocol, such as TCP—thus the name "lightweight." The TCP/IP protocol suite is installed on many desktops that connect to the Internet or other IP-based networks, so it makes sense for LDAP to take advantage of a widely used protocol stack.

LDAP Overview

To reduce overhead and costs further, LDAP omits some of the less frequently used features of X.500, encodes the data differently, and represents the data more simply. However, because LDAP doesn't include information as to how the directory service is structured, it's still necessary to use it in conjunction with X.500 as opposed to as a replacement for it.

For an LDAP client to communicate with an X.500 DSA, most implementations include an LDAP server that functions something like a gateway between the LDAP client and the X.500 DSA. At some point, with X.500 DSAs still maintaining a high overhead and cost, LDAP servers took on more functionality to attempt to replace the need for an X.500 DSA. However, it's important to remember that LDAP was designed originally not as a full directory service standard, but as a streamlined method for accessing X.500 directories.

One of the main reasons LDAP has become so popular is its acceptance by some of the major networking companies, such as Novell and Banyan, as well as browser companies such as Netscape.

The Connectionless Lightweight Directory Access Protocol

This protocol is so "lightweight" that it can only perform read activity on an X.500 directory. Although it's derived from LDAP, CLDAP doesn't allow the user to change or write any information. CLDAP requires another connectionless-oriented protocol, such as UDP, to "transport" it. Many client workstations now include the TCP/IP protocol stack, so UDP is accessible.

Practice Questions

Question 1

> Which of the following statements best describe X.500 Directory
> Services? [Choose the two best answers]
>
> ❑ a. Provides a distributed database of user information and
>   services
>
> ❑ b. Provides a centralized database of user information and
>   services
>
> ❑ c. Defines processes at the Session layer of the OSI model
>
> ❑ d. Provides a replication of its database

The correct answers are a and d. X.500 Directory Services is a distributed
database that provides for replication. Answer b is incorrect because it refers to
a *centralized* database. Answer c is incorrect because X.500 defines processes at
the Application layer of the OSI model, not the Session layer.

Question 2

> The DIT information is stored in which of the following databases?
>
> ○ a. Management Information Base (MIB)
>
> ○ b. Directory Information Base (DIB)
>
> ○ c. Library Information Base (LIB)
>
> ○ d. White Pages Information Base (WPIB)

The correct answer is b. All the DIT information is stored in the DIB. Answer
a is the trick part of the question and is incorrect because although MIB is a
database that stores information, it's used by the SNMP protocol, not the X.500
structure. Answers c and d are incorrect because LIB and WPIB do not exist in
the X.500 structure.

Question 3

> Which of the following are features of the X.500 directory structure? [Choose the three best answers]
>
> ❑ a. Replication
>
> ❑ b. Scalable
>
> ❑ c. Distribution
>
> ❑ d. Synchronization

The correct answers are a, b, and d. Replication of the X.500 tree to other servers or locations provides for the distributed nature of the database. Therefore, answer a is correct. Because X.500 is distributed, it's scalable. Therefore, answer b is correct. Synchronization is a feature included to make sure all copies of the database are updated and contain the latest changes. Therefore, answer d is correct. There's no feature called distribution—it's *distributed*. Therefore, answer c is incorrect.

Question 4

> Beginning at the top of the tree, what's the correct object order for an X.500 directory DIT?
>
> ○ a. Root, Country, Organization, Organization Unit, Common Name
>
> ○ b. Root, Organization Unit, Country, Organization, Common Name
>
> ○ c. Common name, Organization Unit, Organization, Country, Root
>
> ○ d. Common name, Country, Organization, Organization Unit, Root

The correct answer is a. Starting at the top of the tree, you have the Root, Country, Organization, Organization Unit, and then Common Name. The X.500 directory is an inverted tree; therefore, the root is at the top of the structure. Answer b is incorrect because the Country object should be right after the Root. Answers c and d are incorrect because they position the Root at the bottom.

Question 5

> The acronym CN stands for which of the following in the X.500 structure?
>
> ○ a. Central Note
>
> ○ b. Central Name
>
> ○ c. Common Name
>
> ○ d. Common Note

The correct answer is c. CN in the X.500 structure stands for *Common Name*. Answers a, b, and d are all incorrect because they do not denote any acronym in the directory structure.

Question 6

> Which of the following requires full use of the OSI stack on the desktop?
>
> ○ a. Directory Access Protocol (DAP)
>
> ○ b. Lightweight Directory Access Protocol (LDAP)
>
> ○ c. Connectionless Lightweight Directory Access Protocol (CLDAP)
>
> ○ d. Heavyweight Directory Access Protocol (HDAP)

The correct answer is a. DAP is the only access protocol in the list that requires the full OSI stack. Answer b is incorrect because LDAP has been scaled down for lighter use, and it uses another protocol for its transport, which allows it to skip the Session and Presentation layers of the OSI model. Answer c is incorrect because CLDAP is a derivative of the LDAP protocol and requires a connectionless protocol for transport. Answer d is incorrect because there's no such thing as an HDAP.

Need To Know More?

 Howes, Tim, PhD. and Mark Smith. *LDAP: Programming Directory-Enabled Applications with Lightweight Directory Access Protocol.* Macmillan Technical Publishing. Indianapolis, IN, 1997. ISBN 1-57870-000-0. This book covers LDAP in complete detail, including the future direction of LDAP.

 Hughes, Jeffrey F. and Blair W. Thomas. *Novell's Four Principles of NDS Design.* Novell Press. San Jose, CA, 1996. ISBN 0-7645-4522-1. This book covers the design of NDS as it relates to NetWare.

 info.internet.isi.edu/7c/in-notes/ is the location on the Internet where you can begin your search on RFCs.

 info.internet.isi.edu/in-notes/rfc/files/rfc1308.txt is where you can find RFC 1308, "Executive Introduction to Directory Services Using the X.500 Protocol," which is a good introduction to X.500.

 info.internet.isi.edu/in-notes/rfc/files/rfc1309.txt will take you to RFC 1309, "Technical Overview of Directory Services Using the X.500 Protocol," which is a more in-depth discussion of X.500 that includes pointers and other information.

 info.internet.isi.edu/in-notes/rfc/files/rfc1777.txt is the address for RFC 1777, "Lightweight Directory Access Protocol," which is a good source for the most recent information and pointers on LDAP.

 info.internet.isi.edu/in-notes/rfc/files/rfc1798.txt is where you can find RFC 1798, "Connectionless Lightweight X.500 Directory Access Protocol," which is a good source for the most recent information and pointers on CLDAP.

 www.datcon.co.uk/press/mdwhite1.htm is a great overview of Directory Services and LDAP, as provided by Data Connection.

Sample Test

In this chapter, we provide pointers to help you develop a successful test-taking strategy, including how to choose proper answers, how to decode ambiguity, how to work within the Novell testing framework, how to decide what you need to memorize, and how to prepare for the test. At the end of the chapter, we include 79 questions on subject matter pertinent to Novell Test 050-632: "Networking Technologies." Good luck!

Questions, Questions, Questions

There should be no doubt in your mind that you're facing a test full of specific and pointed questions. Networking Technologies is a form exam that consists of 79 questions that you can take up to 105 minutes to complete. This means you must study hard so you can answer as many questions as possible correctly, without resorting to guesses.

> *Note:* *We expect Novell to change this test to adaptive format eventually. Please see Chapter 1 for more information on adaptive testing.*

For this exam, questions belong to one of seven basic types:

➤ Multiple-choice questions with a single answer

➤ Multiple-choice questions with multiple answers

➤ Multipart questions with a single answer

➤ Multipart questions with multiple answers

➤ Pick one or more spots on a graphic

Always take the time to read each question at least twice before selecting an answer, and always look for an Exhibit button as you examine each question. Exhibits include graphic information related to a question. An exhibit is usually a screen capture of program output or GUI information that you must examine to analyze the question's contents and formulate an answer. The Exhibit button brings up graphics and charts used to help explain a question, provide additional data, or illustrate page layout or program behavior.

Not every question has only one answer; many questions require multiple answers. Therefore, it's important to read each question carefully to determine how many answers are necessary or possible, as well as to look for additional hints or instructions when selecting answers. Such instructions often occur in brackets, immediately following the question itself (as they do for all multiple-choice, multiple-answer questions).

Picking Proper Answers

Obviously, the only way to pass any exam is to select enough of the right answers to obtain a passing score. However, Novell's exams are not standardized like the SAT and GRE exams, and they can sometimes be quite a bit more challenging. In some cases, questions can be hard to follow or filled with technical vocabulary, and deciphering them can be difficult. In those cases, you

may need to rely on answer-elimination skills. Almost always, at least one answer out of the possible choices for a question can be eliminated immediately
because it matches one of these conditions:

➤ The answer does not apply to the situation.

➤ The answer describes a nonexistent issue, an invalid option, or an
imaginary state.

➤ The answer may be eliminated because of the question itself.

After you eliminate all answers that are obviously wrong, you can apply your
retained knowledge to eliminate further answers. Look for items that sound
correct but refer to actions, commands, or features that are not present or not
available in the situation that the question describes.

If you're still faced with a blind guess among two or more potentially correct
answers, reread the question. Try to picture how each of the possible remaining
answers would alter the situation. Be especially sensitive to terminology; sometimes the choice of words ("remove" instead of "disable") can make the difference
between a right answer and a wrong one.

Only when you've exhausted your ability to eliminate answers, and you're still
unclear about which of the remaining possibilities is correct, should you guess
at an answer (or answers). Guessing gives you at least some chance of getting a
question right; just don't be too hasty when making a blind guess.

Decoding Ambiguity

Novell exams have a reputation for including straightforward questions. You
won't have to worry much about deliberate ambiguity, but you will need a good
grasp of the technical vocabulary involved with networking technologies to
understand what some questions are trying to ask. In our experience with numerous Novell tests, we've learned that mastering the lexicon of Novell's
technical terms pays off on every exam. The Novell tests are tough but fair, and
they're deliberately made that way.

However, you need to brace yourself for one set of special cases. Novell tests are
notorious for their use of double negatives and similar circumlocutions, such as
"What item is not used when creating a <insert your favorite task here>?" Our
guess is that Novell includes such Byzantine language in its questions because
it wants to make sure examinees can follow instructions to the letter, no matter
how strangely worded those instructions might be. Although this may seem
like a form of torture, it's actually good preparation for those circumstances
where you have to follow instructions from technical manuals or training materials, which are themselves not quite in the same ballpark as "great literature"

or even "plain English." Even though we've been coached repeatedly to be on the lookout for this kind of stuff, it still fools us anyway from time to time. So you need to be on the lookout yourself and try to learn from our mistakes.

The only way to beat Novell at this game is to be prepared. You'll discover that many exam questions test your knowledge of things that are not directly related to the issue raised by a question. This means that the answers you must choose from, even incorrect ones, are just as much a part of the skill assessment as the question itself. If you don't know something about most aspects of the various networking technologies, you may not be able to eliminate obviously wrong answers because they may relate to a different technology than the one that's addressed by the question at hand. In other words, the more you know about networking technologies in general, the easier it will be for you to tell a right answer from a wrong one.

Questions often give away their answers, but you have to read carefully to see the clues that point to those answers. Often, subtle hints appear in the question text in such a way that they seem almost irrelevant to the situation. You must realize that each question is a test unto itself and that you need to inspect and successfully navigate each question to pass the exam. Look for small clues, such as the mention of utilities, services, and configuration settings. Little things like these can point at the right answer if properly understood; if missed, they can leave you facing a blind guess.

Because mastering the technical vocabulary is so important to testing well for Novell, be sure to brush up on the key terms presented at the beginning of each chapter. You may also want to read through the Glossary at the end of this book the day before you take the test.

Working Within The Framework

The test questions appear in random order, and many elements or issues that receive mention in one question may also crop up in other questions. It's not uncommon to find that an incorrect answer to one question is the correct answer to another question, or vice versa. Take the time to read every answer to each question, even if you recognize the correct answer to a question immediately. That extra reading may spark a memory or remind you about a networking technology that helps you on another question later in the exam.

Review each question carefully; test developers love to throw in a few tricky questions. Often, important clues are hidden in the wording or special instructions. Do your best to decode ambiguous questions; just be aware that some questions will be open to interpretation.

You might also want to jot some notes on your piece of paper or plastic sheet about questions that contain key information.

 Don't be afraid to take notes on what you see in various questions. Sometimes, what you record from one question—especially if it isn't as familiar as it should be or reminds you of the name or use of some protocol or service details—can help you with other questions later in the test.

Deciding What To Memorize

The amount of memorization you must undertake for an exam depends on how well you remember what you've read and how well you know the various aspects of networking by heart. If you're a visual thinker, and you can see network setups and protocol stacks in your head, you won't need to memorize as much as someone who's less visually oriented. The tests will stretch your recollection of the various networking technologies and protocols and the OSI model.

At a minimum, you'll want to memorize the following types of information:

➤ The OSI model's layers and their uses

➤ Which protocols operate at which layer of the OSI model

➤ The characteristics and components of the TCP/IP and IPX/SPX protocol suites

➤ The various connectivity devices used in networking technologies

➤ The different acronyms used for the various networking technologies

If you work your way through this book and try learn the various technologies that are covered throughout, you should have little or no difficulty mastering this material. Also, don't forget that The Cram Sheet at the front of the book is designed to capture the material that's most important to memorize; use this to guide your studies as well. Finally, don't forget to obtain and use Novell's Test Objectives for Course 565 as part of your planning and preparation process (**education.novell.com/testinfo/objectives/565tobj.htm**).

Preparing For The Test

The best way to prepare for the test—after you've studied—is to take at least one practice exam. We've included one here in this chapter for that reason; the test questions are located in the following pages. (Unlike the preceding chapters in this book, the answers don't follow the questions immediately; you'll have to flip to Chapter 21 to review the answers separately.)

Give yourself no more than 105 minutes to take the exam, keep yourself on the honor system, and don't look at earlier text in the book or jump ahead to the answer key. When your time is up, or you've finished the questions, you can check your work in Chapter 21. Pay special attention to the explanations for the incorrect answers; these can also help to reinforce your knowledge of the material. Knowing how to recognize correct answers is good, but understanding why incorrect answers are wrong can be equally valuable.

Taking The Test

Relax. Once you're sitting in front of the testing computer, there's nothing more you can do to increase your knowledge or preparation. Take a deep breath, stretch, and start reading that first question.

There's no need to rush; you have plenty of time. If you can't figure out the answer to a question after a few minutes, though, you may want to guess and move on to leave more time for remaining unanswered questions. Remember that both easy and difficult questions are intermixed throughout the test in random order. Because you're taking a form test, you should watch your time carefully: try to be one-quarter of the way done (20 questions) in at least 26 minutes, halfway done (40 questions) in at least 52 minutes, and three-quarters done (60 questions) in 78 minutes.

Set a maximum time limit for questions and watch your time on long or complex questions. If you hit your time limit, you need to guess and move on. Don't deprive yourself of the opportunity to see more questions by taking too long to puzzle over answers, unless you think you can figure out the correct answer. Otherwise, you're limiting your opportunities to pass.

That's it for pointers. Here are some questions for you to practice on.

Sample Test

Question 1

What does the acronym CN stand for in the X.500 structure?

- ○ a. Common name
- ○ b. Central node
- ○ c. Common node
- ○ d. Certified name

Question 2

Routers are able to interconnect networks with varied architectures. Which of the following statements accurately reflects the fundamental reason that they are able to route packets without regard for the underlying network architecture?

- ○ a. Routers utilize split horizon algorithms to provide connectivity options between varied network architectures.
- ○ b. Routers include networking algorithms that provide the capability to translate between differing networking architectures.
- ○ c. Routers are cognizant of the physical addresses of the networking devices and operate without regard for the upper-layer protocols involved.
- ○ d. Routers operate above the Physical and Data Link layers and are therefore unaware of the underlying network architectures.

Question 3

How is the count-to-infinity problem handled by OSPF routers?

- ○ a. OSPF networks do not suffer from the count-to-infinity problem.
- ○ b. OSPF uses poison reverse to eliminate the count-to-infinity problem.
- ○ c. OSPF uses split horizon to eliminate the count-to-infinity problem.
- ○ d. OSPF increases infinity from 16 to 65,535 to eliminate the count-to-infinity problem.

Question 4

In the event that two bridges have been assigned the same bridge ID and are both eligible to be the root bridge, which of the following fields is used as a "tie-breaker" to determine the root bridge?

- ○ a. Port name
- ○ b. Port ID
- ○ c. Port state
- ○ d. Port cost

Question 5

Which connectivity device can be used to establish VLANs at both the Data Link and Network layers?

- ○ a. Repeater
- ○ b. Active hub
- ○ c. Switch
- ○ d. Router

Question 6

Which of the following protocols cannot be routed through an internetwork? [Choose the two best answers]

❑ a. IPX

❑ b. NetBEUI

❑ c. IP

❑ d. LAT

Question 7

Which of the following would not be considered a step used in building a SAP services table? [Choose the two best answers]

❑ a. A router broadcasts a service request.

❑ b. A server queries the SNMP manager for the most current MIB updates.

❑ c. Routers and servers respond to service queries from other SAP devices.

❑ d. Routers and servers respond to MIB updates by updating their services tables.

❑ e. SAP devices fill in their services tables with information from SAP service responses.

Question 8

What is the upper limit to the number of hostnames allowed in a single host table?

○ a. Less than 255.

○ b. No more than 255 per host table, excluding aliases.

○ c. No more than 255 per host table, including aliases.

○ d. The number of hostnames per table is unlimited.

Question 9

Which of the following series of numbers and/or letters is reserved and cannot be used when assigning IPX network addresses?

○ a. FFFFFFFE

○ b. 11111111

○ c. BA5EBA11

○ d. EEEEEEEE

Question 10

Which of the following events could trigger both a hosts table lookup and the DNS name-to-address resolution process?

○ a. A name server searches its local database to start the process.

○ b. A client requests an IP address from a name server in the local domain.

○ c. A user addresses a network communication with a hostname instead of an IP address.

○ d. A client requests an IP address from the root domain server in the local domain.

Question 11

What happens when the system encounters a pound sign when reading a line in a host table?

○ a. Anything else on that line is ignored and the system resumes reading at the start of the next line.

○ b. The command following the pound sign is executed.

○ c. The system jumps to the host table number that follows the pound sign.

○ d. Names to the right of the pound sign are treated as aliases.

Question 12

Which WAN protocol is designed to overcome the shortcomings
of SLIP and includes the following features:

➤ Dynamic IP addressing

➤ Login authentication

➤ Multiple, concurrent protocol support

➤ Error control

○ a. X.25

○ b. ATM

○ c. PPP

○ d. Frame relay

Question 13

Which of the following describes the function of the IN-ADDR.ARPA
zone type?

○ a. Resolves names to IP addresses

○ b. Resolves IP addresses to names

○ c. Resolves domain names to IPv6 IP addresses

○ d. None of the above

Question 14

Which of the following IP addresses could be assigned on a Class
C network? [Choose the two best answers]

❑ a. 11010010.00101101.00111010.11011110

❑ b. 206.77.77.31

❑ c. 10111111.11111011.10101100.11110001

❑ d. 129.33.33.61

❑ e. 11110001.10011011.10101100.11110001

Question 15

Which of the following IP addresses might you find on a private network that's connected to the Internet? [Choose the two best answers]

❏ a. 10.245.200.11

❏ b. 206.77.77.31

❏ c. 172.32.0.1

❏ d. 192.168.170.33

Question 16

Which of the following types of routers is used to connect a stub area to the backbone?

○ a. AS

○ b. RIP II

○ c. ASBR

○ d. ABR

Question 17

Which of the following features are associated with X.500 Directory Services? [Choose the three best answers]

❏ a. Scalability

❏ b. Hierarchical structure

❏ c. Synchronization

❏ d. Replication

Question 18

Which of the following X.500 protocols is specifically targeted at simple management and browser applications, and is used when simple read/write interactive access to the directory is required?

- ○ a. Directory Access Protocol (DAP)
- ○ b. Lightweight Directory Access Protocol (LDAP)
- ○ c. Connectionless Lightweight Directory Access Protocol (CLDAP)
- ○ d. Heavyweight Directory Access Protocol (HDAP)

Question 19

Data encryption and decryption only occur at which layer of the OSI model?

- ○ a. Transport layer
- ○ b. Session layer
- ○ c. Presentation layer
- ○ d. Application layer

Question 20

Which of the following connectivity devices inserts its hardware address in the source address fields of the Data Link header for every frame it transmits?

- ○ a. Router
- ○ b. Network board
- ○ c. Active hub
- ○ d. Repeater

Question 21

When it isn't provided by lower-layer protocols, which OSI layer is commonly depended on to provide end-to-end control and error checking?

O a. Session layer

O b. Presentation layer

O c. Transport layer

O d. Physical layer

Question 22

At which of the following layers of the OSI model do ISDN processes operate? [Choose the three best answers]

❑ a. Physical

❑ b. Data Link

❑ c. Network

❑ d. Session

❑ e. Presentation

Question 23

During the source route discovery process, how does an intermediate bridge handle a hello frame?

O a. It appends its address to the current route information and forwards this to all ports except the one on which the hello frame was received.

O b. It forwards the frame to the destination network port only.

O c. It returns the frame to the source device after verifying the end router hardware address.

O d. It records the current route information in its bridge table so when the response packet from the destination device arrives, it can update the packet appropriately for future forwarding.

Question 24

The Process/Application layer protocol that enables you to monitor a network from a single station called an _____ manager is

_____.

○ a. ICMP

○ b. MIB

○ c. SMTP

○ d. SNMP

Question 25

On an IP network that uses RIP, what would be the effect of manually assigning a cost metric of 16 to a particular route?

○ a. The route would be selected only as a last resort.

○ b. Only OSPF routers could use the route.

○ c. The route would be considered unreachable.

○ d. The router would reset the hop count to the proper value
in 30 seconds or less.

Question 26

You want to connect your corporate IP network to the Internet.
The company intranet currently includes 7 networks with between
60 and 150 users on each network. You have a registered Class B
IP address. Which of the following subnet masks will support
enough subnets to meet your current network needs? [Choose
the three best answers]

❑ a. 11111111.11111111.11111111.00000000

❑ b. 255.255.192.0

❑ c. 255.255.240.0

❑ d. 255.255.248.0

Question 27

A stub area with 5 regular OSPF routers is connected to a back-bone that has 11 regular OSPF routers. How many routers exchange LSUs in the stub area?

○ a. 5

○ b. 6

○ c. 16

○ d. 17

Question 28

Which of the following TCP/IP protocols provide address resolution? [Choose the three best answers]

❑ a. UDP

❑ b. ARP

❑ c. BOOTP

❑ d. RARP

❑ e. NDS

Question 29

Which of the following IP addresses is used to refer to the default route?

○ a. 0.0.225.225

○ b. 0.0.0.0

○ c. 225.225.225.225

○ d. 225.225.0.0

Question 30

Which of the following statements are true of domain names?
[Choose the three best answers]

☐ a. Domain names are case-sensitive.

☐ b. A domain name can be up to 255 characters long.

☐ c. The full name for any domain is constructed by listing all
the labels in the path, from the domain to the root.

☐ d. A period is used between the labels in the domain name.

Question 31

Which of the following does not represent an element of IPX
addressing?

○ a. Node address

○ b. Socket number

○ c. Internal network address

○ d. Virtual circuit ID

Question 32

Which aspect of connection services would be associated with
frames that do not contain sequence numbers?

○ a. Connectionless

○ b. Nonreliable

○ c. Connection oriented

○ d. Reliable

Question 33

On a TCP/IP network, which table is maintained on each system to map IP addresses to hardware addresses?

○ a. Host table

○ b. ARP table

○ c. DNS table

○ d. RARP table

Question 34

Which of the following statements is true about an OSPF router that has a priority of zero?

○ a. The router is functioning as a backup designated router (BDR).

○ b. The router is ensured of becoming the designated router (DR) if a full-state change occurs.

○ c. The router will advertise all routes as unreachable.

○ d. The router is not eligible to become the BDR.

Question 35

Which two types of packets are used by RIP?

○ a. Broadcast and response

○ b. Request and respond

○ c. Query and response

○ d. Query and repeat

Question 36

Which of the following routing protocols is an enhancement of EGP, and was designed to give administrators more control over their routing environments and better scalability in large internetworks?

○ a. OSPF

○ b. ASBR

○ c. BGP

○ d. RIP II

Question 37

When do IPX routers using RIP broadcast that all routes are unreachable?

○ a. When a router boots and initializes

○ b. When poison reverse is enabled at the same time that split horizon is enabled

○ c. When a router detects that its neighbor is down

○ d. When a router is downed

Question 38

What is the object hierarchy, starting at the [Root], for an X.500 directory DIT?

○ a. Common Name, Country, Organization, Organization Unit, [Root]

○ b. [Root], Organization Unit, Country, Organization, Common Name

○ c. Common Name, Organization Unit, Organization, Country, [Root]

○ d. [Root], Country, Organization, Organization Unit, Common Name

Question 39

Which 802.x standard uses a data transfer technology called Distributed Queue Dual Bus (DQDB) that allows both synchronous and asynchronous traffic for supporting voice, video, and data transmissions?

○ a. 802.3

○ b. 802.5

○ c. 802.6

○ d. 802.11

Question 40

What does the IEEE 802.9 standard define?

○ a. A token-passing bus logical topology

○ b. Standards for wireless LAN implementations, such as spread-spectrum and infrared devices

○ c. A standard for securely exchanging data using encryption mechanisms

○ d. Isochronous Ethernet (also known as *IsoEnet*), focusing on the integration of voice transmissions with data transmissions to support both sporadic and patterned traffic

Question 41

Which IEEE 802.3 standard supports a data rate of 10Mbps on 50 ohm coaxial cable for distances up to 500 meters?

○ a. 10Base2

○ b. 10Base5

○ c. 1Base5

○ d. 10BaseT

Question 42

A completed application template requesting a registered domain name under the country code domain for Italy should be sent to which of the following addresses?

○ a. hostmaster@internic.net

○ b. iana@iana.org

○ c. NIC.MASTER.SP

○ d. NIC.MASTER.IT

Question 43

Which physical topology has every device connected to every other device on the network using point-to-point connections?

○ a. Cellular

○ b. Ring

○ c. Mesh

○ d. Bus

Question 44

Which of the following statements concerning the relationships between layer processes is true?

○ a. Network layer processes depend on Transport layer processes for their operation.

○ b. Network layer processes handle service requests made by the Data Link layer.

○ c. Transport layer processes request Network layer services.

○ d. Transport layer processes provide services to the Network layer.

Question 45

Which of the following connectivity devices is used to extend a network on a purely mechanical basis?

○ a. Active hub

○ b. Router

○ c. Switch

○ d. Gateway

Question 46

Bridge latency is less when using bridges that support which of the following modes?

○ a. Blocking mode

○ b. Forwarding mode

○ c. Store-and-forward mode

○ d. Cut-through mode

Question 47

Load balancing can be used with which of the following routing algorithms? [Choose the two best answers]

❑ a. Source routing

❑ b. Cut-through

❑ c. Link state

❑ d. Distance vector

Question 48

Which of the following represents an advantage of a router over a switch?

○ a. Less configuration is required.

○ b. The ability to quickly adapt to network configuration changes.

○ c. More cost effective in terms of packets forwarded per second.

○ d. Operates independent of upper-layer protocols, thus allowing nonroutable protocols to be forwarded.

Question 49

Which of the following IP addresses is the dotted decimal equivalent of 11001101.01001011.10100011.00000100?

○ a. 206.75.175.5

○ b. 206.77.177.41

○ c. 217.75.175.5

○ d. 128.33.33.61

○ e. 205.75.163.4

Question 50

Which routing protocol defines a pseudonode to which all other routers on the network connect?

○ a. OSPF

○ b. IPX

○ c. NLSP

○ d. RIP

Question 51

Which of the following network classes is reserved for multicast addresses only?

○ a. Class A

○ b. Class B

○ c. Class C

○ d. Class D

○ e. Class E

Question 52

Which of the following TCP/IP protocols operate at the Internet layer of the DoD model and, therefore, map to the Network layer of the OSI model? [Choose the three best answers]

❑ a. ICMP

❑ b. HTTP

❑ c. FTP

❑ d. IP

❑ e. ARP

Question 53

Which TCP/IP protocol handles fragmentation and reassembly of transport protocol data units (TPDUs) when necessary, using sequence numbers to ensure proper reassembly at the destination?

○ a. TCP

○ b. IP

○ c. SMTP

○ d. FTP

Question 54

Which of the following protocols allows routers to communicate within an autonomous system?

○ a. AS

○ b. IGP

○ c. ASRP

○ d. EGP

Question 55

Under what condition does an OSPF router send an LSU after a 30-minute hold-down interval?

○ a. If there are no network updates.

○ b. If there are network updates to report.

○ c. The default "hello" time is over 30 minutes.

○ d. Never; all updates are within 30 seconds.

Question 56

Which of the following statements correctly describe an advantage of link-state routing? [Choose the three best answers]

❑ a. Faster convergence than distance vector routing networks.

❑ b. Easier implementation than distance vector routing networks.

❑ c. Utilizes first-hand information.

❑ d. Routing status of the network can be obtained by querying a single router.

Question 57

Which of the following fields will typically change as a packet is routed through an internetwork? [Choose the two best answers]

❏ a. The source hardware address in the Data Link header

❏ b. The network source address in the Network header

❏ c. The destination service port in the LLC sublayer information of the Data Link header

❏ d. The destination hardware address in the Data Link header

Question 58

Some protocols are considered to be technically nonroutable. Which of the following statements best describes the most common reason why a protocol would be considered nonroutable?

○ a. It does not contain the appropriate Data Link layer information required by routers.

○ b. It uses advanced Transport layer services to move across the Internet and avoids the routing overhead required by the more primitive networking protocols.

○ c. It defines Physical layer network addresses for internal routing.

○ d. It does not specify the Network layer addresses required by routers.

Question 59

To what does the IP address 0.0.0.45 refer?

○ a. Node 45 on network 0.0.0

○ b. The multicast node 45 address

○ c. Any host on network 45

○ d. Node 45 on "this" network

Question 60

Which type of connection service would be associated with putting frames out on the media without first exchanging setup messages to determine whether the receiving end is ready?

O a. Connectionless

O b. Nonreliable

O c. Connection oriented

O d. Reliable

Question 61

Which of the following protocols defines the standard interface to packet-switched networks that's the most popular interface currently used for WANs?

O a. X.25

O b. ATM

O c. PPP

O d. Frame Relay

Question 62

Which connection device increases the total throughput of a LAN by keeping frames on the local segment local and filtering frames that belong on other LAN segments?

O a. Bridge

O b. Router

O c. Repeater

O d. Active hub

Question 63

Which term is applied to the situation in which data packets circle in an endless loop between two redundant bridges and are never correctly routed to their destinations?

○ a. Count-to-infinity

○ b. Split horizon

○ c. Bridging loop

○ d. Poison reverse

Question 64

To which address should BPDUs be addressed?

○ a. The hardware address of each individual bridge

○ b. A multicast address assigned to bridges

○ c. The network address of the bridge

○ d. A broadcast address used by all routers

Question 65

What is the most important performance benefit of token ring switches?

○ a. They are truly "plug and play."

○ b. They reduce collisions by isolating rings on their own ports.

○ c. They eliminate the campus-wide bottleneck caused by backbone rings.

○ d. They raise the backbone speed to 100Mbps.

Question 66

Some older WAN protocols provide connection-oriented services to compensate for the lack of reliability in the underlying media. At which layer of the OSI model do these services operate?

○ a. Network layer

○ b. Data Link layer

○ c. Transport layer

○ d. Physical layer

Question 67

Which Class E address is commonly used on networks?

○ a. 1110111.00000000.00000000.00000001

○ b. 255.255.255.255

○ c. 11.FF.FF.FE

○ d. Class E addresses are reserved and are not used on networks.

Question 68

Where is the authoritative database for a zone maintained?

○ a. In the zone hosts table

○ b. At **INTERNIC.NET**

○ c. On the master name server for the zone

○ d. In the hosts table in the MIB

Question 69

What is the process of downloading the authoritative database from the master name server to the replica name server called?

○ a. Zone transfer

○ b. Replication

○ c. Backup

○ d. Migration

Question 70

Which of the following represents a valid reason to subnet a network?

○ a. To use multiple media

○ b. To extend the network

○ c. To reduce congestion

○ d. To improve security

○ e. All of the above

Question 71

You have a Class C IP address. You need to subnet your network to support 15 subnets with no more than 10 hosts per subnet. Your routers support subnet zero. What is the least number of bits you can mask and still create the necessary number of subnets?

○ a. Two bits

○ b. Three bits

○ c. Four bits

○ d. A Class C IP address will not support this configuration.

Question 72

What is the minimum mask required to supernet enough Class C IP addresses to support 2,000 hosts on a single network?

○ a. 255.255.255.224

○ b. 255.255.240.0

○ c. 255.255.255.0 /21

○ d. 255.255.248.0

Question 73

Which routing process makes it possible to route to classless IP addresses between domains across the Internet?

○ a. RIP

○ b. CIDR

○ c. Source routing

○ d. None of the above

Question 74

Which of the following TCP/IP protocols maps to the Network Access layer of the DoD model?

○ a. ARP

○ b. ICMP

○ c. Ethernet

○ d. FDDI

○ e. None of the above

Question 75

Which of the following TCP/IP protocols works with IP to notify a ULP when a packet's time to live (TTL) has expired?

○ a. ICMP

○ b. ARP

○ c. SPX

○ d. LSU

○ e. None of the above

Question 76

Devices that can connect dissimilar systems are referred to as what?

○ a. Bridges

○ b. Switches

○ c. Routers

○ d. Gateways

Question 77

Which of the following types of commands are defined within the SNMP protocol?

○ a. **GetRequest**

○ b. **GetResponse**

○ c. **GetNextRequest**

○ d. **Trap**

○ e. Answers a and b only

○ f. Answers a, b, c, and d

Question 78

In which TCP/IP specification is an Anycast address defined?

○ a. IPv6

○ b. OSPF

○ c. DNS

○ d. RIP II

Question 79

Which service assigns and tracks IPX network addresses and organization names?

○ a. ARIN

○ b. InterNIC

○ c. The Novell Network Registry

○ d. DNS

Answer Key

1. a	21. c	41. b	61. a
2. d	22. a, b, c	42. b	62. a
3. a	23. a	43. c	63. c
4. b	24. d	44. c	64. b
5. c	25. c	45. a	65. c
6. b, d	26. a, c, d	46. d	66. b
7. b, d	27. b	47. c, d	67. b
8. d	28. b, c, d	48. b	68. c
9. a	29. b	49. e	69. a
10. c	30. b, c, d	50. c	70. e
11. a	31. d	51. d	71. c
12. c	32. b	52. a, d, e	72. d
13. b	33. b	53. b	73. b
14. a, b	34. d	54. b	74. e
15. a, d	35. b	55. b	75. a
16. d	36. c	56. a, c, d	76. d
17. a, c, d	37. d	57. a, d	77. f
18. b	38. d	58. d	78. a
19. c	39. c	59. d	79. c
20. b	40. d	60. a	

Question 1

The correct answer is a. In the X.500 structure, CN stands for *common name*. Answers b, c, and d are incorrect because none of the answers denotes an acronym in the X.500 directory structure.

Question 2

The correct answer is d. Because routers are Network layer devices, their operation is independent of the protocols operating at the Physical and Data Link layers. The Data Link and Physical layer protocols define processes that deal with network architecture issues. Answer a is incorrect because the split horizon algorithm is used by routers to reduce the time for convergence. Answer b is incorrect because it describes the function of a gateway—not a router. Answer c is incorrect because it describes a Data Link layer process and routers only operate at the Network layer.

Question 3

The correct answer is a. OSPF networks are not affected by the count-to-infinity problem. RIP networks can use either split horizon or poison reverse to reduce the effects of count-to-infinity, but they are not necessary on OSPF networks. Therefore, answers b and c are incorrect. Although the maximum cost of an OSPF route is 65,535, this is not a solution for count-to-infinity (in fact, a count-to-infinity will take considerably longer if infinity is 65,535 instead of 16). Therefore, answer d is incorrect.

Question 4

The correct answer is b. The port ID is used as the "tie-breaker" to determine which bridge will become the root bridge when two eligible bridges have the same bridge ID. Port name and port state are not fields included in the bridge protocol data unit (BPDU). Therefore, answers a and c are incorrect. The port cost, on the other hand, is used to determine which bridge will be the designated bridge. Therefore, answer d is incorrect.

Question 5

The correct answer is c. Depending on the type of switch used, VLANs can be established at either the Data Link or Network layer. Both repeaters and active hubs are Physical layer devices. Therefore, answers a and b are incorrect. Routers only function at the Network layer. Therefore, answer d is incorrect.

Question 6

The correct answers are b and d. NetBEUI and LAT are considered nonroutable protocols because they contain no Network layer addressing information. Both IPX and IP are routable protocols and do not have to be bridged to be sent through an internetwork. Therefore, answers a and c are incorrect.

Question 7

The correct answers are b and d. A SAP services table does not contain MIB information. Therefore, answers b and d would not be involved in building a SAP services table. Answers a, c, and e describe steps used in building a SAP services table and are therefore incorrect.

Question 8

The correct answer is d. The number of hostnames in a host table is unlimited (although very large host tables are impractical in most environments). Answers a, b, and c are incorrect because they specify an upper limit.

Question 9

The correct answer is a. The numbers and letters 00000000, FFFFFFFE, and FFFFFFFF are reserved and cannot be used when assigning IPX network addresses. The numbers in answers b, c, and d all fall within the valid range of numbers that can be used for addressing IPX networks. Therefore, answers b, c, and d are incorrect.

Question 10

The correct answer is c. If a user addresses a network communication with a hostname instead of an IP address, the local hosts table (if it exists) will be searched. If the name-to-address resolution can't be handled locally, clients will usually request IP addresses from name servers in their local domain. Answer a is incorrect because the name server searches its database after receiving a request for name resolution and no hosts table is involved. Answer b is incorrect because no hosts table is involved in the name-to-address resolution. Answer d is incorrect because root domain servers do not reside in local domains.

Question 11

The correct answer is a. When the system encounters a pound sign on a line in a hosts table, it ignores anything else on the line and moves to the start of the next line. Answers b, c, and d are all incorrect because the system would ignore anything else on the line.

Question 12

The correct answer is c. The Point-to-Point Protocol (PPP) includes the features in the bulleted list and is specifically designed to address the shortcomings of SLIP. Therefore, answers a, b, and d are incorrect.

Question 13

The correct answer is b. An IP address in an IN-ADDR.ARPA zone has the dotted octet order reversed and is used to resolve IP addresses to names. Standard DNS zones resolve names to IP addresses. Therefore, answer a is incorrect. IP6.INT zones resolve domain names to IPv6 IP addresses. Therefore, answer c is incorrect. Answer d is incorrect because answer b is correct.

Question 14

The correct answers are a and b. The value of the first byte of the IP address on a Class C network is in the range 192 to 223, and the first zero in the byte is in the third position from the left (110). In answer c, the first zero in the first byte is in the second position. Therefore, answer c is incorrect. In answers d and e, the first bytes are outside of the range 192 to 223. Therefore, answers d and e are incorrect.

Question 15

The correct answers are a and d. InterNIC has reserved blocks of IP addresses for private networks in the following ranges:

➤ 10.0.0.0 to 10.255.255.255

➤ 172.16.0.0 to 172.31.255.255

➤ 192.168.0.0 to 192.168.255.255

Answers a and d have addresses that fall within one of these ranges. The addresses in answers b and c are not in the range of any of the reserved blocks and are therefore incorrect. The addresses in the reserved ranges are ignored by

Internet routers, making it possible for the private networks using these numbers to connect to the Internet.

Question 16

The correct answer is d. An area border router (ABR) is used to connect transit areas and stub areas to the backbone area. Autonomous systems (AS) are connected to other autonomous systems with autonomous system border routers (ASBR). Therefore, answers a and c are incorrect. RIP II is a vector routing protocol that does not support areas. Therefore, answer b is incorrect.

Question 17

The correct answers are a, c, and d. X.500 Directory Services defines a distributed (scalable), replicated database that's synchronized to ensure accuracy across all replicas. Answer b is incorrect because the hierarchical structure of the directory is not considered a feature.

Question 18

The correct answer is b. LDAP specifically targets simple management and browser applications and is designed for use when simple read/write interactive access to the directory is required. DAP supports read, search, and modify access. Therefore, answer a is incorrect. CLDAP is a protocol derived from LDAP that only allows read activity on an X.500 directory. Therefore, answer c is incorrect. There's no HDAP defined within X.500 Directory Services. Therefore, answer d is incorrect.

Question 19

The correct answer is c. Data transformation occurs at the Presentation layer only. Because answer c is correct, answers a, b, and d are incorrect.

Question 20

The correct answer is b. A network board is a Data Link layer device that inserts its hardware address in the source address fields of the Data Link header for every frame it transmits. A router is a Network layer device and as such does not have access to Data Link headers. Therefore, answer a is incorrect. Active hubs and repeaters operate at the Physical layer and deal with a bit stream that isn't organized into logical frames. Therefore, answers c and d are incorrect.

Question 21

The correct answer is c. The Transport layer processes perform tasks associated with ensuring reliability. Processes above the Transport layer assume that reliability is handled at the lower layers. Therefore, answers a and b are incorrect. Layers below the Transport layer are generally characterized as "connectionless" and "unreliable." Therefore, answer d is incorrect.

Question 22

The correct answers are a, b, and c. ISDN includes processes that operate at the Physical, Data Link, and Network layers. ISDN doesn't include Session or Presentation layer processes. Therefore, answers d and e are incorrect.

Question 23

The correct answer is a. During route discovery, each intermediate bridge appends its own address to the hello frame to build a complete list of bridges between the source and destination devices, and then forwards the frame to all segments except the one on which the frame was received. The processes described in answers b, c, and d are not part of the source route discovery process and are therefore incorrect.

Question 24

The correct answer is d. The Simple Network Management Protocol (SNMP) allows you to monitor a network from a single workstation called an SNMP manager. Internet Control Message Protocol (ICMP) works with IP at the Internet layer. Therefore, answer a is incorrect. The Management Information Base (MIB) is part of the SNMP protocol, but does not enable the management feature. Therefore, answer b is incorrect. Simple Mail Transfer Protocol (SMTP) is the Process/Application layer protocol that serves as the foundation for email applications. Therefore, answer c is incorrect.

Question 25

The correct answer is c. IP RIP uses a route cost of 16 to designate an unreachable network. An unreachable route is not selected as a route to a network. Therefore, answer a is incorrect. OSPF is not part of RIP. Therefore, answer b is incorrect. A manually assigned cost metric overrides hop count information gathered from RIP broadcasts. Therefore, answer d is incorrect.

Question 26

The correct answers are a, c, and d. Using the general formula ($2^n - 2$ = number of subnets) to calculate the number of networks possible by borrowing bits from the host portion of the IP address makes answers a, c, and d correct. They provide for 254, 14, and 30 subnets, respectively. Only answer b (with two possible subnets) fails to provide at least seven possible subnets. Therefore, answer b is incorrect.

Question 27

The correct answer is b. A stub area is connected to the backbone by only one router, an ABR. Because all routers in an area exchange LSUs, the five regular routers and the ABR in the stub area exchange LSUs. Answer a does not include the ABR router and is therefore incorrect. Answers c and d are incorrect because regular routers in different areas do not exchange LSUs.

Question 28

The correct answers are b, c, and d. ARP provides IP-address-to-hardware-address resolution, and BOOTP and RARP provide hardware-address-to-IP-address resolution. UDP is a transport protocol. Therefore, answer a is incorrect. Novell Directory Services (NDS) is not part of the TCP/IP protocol suite. Therefore, answer e is incorrect.

Question 29

The correct answer is b. Network 0.0.0.0 is used to refer to the default route to simplify IP routing tables. The address 0.0.225.225 refers to all hosts on "this" network. Therefore, answer a is incorrect. The address 255.225.255.255 refers to "all" hosts. Therefore, answer c is incorrect. The address 225.225.0.0 refers to the network itself. Therefore, answer d is incorrect.

Question 30

The correct answers are b, c, and d. Each of these statements is true of domain names. Answer a is incorrect because domain names are not case-sensitive.

Question 31

The correct answer is d. The virtual circuit ID is not an IPX addressing element. IPX addressing elements include the network address, node address, socket number, and internal network address. Therefore, answers a, b, and c are incorrect.

Question 32

The correct answer is b. Nonreliable means that frames do not contain the reliability features usually associated with sequence numbers. The reliability is assumed to be handled by processes operating in upper layers. Therefore, answer b is correct and d is incorrect. Connectionless and connection oriented refer to whether messages are exchanged at the beginning of a session. Therefore, answers a and c are incorrect.

Question 33

The correct answer is b. An ARP table is maintained by each system on a TCP/IP network to map IP addresses to hardware addresses. Host tables are used for name-to-address resolution. Therefore, answer a is incorrect. DNS information is not maintained on local systems. Therefore, answer c is incorrect. RARP is used to resolve hardware addresses to IP addresses for diskless workstations. Therefore, answer d is incorrect.

Question 34

The correct answer is d. An OSPF router that has a priority of zero is not eligible to become the DR or BDR; in other respects, however, it functions as any other OSPF router. Therefore, answer d is correct and answers a and b are incorrect. OSPF routers do not advertise routes as unreachable. Therefore, answer c is incorrect.

Question 35

The correct answer is b. The request and respond packet types are identical except for the Packet Type field, which indicates either the request or respond type. Broadcast, response, query, and repeat are not valid RIP packet type names. Therefore, answers a, c, and d are incorrect.

Question 36

The correct answer is c. The Border Gateway Protocol (BGP) is an enhancement of EGP. It's one of several new interdomain routing protocols designed to give administrators more control and better scalability in large internetworks.

OSPF and RIP II are interior gateway protocols. Therefore, answers a and d are incorrect. An ASBR is a router type used to connect autonomous systems using either EGP or BGP. Therefore, answer b is incorrect.

Question 37

The correct answer is d. When a router is downed, it broadcasts a message that all routes through it are unreachable. Answer b is incorrect because poison reverse and split horizon cannot be enabled concurrently (poison reverse is actually "split horizon *with* poison reverse"). Routers do not broadcast a metric of 16 for all routes (meaning all routes are unreachable) when they join a network or when they detect that a neighboring router is down. Therefore, answers a and c are incorrect.

Question 38

The correct answer is d. Starting at [Root], the proper hierarchical sequence is [Root], Country, Organization, Organization Unit, and then Common Name. The X.500 directory is an inverted tree; therefore, [Root] is at the beginning of the structure. Answer b is incorrect because the Country object should be right after the [Root] object. Answers a and c are incorrect because they position [Root] at the bottom of the tree.

Question 39

The correct answer is c. The 802.6 standard defines Distributed Queue Dual Bus (DQDB), which allows both synchronous and asynchronous traffic for supporting voice, video, and data transmissions. The 802.3 standard describes the CSMA/CD protocol. Therefore, answer a is incorrect. The 802.5 standard uses a token passing sequentially from one connected node to another at speeds of 1, 4, or 16Mbps. Therefore, answer b is incorrect. The 802.11 standard defines wireless LAN implementations such as spread-spectrum and infrared devices. Therefore, answer d is incorrect.

Question 40

The correct answer is d. Isochronous Ethernet is defined by the IEEE 802.9 standard. A token-passing bus logical topology is defined by IEEE 802.4. Therefore, answer a is incorrect. The standards for wireless LAN implementations, such as spread-spectrum and infrared devices, are defined by IEEE 802.11. Therefore, answer b is incorrect. A standard for securely exchanging data using encryption mechanisms is defined by IEEE 802.10. Therefore, answer c is incorrect.

Question 41

The correct answer is b. The 10Base5 802.3 standard allows a 10Mbps data rate over a maximum distance of 500 meters using 50 ohm coaxial cable. The distance limit for 10Base2 is 185 meters. Therefore, answer a is incorrect. 1Base5 is limited to a data rate of 1Mbps. Therefore, answer c is incorrect. 10BaseT is for twisted-pair media. Therefore, answer d is incorrect.

Question 42

The correct answer is b. Requests for registered domain names outside the U.S. are submitted to **iana@iana.org**. Only requests for registered domain names inside the U.S. are submitted to **hostmaster@internic.net**. Therefore, answer a is incorrect. Answers c and d are not valid addresses and are therefore incorrect.

Question 43

The correct answer is c. In a mesh topology, every device is directly connected to every other device via a point-to-point connection. Both the cellular and bus topologies use multipoint connections. Therefore, answers a and d are incorrect. A ring topology uses point-to-point connections to attach a device to the devices on either side, not to every other device. Therefore, answer b is incorrect.

Question 44

The correct answer is c. The relationship between layers requires that the processes in a layer request services from the layer below and provide services to the layer(s) above. The statement in answer c supports this relationship. The Network layer is below the Transport layer; it does not request services from the layer above. Therefore, answer a is incorrect. The Network layer is above the Data Link layer; it does not provide services to the layer below. Therefore, answer b is incorrect. The Transport layer is above the Network layer; it does not provide services to the layer below. Therefore, answer d is incorrect.

Question 45

The correct answer is a. Active hubs operate at the Physical layer on a purely mechanical basis. Routers, switches, and gateways are capable of recognizing addresses and require some intelligence. Therefore, answers b, c, and d are incorrect.

Question 46

The correct answer is d. A bridge operating in cut-through mode forwards a frame once the header is read without waiting for the entire frame to arrive. This greatly reduces bridge latency. The blocking and forwarding states have no effect on latency. Therefore, answers a and b are incorrect. The bridge latency associated with store-and-forward mode is greater than that of cut-through mode. Therefore, answer c is incorrect.

Question 47

The correct answers are c and d. Both link-state routing and distance vector algorithms can be configured to support load balancing (although it's a bit easier to configure on link-state routers). Source routing and cut-through are bridging and switching operations, respectively; they are not routing operations. Therefore, answers a and b are incorrect.

Question 48

The correct answer is b. Routers are much faster in situations that require reconfiguration and are able to continue forwarding packets while the reconfiguration takes place. This is not the case for bridges and switches. All other statements represent advantages of switches over routers. Therefore, answers a, c, and d are incorrect.

Question 49

The correct answer is e. Within each octet, adding the decimal values of the place positions occupied by 1 yields the values 205, 75, 163, and 4 for the octets. Only answer e has these decimal values for the octets. Therefore, answers a, b, c, and d are incorrect.

Question 50

The correct answer is c. The designated router in the NLSP protocol creates a pseudonode to which all other routers on the network attach. OSPF, IPX, and RIP do not define a pseudonode. Therefore, answers a, b, and d are incorrect.

Question 51

The correct answer is d. Class D networks are reserved for multicast addresses. Class A, B, and C networks contain assignable addresses, and Class E networks are reserved for future and experimental use as well as for broadcasts. Therefore, answers a, b, c, and e are incorrect.

Question 52

The correct answers are a, d, and e. ICMP, IP, and ARP are all DoD Internet layer protocols that can be mapped to the Network layer of the OSI model. Answers b and c are incorrect because both HTTP and FTP operate at the Process/Application layer of the DoD model.

Question 53

The correct answer is b. IP can handle fragmentation and reassembly of TPDUs when necessary, although it's thought of primarily as the connectionless, unreliable transport for TCP. Answer a is incorrect because TPDUs are built and delivered to IP by TCP. Answer c is incorrect because SMTP is for mail information. Answer d is incorrect because FTP operates at the upper layers of the OSI model to handle file transfers.

Question 54

The correct answer is b. An interior gateway protocol, such as RIP or OSPF, allows routers in an autonomous system (AS) to communicate. An AS is a logical component of a hierarchical routing scheme (not a protocol) and does not allow or disallow communication. Therefore, answer a is incorrect. ASRP is not defined within the TCP/IP suite. Therefore, answer c is incorrect. An exterior gateway protocol, such as EGP or BGP, is used to communicate between autonomous systems. Therefore, answer d is incorrect.

Question 55

The correct answer is b. Routers using OSPF send LSUs every 30 minutes if there are changes to the network. OSPF routers will periodically "flood" LSUs for the entries for which they're responsible if no network changes have occurred. Therefore, answer a is incorrect. The default "hello" time interval is 10 seconds. Therefore, answer c is incorrect. OSPF routers do not send updates every 30 seconds (the default for IP RIP is 30 seconds). Therefore, answer d is incorrect.

Question 56

The correct answers are a, c, and d. Faster convergence, first-hand information, and ease of obtaining network status are all advantages of link-state routing networks. Ease of implementation is the biggest advantage of a distance vector routing network. Therefore, answer b is incorrect.

Question 57

The correct answers are a and d. The physical source and destination fields typically change to reflect the hardware addresses of the routers involved in moving a packet across the internetwork. The network and service port addresses are defined by protocols at the Network layer and above, and they would not be changed to reflect changes in the underlying hardware as a packet moves across the internetwork. Therefore, answers b and c are incorrect.

Question 58

The correct answer is d. Nonroutable protocols do not contain Network layer information, which means that routers cannot interpret their addresses. Routers are not concerned with Data Link layer information. Therefore, answer a is incorrect. Transport layer protocols require the services of a routing protocol to move data across an internetwork. Therefore, answer b is incorrect. Addresses are not definable at the Physical layer because data is in the form of a raw bit stream. Therefore, answer c is incorrect.

Question 59

The correct answer is d. An IP address with all network bits set to 0 refers to "this" (or the local) network. A node ID would represent that node on the local network. Therefore, answers a, b, and c are incorrect.

Question 60

The correct answer is a. Connectionless refers to a service that does not exchange messages at the beginning of a session to ensure that the receiver is available and ready to receive frames. Nonreliable refers to frames that do not contain sequence numbers. Therefore, answer b is incorrect. Connection oriented refers to a service that first exchanges messages to be sure the receiver is available and ready. Therefore, answer c is incorrect. Reliable refers to frames that contain sequence numbers. Therefore, answer d is incorrect.

Question 61

The correct answer is a. X.25 provides the standard interface to packet-switched networks that's the most widely used interface for WANs. ATM, PPP, and Frame Relay are all WAN protocols, but none of them defines a standard interface to packet-switched networks. Therefore, answers b, c, and d are incorrect.

Question 62

The correct answer is a. Bridges build tables that map hardware addresses to their bridge ports, which allows them to isolate local traffic on individual segments and increase total throughput on a LAN. Routers do not filter frames between segments on a network. Therefore, answer b is incorrect. Repeaters and active hubs work on a purely mechanical level and are unable to perform filtering functions. Therefore, answers c and d are incorrect.

Question 63

The correct answer is c. When the spanning tree protocol is not used, redundant bridges are susceptible to bridging loops in which data packets circle in an endless loop between two bridges. Answers a, b, and d are all associated with the distance vector routing algorithm. Therefore, answers a, b, and d are incorrect.

Question 64

The correct answer is b. Bridges use BPDUs to communicate. To conform to IEEE specifications, BPDUs should be addressed to a multicast address assigned to bridges. Because any BPDU should be able to be read by any bridge, the bridge hardware address shouldn't be specified. Therefore, answer a is incorrect. Bridges cannot interpret Network layer information. Therefore, answers c and d are incorrect.

Question 65

The correct answer is c. The switch allows each ring to be no more than one hop from any other ring, thus allowing full 16Mbps connections between any two rings at any time. Although token ring switches are "plug and play," this is not a key performance benefit. Therefore, answer a is incorrect. Token-passing media access schemes do not experience collisions. Therefore, answer b is incorrect. Even full-duplex token ring speed cannot exceed 32Mbps. Therefore, answer d is incorrect.

Question 66

The correct answer is b. Although most LAN protocols at the Data Link layer are connectionless, the older WAN protocols and some of the newer WAN protocols are connection oriented and reliable. Connection-oriented services compensating for media unreliability do not operate at the Network, Transport, or Physical layer. Therefore, answers a, c, and d are incorrect.

Question 67

The correct answer is b. The Class E address 255.255.255.255 is used for broadcasts to address all hosts. Answers a and c do not show Class E addresses and are therefore incorrect. Answer d is incorrect because answer b is correct.

Question 68

The correct answer is c. The master name server maintains the names and IP addresses of all hosts in a zone. The information is called the *authoritative database* for the zone. There is no zone hosts table, nor is there a hosts table in the MIB. Therefore, answers a and d are incorrect. The InterNIC has no responsibility for maintaining the authoritative databases for individual zones. Therefore, answer b is incorrect.

Question 69

The correct answer is a. In a zone transfer, a copy of the authoritative database is downloaded to the replica name server. Answers b, c, and d refer to different file management processes and are therefore incorrect.

Question 70

The correct answer is e. All of the reasons listed in answers a, b, c, and d are valid reasons to subnet a large network into smaller subnetworks.

Question 71

The correct answer is c. Masking 4 bits allows 15 subnets ($2^4 - 1 = 15$) with 14 hosts per subnet. Masking 2 bits allows 3 subnets, and masking 3 bits allows 7 subnets. Therefore, answers a and b are incorrect. Answer d is incorrect because answer c is correct.

Question 72

The correct answer is d. Borrowing 3 bits from the default mask of 255.255.255.0 leaves 5 bits in the third octet masked to give a supernet mask of 255.255.248.0. This mask allows up to 2,048 hosts on a single network by combining 8 contiguous Class C addresses. Answer b provides for more than the needed hosts (up to 4,096) but requires 16 contiguous Class C addresses. Therefore, answer b is incorrect. Answers a and c do not represent masks for supernetting. Therefore, answers a and c are incorrect.

Question 73

The correct answer is b. Classless InterDomain Routing (CIDR) allows blocks of contiguous IP addresses representing multiple Class C addresses to be advertised as a single address for routers to forward packets to. RIP does not support classless interdomain routing. Therefore, answer a is incorrect. Source routing is a bridging protocol. Therefore, answer c is incorrect. Answer d is incorrect because answer b is correct.

Question 74

The correct answer is e. The TCP/IP protocol suite does not include processes that operate below the Internet layer of the DoD model. Therefore, answers a, b, c, and d are incorrect.

Question 75

The correct answer is a. The Internet Control Message Protocol (ICMP) works with IP to provide network error and control information to upper-layer protocols such as TCP. ARP is concerned with address resolution. Therefore, answer b is correct. SPX is not a TCP/IP protocol. Therefore, answer c is incorrect. LSUs are link-state routing update packets. Therefore, answer d is incorrect. Because answer a is correct, answer e is incorrect.

Question 76

The correct answer is d. Gateways are devices that can be used to connect dissimilar systems. Bridges and switches are used to connect segments on a network. Therefore, answers a and b are incorrect. Routers are used to connect networks to networks. Therefore, answer c is incorrect.

Question 77

The correct answer is f. Only five types of commands are defined within the SNMP protocol. (The type of command not listed as an answer is **SetRequest**.) All the types of commands listed in answers a through d are defined within SNMP. Therefore, answer e is incorrect.

Question 78

The correct answer is a. The newest version of IP specifies an Anycast address, which is defined to address a set of nodes, where a packet can be delivered to any one of the nodes. The Anycast address is new and is not defined in any of the existing TCP/IP protocols. Therefore, answers b, c, and d, which are all existing TCP/IP protocols, are incorrect.

Question 79

The correct answer is c. The Novell Network Registry ensures that IPX network numbers are unique, much like the registration of IP addresses ensures their uniqueness. ARIN, InterNIC, and DNS are all associated with IP addressing and have nothing to do with IPX network address registration. Therefore, answers a, b, and d are incorrect.

Glossary

active hub—A Network layer connectivity device used to amplify transmission signals and connect additional nodes and network segments to a network.

alias—A name that can be used in place of a hostname to reference the same IP address that the hostname references. In a hosts table, an alias is listed on the same line with, and to the right of, the hostname.

American National Standards Institute (ANSI) standard—A standard recognized by the American National Standards Institute. ANSI is the U.S. standards body responsible for many current terminal and data communications standards. It represents the U.S. on the Consultative Committee for International Telegraphy and Telephony (CCITT) and the International Standards Organization (ISO).

American Registry for Internet Numbers (ARIN)—A nonprofit organization established to administer IP address assignments handled by the InterNIC.

American Standard Code for Information Interchange (ASCII)—A seven-bit character code commonly used in local area networks (LANs) for interchanging data between communicating devices. ASCII is recognized as a U.S. standard.

amplifier—A Network layer connectivity device used to boost analog signals.

Application layer—The top layer of the Open Standards Interconnection (OSI) model. The Application layer serves as the user interface to network applications and services, such as file transfer and print services.

area border router (ABR)—A router that connects an Open Shortest Path First (OSPF) area to the backbone area.

Asynchronous Transfer Mode (ATM)—A packet-switched networking architecture based on Broadband Integrated Services Digital Network (B-ISDN) technology. ATM provides connection-oriented nonreliable service over virtual circuits using fixed-length (53 byte) packets called *cells*.

ATM Adaptation Layer (AAL)—A functional grouping of the Asynchronous Transfer Mode (ATM) processes responsible for converting information to cells and determining data stream requirements. Processes in this functional group map to the Network layer of the OSI model.

attenuation—The reduction in the strength of an electrical signal over distance.

attribute—A unique value or property associated with an individual terminating object in an X.500 directory structure.

authoritative database—A database maintained on the master name server for a DNS zone. The database includes the names and addresses of all IP hosts within the domain, the names of all subdomains and the name servers for those domains, and the addresses of the name servers for the root domain and any other domains necessary to link to the existing DNS hierarchy.

AutoNegotiation—The process used by 10 and 100Mbps Fast Ethernet adapters to negotiate the fastest supported data rate in a mixed system.

autonomous system—A logical grouping of routers and networks maintained under a single administrative control but linked to a larger network, such as the Internet. Routers within an autonomous system communicate using an interior gateway protocol (IGP) such as Open Shortest Path First (OSPF).

autonomous system border router (ASBR)—Also called *autonomous system boundary router.* A router that communicates with and exchanges routing information with routers belonging to other autonomous systems (AS). ASBRs use an exterior gateway protocol (EGP) for communication.

Autonomous Unit Interface (AUI)—A type of universal media connector for Ethernet cables.

backbone—A cable used to form the main trunk of a network.

baseband—A signaling technology that uses an unmodulated, single-carrier frequency on a given network medium.

Basic Rate Interface (BRI)—One of the standard interfaces available between an ISDN switch and a subscriber. The BRI interface contains two 64Kbps channels for voice and data and one 16Kbps channel for connection control information.

beaconing—A signaling process employed by nodes on a token ring network to indicate that a serious error has occurred. The error may involve the node itself or it may involve the node's nearest active upstream neighbor (NAUN). The beaconing process causes all normal network transmissions to be suspended until the error condition is corrected.

B-ISDN (Broadband ISDN)—An extension of ISDN that offers enhanced data rates (multiples of 155Mbps as opposed to 64Kbps) because it uses fiber-optic transmission media.

bit—The basic unit of data in computer system communications. A single bit has a binary equivalent of either 0 or 1.

bridge—A hardware device that connects two or more physical network segments. A bridge forwards frames between the connecting networks on the basis of information contained in the data-link header.

bridge port—The media interface on a bridge that connects the bridge to a LAN segment.

bridge protocol data unit (BPDU)—A hello packet in a spanning tree protocol.

bridging loop—A critical error condition in which data packets circle in a loop between two redundant bridges and are never routed to their destinations correctly. The term *bridging loop* is also applied to the broadcast storms that occur when the spanning tree protocol is not used.

broadband—A transmission technology that multiplexes several independent network carriers onto a single cable. Broadband networking allows multiple networks to coexist on a single cable. Each network conducts conversations on a different frequency; traffic from one network does not interfere with traffic from the others.

broadband network—A network employing broadband technology to transmit multiple streams of information over long distances over the same cable.

broadband transmission—An analog communication technique that uses several communications channels simultaneously.

broadcast storm—A condition in which one workstation triggers several other workstations to transmit large numbers of frames at the same time.

brouter (bridging router)—A hardware device that routes some protocols and bridges others. A brouter can operate at either the Data Link layer (layer 2) or Network layer (layer 3) of the OSI model.

Carrier Sense—The process of checking the media for carrier signals before transmitting. Used in Carrier Sense Multiple Access/Collision Avoidance (CSMA/CA) and Carrier Sense Multiple Access/Collision Detection (CSMA/CD) media access schemes.

Carrier Sense Multiple Access/Collision Detection (CSMA/CD)—A method in which collisions are detected by monitoring the transmission line for a special signal that indicates a collision has occurred.

checksum—A calculation that keeps a running total of the bits of a transmitted message as a means of detecting errors in transmission. This value is transmitted and compared with the value of the receiving computer. This can detect most errors in a packet, although it's not as accurate as a cyclic redundancy check (CRC) calculation.

classful hierarchy—An addressing hierarchy in which the IP addresses conform to the standard number of bits for the network address and host address for each type of class.

Classless InterDomain Routing (CIDR)—A routing strategy that allows organizations that have more than 256 nodes but fewer than 65,536 nodes on a network to be able to use a special Class C Internet address. This strategy allows the assignment of consecutive Class C addresses in a way that makes them appear to be a single address to Internet routers.

coaxial cable—A type of cable that uses a central solid wire surrounded by insulation. A braided-wire conductor sheath surrounds the insulation, and a plastic jacket surrounds the sheath. This cable can accommodate high bandwidth and is resistant to interference.

collision detection—A media access protocol for dealing with the effects of packet collision. This occurs when two data packets are sent at the same time and are therefore discarded and must be resent. Collisions are detected by checking the direct current (DC) voltage level on the line. If the level is higher than expected, a collision is occurring.

constant bit rate (CBR)—A type of ATM connection under the Class A Quality of Service (QoS) level. CBR is typically reserved for voice or video, or other data that must be transmitted at a constant rate.

convergence—The process of synchronizing routing databases across all routers within the internetwork.

count-to-infinity problem—An artifact that can occur in distance vector routing. A count-to-infinity condition occurs if a network becomes unreachable because routers are relying on and advertising incorrect information.

Data Link layer—The second layer in the seven-layer OSI model, the Data Link layer packages and addresses data (using hardware-level addresses) and controls transmission flow over communication lines.

database description packet (DDP)—A NetWare Link Services Protocol (NLSP) packet containing summary information that's sent to the designated router (DR) and backup designated router (BDR) by regular OSPF routers.

datagram—A packet containing information and address information. A datagram is a type of packet routed through a packet-switching network. The information held by the datagram is referred to as the *payload*, and the address information is usually contained in a header. Datagrams do not need to arrive in consecutive order because they have address information. Datagrams are used in connectionless transmission mechanisms.

Department of Defense (DoD) model—A four-layer model for networking computers that was designed by the Department of Defense.

designated router (DR)—An NLSP router responsible for exchanges of link-state information between all other NLSP routers on a local area network (LAN). The DR has the highest priority of the routers. In Open Shortest Path First (OSPF) protocol networks, the DR is a router that generates a link-state advertisement for a multiaccess network, and it reduces the number of adjacencies required on a multiaccess network.

Digital Equipment Corporation Local Area Transport (DEC LAT)—A nonroutable network communication protocol.

Directory Access Protocol (DAP)—An X.500 Directory Services protocol. The DAP establishes communications between a Directory User Agent (DUA) and a Directory System Agent (DSA).

Directory Information Base (DIB)—The database that stores the Directory Information Tree (DIT) information in an X.500 Directory Services implementation.

Directory Information Tree (DIT)—The structure that organizes the information for a DIB in the X.500 Directory Services model. The DIT does not hold the actual data but rather information on where the data can be located.

Directory Service Agent (DSA)—The process running on a local server that allows access to the DIB.

Directory Services (DS)—A global, distributed, replicated database that retains information about all resources in a network. This can manage any size network through a hierarchical, tree-like representation. Also called X.500 Directory Services.

Directory User Agent (DUA)—A program used in the X.500 Directory Services model for accessing directory services. A DUA establishes an interface between an end user and a Directory System Agent (DSA), which retrieves the requested services.

distance vector algorithms—The class of routing algorithms that broadcasts routing information periodically instead of sending information only when a change occurs in a route.

distance vector routing—A dynamic routing scheme that uses hop counts to determine route selections and relies on second-hand information to build the routing database.

distinguished name (DN)—The complete path from an object to the [Root] of the Novell Directory Services (NDS) directory tree. A DN is a combination of an object's common name and context.

distributed database—A database that provides services to all network applications and users over different platforms. The distributed database can be stored on different hard drives in different locations.

DNS resolver—A program that converts a domain name into an IP address that the name represents.

DNS zone—A logical partition or subdivision of the Domain Name System (DNS) namespace. Also called a *subdomain*, a zone begins at a specified domain and extends downward until either an end node is reached or another subdomain begins.

domain—This term refers to an administrative element of the Domain Name System (DNS) naming hierarchy.

Domain Name System (DNS)—A distributed naming service that provides information about the Internet Protocol addresses and domain names of all computers on a network.

Dynamic Host Configuration Protocol (DHCP)—A protocol that dynamically assigns IP addresses to Windows-based personal computers in a LAN. DHCP allows each client to request an IP address from the server and return the address when it's done.

encapsulation—When one protocol is enveloped within another protocol for transmission.

encryption—A process in which text is changed into an unreadable form that can only be deciphered by a computer that has the proper decryption algorithms.

Ethernet—A type of shared-media LAN that uses a bus or star topology and packet switching, and is based on contention-oriented media access.

Ethernet hub—A Physical layer device on an Ethernet network that functions as a multiport repeater.

Exterior Gateway Protocol (EGP)—A protocol used by gateways in an internetwork to provide a method of communication between routers at the edges of their respective autonomous systems. EGP is used in the Internet core system and is part of TCP/IP.

Fast Ethernet—Ethernet that operates at 100Mbps by limiting the time it takes for a bit to be sent. Fast Ethernet can't be run on a cable longer than 100 meters between the repeater and the sender. Also, there can be no more than two repeater hops.

Fiber Distributed Data Interface (FDDI)—A high-speed LAN protocol that uses fiber-optic cable that can transmit light and operate at data rates of 100Mbps. Most fiber-optic LANs use a token-passing mechanism as well as a duel-ring topology.

flooding—A process used by a link-state router to build and maintain a logical network by sending a packet with information about its links to all other link-state routers on the network. Each router then combines its own information with the information gained from the other routers.

frame—A packet data format consisting of streams of bits. A frame includes start bits, data bits, and stop bits in addition to the payload.

Frame Relay—A protocol specification and a type of public data network service that provides efficient Data Link layer functions on permanent and switched virtual circuits.

full-duplex mode—When two data streams flow in opposite directions simultaneously. In full-duplex mode, the recipient node can send control data back to the sender while the sender continues to send data.

gateway—A link between two dissimilar networks that acts as a translator between the systems.

graphical user interface (GUI)—An operating environment that uses icons and buttons rather than commands to perform certain functions.

half-duplex mode—A communication mode that allows communication in both directions but not at the same time.

hello frame—A packet type transmitted on a source-routing network as part of the route-determination process.

hexadecimal number—A base-16 number system in which the numbers 1 to 9 are represented by numbers and 10 to 15 are represented by the letters A to F.

hop—The distance traveled by a packet between routers or other network devices as it moves along to its final destination.

host—A central computer to which other nodes, storage devices, or controllers are attached.

host table—A locally maintained table that lists the TCP/IP hosts on a network along with their network addresses.

hostname—An Internet term for a machine's name. The hostname is part of the fully qualified domain name (FQDN).

hybrid network—A network that mixes two or more network topologies.

IN-ADDR.ARPA zone—A DNS zone type that performs address-to-name resolution (as opposed to name-to-address resolution performed by a regular DNS zone).

Institute of Electrical and Electronics Engineers (IEEE)—A networking organization that establishes standards for networks and network components.

Integrated Services Digital Network (ISDN)—A digital communication service that uses special adapters on regular phone lines that can differentiate between digital and other types of data transfer. ISDN lines can transfer data at up to 1.536Mbps.

interior gateway protocols (IGPs)—Protocols used to exchange routing table information between routers within the intranet.

International Standards Organization (ISO)—A Geneva-based organization that sets standards for data communication.

Internet Control Message Protocol (ICMP)—A TCP/IP protocol that works with IP and is used to handle link-level error and control messages.

Internet Engineering Task Force (IETF)—A team that addresses short-term engineering concerns of the Internet.

Internet Protocol (IP)—A DoD Internet layer protocol that provides connectionless, nonguaranteed service to move packets across an internetwork.

Internet Service Provider (ISP)—A commercial organization that provides customers access to the Internet, usually for a fee.

Internetwork Packet Exchange (IPX)—The Novell communications protocol that operates at the Network layer of the OSI model. It's used to route data packets to a requested internetwork destination.

InterNIC (Internet Network Information Center)—A central organization responsible for allocating and maintaining World Wide Web domain names. This organization is a cooperative effort between AT&T, the National Science Foundation (NSF), and Network Solutions, Inc.

IP Registry—An organization authorized to assign registered IP addresses.

ITU-Telecommunications Standards Sector—A United Nations company that develops international telecommunications standards.

leaf object—A Directory Services object that resides at an endpoint in the Directory Information Tree (DIT) and does not contain any other objects.

Lightweight Directory Access Protocol (LDAP)—A protocol designed to provide client access to the X.500 directory. It's used when simple read/write interactive access to the directory is required. It's specifically targeted at simple management and browser applications.

Link Access Procedures-Balanced (LAPB)—A bit-oriented, Data Link layer protocol from the CCITT used for communications between devices designated as data circuit-terminating equipment (DCE) and data terminating equipment (DTE).

Link State Packet (LSP)—The link-state database for a router in a link-state routing environment. The packet contains information about all the connections for a router.

link state update (LSU) packet—A packet used to relay link-state changes to neighboring routers.

load balancing—A scheme that distributes network traffic among parallel paths, thus providing redundancy while efficiently using available bandwidth.

local area network (LAN)—A group of computers linked together to share files and resources.

Logical Link Control (LLC) sublayer—A protocol and packet format commonly used in Systems Network Architecture (SNA) networks and more widely supported than the Synchronous Data Link Control (SDLC) protocol.

Management Information Base (MIB)—A database of network-management information and objects used by the Common Management Information Protocol (CMIP) and the Simple Network Management Protocol (SNMP).

master name server—The server in a DNS zone that stores and manages the authoritative database for the zone.

Media Access Control (MAC) sublayer—The lower sublayer of the OSI Data Link layer. This layer includes functions that control access to the network media.

Media Independent Interface (MII)—Part of the 802.3u specification that allows Fast Ethernet to use any one of three Physical layer transceivers to connect to the network.

multiport repeater—An Ethernet network repeater that connects multiple network nodes in parallel.

Multistation Access Unit (MSAU)—A multiport wiring hub used on token ring networks that can connect as many as eight nodes.

nearest active upstream neighbor (NAUN)—A token ring node from which another node receives packets and the token.

NetWare Core Protocol (NCP)—The protocol used by a server's NetWare operating system to accept and respond to workstation requests.

NetWare Link Services Protocol (NLSP)—Novell's iteration of the IS-IS link-state routing protocol.

network board—A circuit board installed in a computer to allow it to communicate with other workstations on a network. Also called a network interface card (NIC), network adapter, network card, and network interface board. Novell uses the term *network board* most often. However, vendors usually call it a NIC.

network ID—The unique address that identifies a specific network on an internetwork.

network interface card (NIC)—See *network board*.

Network layer—The third layer of the OSI model. The Network layer ensures that information moving across an internetwork arrives at its intended destination.

node address—Another name for the MAC address or hardware address for a network station.

Novell's Network Registry—A Novell service that assigns and tracks IPX network addresses and organization names. The Registry enables participating organizations to share data between interconnected NetWare networks without name and address conflicts.

object—A structure in NDS that stores information about a network resource. An object consists of categories of information as well as the data in those properties.

Open Shortest Path First (OSPF)—A link-state internal gateway protocol (IGP) that's part of the TCP/IP protocol suite. OSPF routers exchange information about the state of their network connections and links. Using this information, OSPF routers determine the shortest path to an intended receiver on the internetwork.

Open Systems Interconnection (OSI) reference model—A seven-layer model that can be used to help better understand the functional requirements and processes involved in creating computer networks. Also called simply the *OSI model*.

operating system—Software that controls a computer's functions.

passive hub—A device that splits a transmission signal and allows more workstations to be added to a network topology.

permanent virtual circuit (PVC)—A communications path between two fixed endpoints that's continuously available; similar to a leased line.

Physical layer—The first layer of the OSI model, the Physical layer defines the rules for transmitting bits of data on a physical medium.

Point-to-Point Protocol (PPP)—An industry-standard protocol developed to provide dial-up access to IP networks.

poison reverse—A vector-routing scheme that's used to shorten the convergence time when the internetwork undergoes a configuration change.

Presentation layer—The sixth layer of the OSI model, the Presentation layer protocols are concerned with issues involving data format. It specifies the processes for managing the negotiation and establishment of the encoded values for the transfer of structured data types.

propagation delay—A value indicating the amount of time required for a signal to pass through a component.

protocol—A rule used to define the procedures to follow as data is transmitted or received.

protocol suite—A collection of networking protocols providing all communications and services required to enable computers to exchange messages and information.

registered address—An IP address that has been assigned by an authorized IP registry.

repeater—A device functioning at the first layer of the OSI model that indiscriminately passes all signals from one network segment to another and reconditions the signals to extend the distance between two hosts.

replica name servers—DNS name servers that act as repositories for a copy of the authoritative database housed on the master name server.

request for comment (RFC)—A procedure in the Internet community that involves the submission of a series of documents containing protocol descriptions, model descriptions, and experimental results for review by experts.

routable protocol—A protocol that can provide the required information to a router that allows it to be routed.

router—Hardware or software designed to handle the exchange of information between network cabling systems.

Routing Information Protocol (RIP)—A routing protocol in which routers use hop count information to determine the most cost-efficient route to a destination.

routing information table—A table that contains information that a router references to determine the best possible route to use when forwarding packets to network destinations.

Routing Table Maintenance Protocol (RTMP)—An Apple routing protocol.

Sequenced Packet Exchange (SPX)—A NetWare protocol that enhances the Novell IPX protocol. SPX adds connection-oriented reliable service to IPX transport.

Serial Line Internet Protocol (SLIP)—An Internet protocol designed to run IP over modems that connect two network systems.

Service Advertising Protocol (SAP)—A Novell protocol used by servers to advertise their services to the network.

Service Advertising Protocol (SAP) filtering—A technique used on IPX/SPX networks to allow only selected SAP packets to be forwarded by routers.

Session layer—The fifth layer of the OSI model, the Session layer manages the dialog between end systems.

shielded twisted pair (STP)—A cable with a foil shield and copper braid surrounding pairs of wires that have a minimum number of twists per foot of cable.

Simple Mail Transfer Protocol (SMTP)—A TCP/IP protocol that provides the specifications for mail system interaction and controls message formats.

Simple Network Management Protocol (SNMP)—A DoD Process/Application layer protocol that specifies a process for collecting network-management data between devices.

Source Node Address—The value in the packet header field that represents the address of the node sending the packet.

stub area—An OSPF area that's connected to the backbone area by a single area border router (ABR).

subnet—A portion or segment of a network.

subnet mask—In the IP addressing scheme, a subnet mask is a group of selected bits that identifies a subnetwork.

subnetting—The process of dividing a network into smaller, connected networks.

supernet—A network created by combining multiple Class C addresses.

switch—A Physical layer device that functions as a high-speed bridge.

switched virtual circuit (SVC)—A circuit established dynamically that remains connected until a user or an application shuts it down.

Synchronous Optical Network (SONET)—A high-speed, fiber-optic network that provides an interface and mechanism for optical transmission of data. Speeds can range from 51.84Mbps to 2.488Gbps.

Thick Ethernet—See *thicknet*.

Thin Ethernet—See *thinnet*.

thicknet—Coaxial cable with a diameter of 1 centimeter, used to connect Ethernet nodes at distances as far away as 1,000 meters.

thinnet—Coaxial cable wire with a diameter of 10 millimeters, used to connect Ethernet nodes at a distance of about 300 meters.

token ring—IBM's version of a LAN, a token ring network consists of stations connected serially, each receiving information sequentially around a closed network ring.

topology—The physical layout of a network, including the cabling, workstation configuration, gateways, and hubs.

transceiver—A device that can transmit data, receive data, and convert between transmission media types.

Transmission Control Protocol/Internet Protocol (TCP/IP)—A suite of networking protocols that enables dissimilar nodes in a heterogeneous environment to communicate with one another.

transparent bridge—A scheme in which bridges pass frames one hop at a time, basing their hops on tables that associate end nodes with bridge ports. The presence of the bridges is transparent to the network's end nodes.

Transport layer—The fourth layer of the OSI model. This layer provides reliable end-to-end delivery of data and detects errors in the sequence of a transmission.

tunneling—The process of encapsulating and de-encapsulating one protocol in another.

unregistered address—An IP address used on a private network that has not been assigned by a registering authority.

unroutable protocol—A communication protocol, such as NetBIOS, that cannot be routed, usually because it lacks Network layer information required by the routing process.

unshielded twisted pair (UTP)—Cable containing two or more pairs of twisted copper wires; the greater the number of twists, the lower the crosstalk.

UTP Ethernet—An Ethernet implementation that uses a cable containing two or more pairs of unshielded, twisted copper wires.

vampire tap—A hardware clamp used to connect one cable segment to another by penetrating the insulation of the cable segment without cutting it.

variable bit rate (VBR)—A connection method used in ATM networks that transmits at varying rates; used for data transmissions whose contents are not time-sensitive.

virtual LAN (VLAN)—A network configuration that can span physical LANs and topologies and is created by software on an as-needed basis.

wide area network (WAN)—A network encompassing a large geographical area.

Xerox Network Systems (XNS)—A multilayer communications protocol originally developed by Xerox that supports a distributed file system in which users can access printers as if they were local.

zone—An arbitrary group of nodes in an AppleTalk network that provides the capability to divide the network into smaller sections.

Index

Bold page numbers indicate sample exam questions.

Connection-oriented services, 15, 17, 18,
  25, 345
Connectivity devices, **22, 25, 329**. *See also*
  Bridges; Combination devices; Repeaters;
  Routers; Switches.
    choosing, 130–133
    nonroutable protocols, 128–129,
      325, 342
    OSI layers and, 19–21, **329**
Constant bit rate. *See* CBR.
Controlling packets, 34
Convergence
  NLSP, 283
  RIP, 204
  routers, 116, 119
Conversation address, X.25, 60
Cost metrics
  NLSP, 272–273, 279, 281
  RIP, 202–203, 261, **331**
  routers, 114, **122**
Counter-rotating rings, 49–50
Count-to-infinity problem. *See also*
  Split horizon.
    OSPF, 215, **218, 324**
    RIP, 204–206
    routers, 116–118, **121**
CRC, 113
CSMA/CD
  Ethernet, 34
  repeaters and, 72
CSNP, 282
Cut-through switches, 99, 102, **104**
Cyclic redundancy check. *See* CRC.

D

DAP, 310, **314**
Data compression, 18, **22**
Data Link Connection Identifiers.
  See DLCIs.
Data Link layer
  ATM, 64–65, **67**
  bridges, 20, 74
  circuit switches, 20
  connectivity devices, 20
  Frame Relay, 62
  frames, 17
  ISDN, 63, **66, 330**
  LAN environment, 17
  network boards, 20, **329**
  packet switches, 20
  PPP, 59
  protocol analyzers and, 297–298
  switches, 20

tasks, 17
virtual LANs and, 100, **107**
Data transformation, 18
Database description packets. *See* DDP.
Databases
  DIB, 307–308
  NLSP, 275, 278–279, 282, 286
  OSPF, 210–211, **217**, 286
  RIP, 202
  SAP, 262, 264–265, **267**
Datagrams, 18. *See also* UDP.
DDP, 209
DEC LAT, 128–129, **325**
Default gateways, 200
Default route IP address, 32, 145, **332**
Delay
  bridges, 87, **338**
  switches, 99, **104**
Designated bridges, 94–95
Designated routers. *See* DR.
DHCP, 227–228, **238**
Dialog, Session layer, 18
Dial-up connections, 59, **68**, 70
DIB, 307–308
Directory Access Protocol. *See* DAP.
Directory Information Base. *See* DIB.
Directory Information Tree. *See* DIT.
Directory services, 315. *See also* X.500
  Directory Services.
Directory structure, X.500, 306–308, **313**
Directory System Agents. *See* DSA.
Directory User Agents. *See* DUA.
Disabled state, 85
Distance vector routing, 115–118, **121**,
  122, 123, 201. *See also* RIP.
Distinguished name. *See* DN.
Distributed Queue Dual Boot.
  See DQDB.
DIT, 306–307, **312, 313**
DLCIs, 62
DN, 309
DNS, 156–160, **163, 164**, 166, **326**
DNS name servers, 160–161
DNS zones, 158–160, **165, 345**
DoD model
  ARP, 191
  BOOTP, 191
  Ethernet, 191
  FDDI, 191
  FTP, 192
  Host-to-Host layer, 192, **194**
  HTTP, 192
  ICMP, 191, 224–225, **347**

CORIOLIS HELP CENTER

Here at The Coriolis Group, we strive to provide the finest customer service in the technical education industry. We're committed to helping you reach your certification goals by assisting you in the following areas.

Talk to the Authors

We'd like to hear from you! Please refer to the "How to Use This Book" section in the "Introduction" of every Exam Cram guide for our authors' individual email addresses.

Web Page Information

The Certification Insider Press Web page provides a host of valuable information that's only a click away. For information in the following areas, please visit us at:

www.coriolis.com/cip/default.cfm

- Titles and other products
- Book content updates
- Roadmap to Certification Success guide
- New Adaptive Testing changes
- New Exam Cram Live! seminars
- New Certified Crammer Society details
- Sample chapters and tables of contents
- Manuscript solicitation
- Special programs and events

Contact Us by Email

Important addresses you may use to reach us at The Coriolis Group.

eci@coriolis.com

To subscribe to our FREE, bi-monthly on-line newsletter, *Exam Cram Insider*. Keep up to date with the certification scene. Included in each *Insider* are certification articles, program updates, new exam information, hints and tips, sample chapters, and more.

techsupport@coriolis.com

For technical questions and problems with CD-ROMs. Products broken, battered, or blown-up? Just need some installation advice? Contact us here.

ccs@coriolis.com

To obtain membership information for the *Certified Crammer Society*, an exclusive club for the certified professional. Get in on members-only discounts, special information, expert advice, contests, cool prizes, and free stuff for the certified professional. Membership is FREE. Contact us and get enrolled today!

cipq@coriolis.com

For book content questions and feedback about our titles, drop us a line. This is the good, the bad, and the questions address. Our customers are the best judges of our products. Let us know what you like, what we could do better, or what question you may have about any content. Testimonials are always welcome here, and if you send us a story about how an Exam Cram guide has helped you ace a test, we'll give you an official Certification Insider Press T-shirt.

custserv@coriolis.com

For solutions to problems concerning an order for any of our products. Our staff will promptly and courteously address the problem. Taking the exams is difficult enough. We want to make acquiring our study guides as easy as possible.

Book Orders & Shipping Information

orders@coriolis.com

To place an order by email or to check on the status of an order already placed.

coriolis.com/bookstore/default.cfm

To place an order through our online bookstore.

1.800.410.0192

To place an order by phone or to check on an order already placed.